access to history

Britain 1951–2007

MICHAEL LYNCH

SECOND EDITION

access to history

Britain 1951–2007

MICHAEL LYNCH

SECOND EDITION

HODDER
EDUCATION
AN HACHETTE UK COMPANY

For Lily May Lynch, born 2007

The Publishers would like to thank Nicholas Fellows and David Ferriby for their contribution to the Study Guide.

The Publishers would like to thank the following for permission to reproduce copyright material:

Photo credits: p3 British Cartoon Archive/Mirrorpix; **p31** Open Government Licence v1.0 (http://www.nationalarchives.gov.uk/doc/open-government-licence/version/3/); **p32** British Cartoon Archive/Solo Syndication; **p42** Solo Syndication; **p60** British Cartoon Archive/Solo Syndication; **p73** 'Roy Jenkins 1977b' by Verhoeff, Bert/Anefo – Dutch National Archives, The Hague, Fotocollectie Algemeen Nederlands Persbureau (ANeFo), 1945–1989, Nummer toegang 2.24.01.05 Bestanddeelnummer 929-0833. Licenced under CC BY-SA 3.0 nl via Wikimedia Commons; **p77** 'Edward Heath Allan Warren' by Allan Warren – Own work. Licenced under CC BY-SA 3.0 via Wikimedia Commons; **p83** Wally Fawkes/*The Observer*/British Cartoon Archive; **p93** Keystone Pictures USA/Alamy; **p118** British Cartoon Archive/Solo Syndication; **p119** Library of Congress LC-DIG-ppmsca-09786; **p161** British Cartoon Archive/Mirrorpix; **p180** 'MSC 2014 Blair Mueller MSC2014 (cropped)' by Müller/MSC. Licensed under CC BY 3.0 de via Wikimedia Commons; **p182** PA/Topfoto; **p222** British Cartoon Archive/Express Newspapers.

Acknowledgements: are listed on page 258.

Every effort has been made to trace all copyright holders, but if any have been inadvertently overlooked the Publishers will be pleased to make the necessary arrangements at the first opportunity.

Although every effort has been made to ensure that website addresses are correct at time of going to press, Hodder Education cannot be held responsible for the content of any website mentioned in this book. It is sometimes possible to find a relocated web page by typing in the address of the home page for a website in the URL window of your browser.

Hachette UK's policy is to use papers that are natural, renewable and recyclable products and made from wood grown in sustainable forests. The logging and manufacturing processes are expected to conform to the environmental regulations of the country of origin.

Orders: please contact Bookpoint Ltd, 130 Milton Park, Abingdon, Oxon OX14 4SB. Telephone: +44 (0)1235 827720. Fax: +44 (0)1235 400454. Lines are open 9.00a.m.–5.00p.m., Monday to Saturday, with a 24-hour message answering service. Visit our website at www.hoddereducation.co.uk

© 2015 Michael Lynch
Second edition © Michael Lynch 2015

First published in 2008 by
Hodder Education
An Hachette UK Company
Carmelite House, 50 Victoria Embankment
London EC4Y 0DZ

Impression number   10 9 8 7 6 5 4 3 2
Year   2019 2018 2017 2016 2015

Cover photo © Bettmann/Corbis
Produced, illustrated and typeset in Palatino LT Std by Gray Publishing, Tunbridge Wells
Printed and bound by CPI Group (UK) Ltd, Croydon CR0 4YY

A catalogue record for this title is available from the British Library

ISBN 978 1471839092

Contents

Dedication

Keith Randell (1943–2002)

The *Access to History* series was conceived and developed by Keith, who created a series to 'cater for students as they are, not as we might wish them to be'. He leaves a living legacy of a series that for over 20 years has provided a trusted, stimulating and well-loved accompaniment to post-16 study. Our aim with these new editions is to continue to offer students the best possible support for their studies.

CHAPTER 1

The Labour Party in power 1945–51

The period 1945–51 was one of the most formative in the whole of the twentieth century. In 1945, the Labour Party came into power with a large majority, following an impressive victory in the first general election after the Second World War. During the next six years it introduced the welfare state and nationalised a significant part of the industrial economy. In doing so, it set a pattern that was largely followed by all succeeding governments up to 1979. This chapter, which serves as an introduction to the whole period 1951–2007, describes the domestic achievements of Clement Attlee's post-war governments and examines the historical debate over those achievements under the following headings:

★ Labour's creation of the welfare state

★ Labour's economic policy 1945–51

★ Foreign affairs

★ Labour's defeat 1951

★ The legacy of the Labour governments 1945–51

Key dates

1945	Overwhelming election victory for Labour		**1948**	Britain began to receive substantial Marshall Aid
	Family Allowances Act		**1949**	Nationalisation of iron and steel
1946	National Insurance Act			Government forced to devalue the pound sterling
	Industrial Injuries Act			
	Nationalisation programme begun		**1950**	Start of Korean War
1947	Government undertook to develop independent nuclear deterrent			Election reduced Labour majority to five
	Independence of India		**1951**	Bevanite rebellion over prescription charges
1948	National Health Service began			Election success for Conservatives, but Labour gained highest popular vote yet
	National Assistance Act			

Labour's creation of the welfare state

> ▶ *How had the Beveridge Report prepared the ground for Labour's introduction of the welfare state?*

Having won an overwhelming victory in the 1945 general election, the Labour Party under Clement Attlee formed the government and proceeded to adopt a radical reforming policy aimed at establishing the welfare state. They based their policy on the Beveridge Report.

The Beveridge Report

In late 1940, although Britain was in the throes of a war that it was not certain of winning, Prime Minister Winston Churchill had asked his officials to consider the preliminary steps that might be taken towards post-war reconstruction in Britain. The outcome was the production of a report by **William Beveridge**, a senior administrator with a long experience in social security provision.

Beveridge believed that it was possible to establish a national minimum level of welfare without recourse to extreme methods. He proposed a universal scheme of insurance which would provide protection against the distress that invariably accompanied sickness, injury and unemployment. Additionally, there would be grants to ease the financial hardships that came with maternity, parenthood and bereavement. The term 'protection from the cradle to the grave', although not Beveridge's own, was an appropriate description of the envisaged scale of welfare provision. The plan was to replace the current unsystematic pattern of welfare with a centrally funded and regulated system.

Insurance was to form the base, with welfare organisations providing the superstructure. Beveridge's 'five giants' (see box) to be defeated on the road to reconstruction were a figurative representation of Britain's major social problems. Beveridge's scheme pointed towards the 'welfare state', a term which pre-dated the report by some ten years but which began to be widely used during the war years. Hardly any of Beveridge's proposals were new. What made them significant in 1942 was their integration into a comprehensive scheme.

The five giants

- Want: to be ended by National Insurance.
- Ignorance: to be ended by an effective education system.
- Disease: to be ended by a comprehensive health service.
- Squalor: to be ended by slum clearance and rehousing.
- Idleness: to be ended by full employment.

SOURCE A

'Beveridge's five giants'. A cartoon first published in 1942.

What was the cartoonist's view in Source A of the problems facing Beveridge?

Beveridge had laid the theoretical foundations for all subsequent developments in the field of social-welfare provision.

Beveridge proposed to take the best aspects of the existing welfare systems and incorporate them into a universal plan. He specifically denied that his plan aimed at 'giving everybody something for nothing'. Freedom from want could not be 'forced on or given to a democracy'; it had to be wanted by the people. Beveridge stressed that a good society depended not on the state but on the individual. He spoke of the retention of 'personal responsibilities'. Individuals would be encouraged to save as private citizens. These ideas were very much in the **Liberal** tradition, as was his belief that his proposals would not involve an increase in government expenditure.

It is notable that at every point, Beveridge assumed the continuation of **capitalism**. His proposals were not socialist. One feature to all forms of **socialism** is a conviction that the capitalist system is exploitative and unjust and, therefore, ultimately indefensible. However, throughout the Beveridge Report there is an implicit understanding that post-war welfare reform will take place within the framework of the continuing capitalist system. It is for that reason that historically the report has to be seen as belonging to liberal, rather than socialist, thinking and planning.

Labour's welfare programme

When Beveridge's report first appeared it was welcomed by all the parties. There was broad agreement that **social reconstruction** would be a post-war necessity in Britain. This showed how much ground had been made in Britain by the principle of **collectivism**, which in turn was evidence of the influence of the moderate socialism that the Labour Party espoused. Yet Churchill did not

 KEY TERMS

Liberal The principles of equality and freedom of the individual.

Capitalism The predominant economic system in the Western world according to which individuals and companies trade and invest for private profit.

Socialism In its British form, a programme for creating equality for all by means of government-led economic and social reforms.

Social reconstruction Shaping society so as to provide protection and opportunity for all its citizens.

Collectivism The people and the state acting together with a common sense of purpose, which necessarily meant a restriction on individual rights.

regard the report as socialist; his reluctance to put the report into practice was on the grounds of cost rather than principle. It was also the case that the Labour members of his wartime **coalition** supported him in 1942 and 1943 in defeating House of Commons' motions calling for immediate implementation of the report.

Now in office after 1945 with a massive majority, the Labour government immediately took steps to put in place the main proposals in the Beveridge Report. Labour's election campaign had promoted the notion that after six years of war effort, the people were entitled to their just reward. It would also be a fitting recompense for the sufferings of the nation during the depression of the inter-war years. The Report had provided the new government with its blueprint for social reconstruction.

The Labour government's strategy for an integrated social-welfare system was expressed in four major measures, which came into effect in the summer of 1948. In a prime-ministerial broadcast on the eve of their introduction, Attlee explained that they were 'comprehensive and available to every citizen' and gave 'security to all members of the family'. The measures to which Attlee referred were:

- The National Insurance Act, which created a system of universal and compulsory government–employer–employee contributions to provide against unemployment, sickness, maternity expenses, widowhood and retirement.
- The National Assistance Act, which complemented National Insurance by establishing National Assistance Boards to deal directly with cases of hardship and poverty.
- The Industrial Injuries Act, which provided cover for accidents that occurred in the workplace.
- The National Health Service Act, which brought the whole population, regardless of status or income, into a scheme of free medical treatment. Drug prescriptions, dental and optical care were included. Under the Act, the existing voluntary and local authority hospitals were co-ordinated into a single, national system, to be operated at local level by appointed health boards. The National Health Service (NHS) would be funded through general taxation and National Insurance.

Two other measures need to be added to the four listed by Attlee: the Education Act of 1944 and the Family Allowances Act of 1945. These were introduced before Labour came into office but were implemented by Attlee's government.

- The Education Act or Butler Act (1944) was introduced by R.A. Butler (see page 21), a Conservative, and may be regarded as the first organised attack on one of Beveridge's five giants: ignorance. It provided compulsory free education within a tripartite secondary education system. At age eleven, in their last year at primary school, pupils were to take the 'eleven plus', an examination to determine whether they were to attend a secondary-grammar (for the academically inclined), a secondary-technical (for the vocationally gifted) or a secondary-modern (for those not fitted for either of the former two categories).

- The Family Allowances Act (1945) provided a weekly payment of five shillings (25p) for every additional child after the first. The money was paid directly to the mother and did not require a means test.

The welfare state: a revolution?

The Labour government's implementation of the welfare state has been described as a social revolution. It was certainly an event of major significance, but it is important to see it in context. It was not a revolution forced on an unwilling people and it was not a revolution that pushed down existing structures. It built on what was already there. It is true that Beveridge had described his plan as a revolution, but he had been keen to stress that it was a 'British revolution', by which he meant it was not destructive but constructive, built on precedent. He said it was 'a natural development from the past'; the nation was ready for such a revolution.

It can now be seen that rather than being the advent of revolutionary socialism, Labour's moves towards a welfare state marked the high point of progressive liberalism. Although the Liberal Party long before 1945 had ceased to be a major political force, it could be argued that the coming of the welfare state marked the final great triumph of liberalism as a set of ideas. It had set the agenda for the foreseeable future. Yet, when due note has been taken of Liberal influence and of the ultimate **consensus** between the parties over welfare, the clear historical fact remains that it was the Labour Party under Attlee that between 1945 and 1951 found the commitment and sense of purpose to turn good intentions into workable and permanent structures. This was often, moreover, achieved in the face of determined opposition.

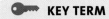

KEY TERM

Consensus Common agreement on major issues.

The NHS

The Act setting up the NHS was passed in 1946 and was intended to come into effect in 1947. However, the resistance of the medical profession meant its introduction was delayed until 1948. A poll of doctors in March 1948 revealed that out of the 80 per cent of the profession who voted, only 4735 supported the NHS scheme while 40,814 were against it.

When it finally came into effect in 1948 the NHS had these main features:

- Primary care would be provided by general practitioners (GPs) who would work as independent contractors and be paid for each patient on their books.
- Dentists and opticians, while providing NHS treatment, would continue to operate as private practitioners.

- Hospitals would be run by fourteen regional boards who would appoint local management committees to oversee matters at local level.
- Community services such as maternity care, vaccinations and the ambulance service were to be provided by local authorities.
- Medical prescriptions would be provided free of charge.
- Private practices and hospitals in which doctors charged their patients fees were to be allowed to continue, thus enabling GPs to be both NHS and private doctors.

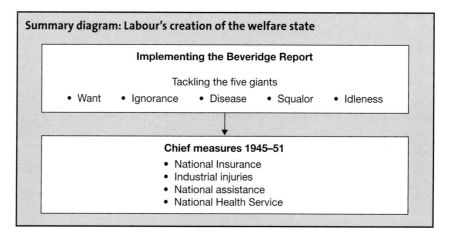

Summary diagram: Labour's creation of the welfare state

Implementing the Beveridge Report

Tackling the five giants

- Want - Ignorance - Disease - Squalor - Idleness

Chief measures 1945–51
- National Insurance
- Industrial injuries
- National assistance
- National Health Service

2 Labour's economic policy 1945–51

▶ *How extensive was the Labour government's restructuring of the economy?*

Keynesianism

KEY FIGURE

John Maynard Keynes (1883–1946)

A director of the Bank of England during the Second World War and the government's chief economic adviser.

Every so often in history, a particular financial or economic theory comes to dominate its time and appears to oblige governments to structure their policies in accordance with it. For most of the period between the late 1940s and the late 1970s, it was Keynesianism that provided the basic frame of reference. **John Maynard Keynes**, a Cambridge academic, believed that economic depressions, such as the one that had afflicted the economy in the 1930s, were avoidable if particular steps were taken. His starting point was demand. He calculated that it was a fall in demand for manufactured products that caused industrial economies to slip into recession. If demand could be sustained, decline could be prevented and jobs preserved.

Keynes maintained that the only agency with sufficient power and influence to keep demand at a high enough level was the government itself. He urged, therefore, that:

- The government should use its budgets and its revenue-raising powers to acquire capital, which it could then reinvest in the economy to keep it at a high level of activity.
- This artificial boost to the economy would lead to genuine recovery and growth. Companies and firms would have full order books and the workers would have jobs and earnings.
- Those earnings would be spent on goods and services, with the result that the forces of supply and demand would be stimulated.
- The government should abandon the practice of always trying to balance the budget between income and expenditure. It should be willing to run **deficit budgets** in the short term, even if this meant borrowing to do so. The government would eventually be able to repay its debts by taxing the companies and workers whose profits and wages would rise in a flourishing economy.

Nationalisation

From its earliest days, the Labour Party had advanced the principle that government had the right to direct the key aspects of economy in order to create efficiency and social justice. Clause IV of the party's constitution committed it to nationalisation, which it defined as 'the common ownership of the means of production, distribution and exchange'. In practice, common ownership meant government control.

> ### Main industries and institutions nationalised under Labour
>
> - 1946: coal, civil aviation, Cable & Wireless, the Bank of England.
> - 1947: road transport, electricity services.
> - 1948: gas.
> - 1949: iron and steel.

Financial problems

The idealism that inspired the government's welfare and nationalisation programmes came at a heavy financial cost, which added to the burdens that it had inherited in 1945. By the end of the war, Britain faced the following problems:

- It had debts of £4198 million.
- The **balance of payments** deficit was £750 million.
- Exports of manufactures had dropped by 60 per cent in wartime.
- **Invisible exports** had shrunk from £248 million in 1938 to £120 million in 1946.
- Costs of maintaining overseas military commitments had quintupled between 1938 and 1946.

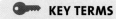

KEY TERMS

Deficit budgets
The government's spending more than it raised in revenue.

Balance of payments
The equilibrium between the cost of imports and the profits from exports; when import costs outstrip income from exports, financial crisis follows.

Invisible exports The sale of financial and insurance services to foreign buyers, traditionally one of Britain's major sources of income from abroad.

Defence costs

A factor that increased Britain's difficulties was that it had agreed with the USA, its **Cold War** ally, to increase its spending on defence from £2.3 billion to £4.7 billion. Despite demobilisation in 1945, Britain, as one of the occupying forces in Europe and as a member of the **UN Security Council**, continued to maintain a large peacetime army of a million men. In addition to the expense entailed by this was the extra financial burden the nation had shouldered when Attlee's government in 1947 committed Britain to the development of its own independent nuclear deterrent. Such developments meant that by the late 1940s Britain was spending 14 per cent of its **GNP** on defence.

Austerity

Faced with these burdens, Hugh Dalton, chancellor of the exchequer (1945–7), and his successor, Stafford Cripps, embarked on a policy of national austerity, whose main features were:

- the continuation of rationing of food and fuel
- tight financial controls to prevent **inflation**
- controls on wages and salaries
- increased taxation on incomes and goods
- restrictions on imports to keep dollar spending to a minimum.

Devaluation

Knowing that austerity alone could not meet the demands on Britain's economy, Dalton had negotiated a loan of $6000 million from the USA and Canada. The government's hope was that, in accordance with Keynesian theory (see page 6), the loan would provide the basis of an industrial recovery. But such recovery as did occur was never enough to meet expectations. A large part of the problem arose from one of the conditions attaching to the loan, which required that the British pound sterling had to be made convertible with the dollar in international trade. However, since the post-war US dollar was much stronger then the pound, the consequence was that Britain began to suffer from what was known as the '**dollar gap**'. US and other international traders could insist that Britain paid for its purchases from them in dollars. This drained Britain of a substantial part of the loan it had negotiated, while at the same time making it harder to meet the repayments.

The consequence of the financial imbalance led to what were known as sterling crises, the two most serious occurring in 1947 and 1949. In both cases the crises took the form of 'a run on the pound', foreign investors withdrawing their money from Britain in large amounts. The crisis in 1947 was deepened by the fact that the year witnessed the worst winter weather yet experienced in Britain in the twentieth century.

Britain eventually survived the 1947 crisis but the drain on its finances continued over the next two years. In 1949 Attlee's government reluctantly took the step that all its deflationary and austerity measures had been intended to avoid; it devalued the pound. The exchange rate of sterling was reduced from $4.03 to $2.80, a fall of 30 per cent. While this certainly made British exports cheaper and boosted overseas sales in the short term, the devaluation was a sure sign that the government's previous policies had not prevented the weakening of the economy.

Marshall Aid

It was something of a paradox that Britain, having been put under severe strain by its indebtedness to the USA, should find that it was the USA that offered it financial salvation. Britain's economic difficulties would have been even greater had it not been for the relief provided by the Marshall Plan, which began to operate from 1948. After 1945, the world's trading nations all experienced severe balance of payments problems. Worried that this would destroy international commerce, the USA, the only economy with sufficient resources, adopted a programme in 1947 to provide dollars to any country willing to receive them in return for granting trade concessions to the USA. Whatever the USA's self-interest may have been, it is difficult to see how Europe could have recovered without a massive inflow of US capital. Under the plan, which bore the name of the US secretary of state, George Marshall, Europe received $15 billion, Britain's share being ten per cent of that.

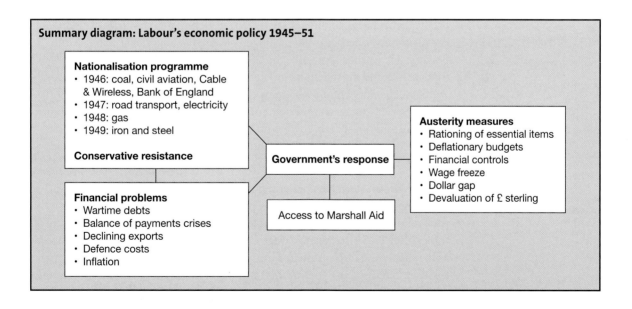

Summary diagram: Labour's economic policy 1945–51

Nationalisation programme
- 1946: coal, civil aviation, Cable & Wireless, Bank of England
- 1947: road transport, electricity
- 1948: gas
- 1949: iron and steel

Conservative resistance

Financial problems
- Wartime debts
- Balance of payments crises
- Declining exports
- Defence costs
- Inflation

Government's response

Access to Marshall Aid

Austerity measures
- Rationing of essential items
- Deflationary budgets
- Financial controls
- Wage freeze
- Dollar gap
- Devaluation of £ sterling

Foreign affairs

▶ *What issues in foreign affairs confronted the Labour government?*

▶ *Why was foreign policy a divisive issue within the Labour Party?*

The question that confronted Britain after 1945 was what role it should play in the post-war international order. The Labour government's answer came in the form of a range of momentous decisions:

- Britain became one of the '**the big five**' members of the UN Security Council.
- Britain chose to side with the USA in the Cold War divide.
- Britain declined to become formally involved in Europe.
- Britain granted India independence.
- Britain became a nuclear power.

These decisions indicated that Britain, led by a Labour government, had opted to remain a world power. By taking on such heavy burdens, Britain, at a time when it was implementing the welfare state at home, subjected itself to chronic economic strain.

Labour and the Cold War

In a speech in March 1946 at Fulton in the USA, Winston Churchill gave a dramatic definition to the Cold War in Europe. He spoke of the occupation of large areas of Eastern Europe by the **Soviet Union** as having created an 'iron curtain' running from the Baltic to the Adriatic. To the west of that line lay the democracies; to the east lay the Soviet-dominated countries of Poland, East Germany, Czechoslovakia, Hungary, Romania, Yugoslavia, Albania and Bulgaria. He warned that while the USSR did not want war it did desire 'the fruits of war and the indefinite expansion of their power and doctrines'. It was, therefore, the duty of the Western world, led by the USA, to unite to prevent further Soviet expansion. Although Attlee pointedly declined to comment on Churchill's Fulton speech, there is little doubt that it coincided in its key points with the pro-American, anti-Soviet attitude that the Labour government had adopted.

It was as British statesmen rather than socialists that Attlee and Ernest Bevin, his foreign secretary, approached the problem of Britain's policies in the post-war world. Their intention was to protect British interests, which in the nature of things after 1945 also meant Western interests, in the face of what they regarded as the threat to Europe presented by the Soviet Union. Joseph Stalin, the Soviet leader, had refused to withdraw his forces from the territories of Eastern Europe which they had occupied during the course of the war. Bevin often said that his natural desire was to be neither anti-Soviet nor pro-American, but that Stalin's stubbornness in occupying half of Europe, and threatening the other half, obliged him to be so.

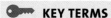 **KEY TERMS**

The big five USA, USSR, Britain, France and China.

Soviet Union Formed in 1922, the Union of Soviet Socialist Republics (USSR, or Soviet Union) was a single-party Communist state that existed until it was dissolved in 1991.

It was in this regard that early in his government Attlee faced a challenge in Parliament over his foreign policy. Interestingly, it came not from the opposition but from within his own party. In 1946 a group of 60 **backbench** Labour MPs, representing the left of the party, introduced an amendment criticising the government for its pro-American stance. Moved by **Richard Crossman**, the amendment called on Attlee's government to co-operate less with the USA and more with the Soviet Union.

Attlee replied by repeating Bevin's claim that the government was not anti-Soviet through prejudice, but simply because the USSR under Stalin was continuing the aggressive, anti-Western approach that had characterised Russian policy since the days of the tsars. This made genuine co-operation with the Soviet Union impossible.

Behind this disagreement between Attlee and the left wing of his party lay a fundamental and lasting difference of opinion as to the real character and purpose of the Labour Party. The mainstream members, typified by Attlee, saw Labour as a radical but non-revolutionary force that was prepared to work within the existing political system to achieve its aim of social reform. In contrast, those on the **Marxist** left believed that Labour's essential role was to work for the replacement of the prevailing capitalist system in Britain with a truly socialist one. They had anticipated that with a Labour Party in power, Anglo-Soviet relations would vastly improve: 'left would understand left'. However, the rapid development of the Cold War after 1945 shattered this hope. Britain found itself siding with the USA against the USSR. The Labour left argued that this was not inevitable; they asserted that, in leaning so heavily on the USA for financial aid, the government was destroying the chance of genuine British independence in international affairs. Desperate though Britain was for Marshall Aid, the left wing of the Labour Party was dismayed by the government's acceptance of it. For many Labour MPs, the financial arrangement tied Britain to the USA in the relationship of beggar and master and so denied the government any chance of acting independently in the post-war world.

Bevin's angry reaction to this was to accuse the left of a total lack of political realism: without the US dollars from the Marshall Aid programme and military support, Britain and Europe could not be sustained. Bevin also angered the left of the party by his contribution to the creation of the **NATO** alliance. Bevin, having played a major role in forming the alliance, then invited the USA to be a member. The USA, which had declared its attitude two years earlier in the **Truman Doctrine**, eagerly accepted the invitation.

The importance of Ernest Bevin as foreign secretary at this critical period was that he established the tradition of post-war British foreign policy: pro-American and anti-Soviet. This was an approach that was to be followed by all the British governments, Labour and Conservative, throughout the existence of the Cold War between 1945 and the early 1990s.

KEY FIGURE

Richard Crossman (1907–74)

Left-wing Labour intellectual who urged the government to follow truly socialist principles.

KEY TERMS

Backbench The area in the House of Commons where MPs sit who hold no official position in the government or opposition.

Marxist The views of Karl Marx, the nineteenth-century revolutionary who believed in the inevitable destruction of capitalism by the workers.

NATO The North Atlantic Treaty Organisation, a defensive alliance formed in 1949 by Britain, France and the Benelux countries as a safeguard against Soviet expansion into Western Europe. The USA became a member by invitation.

Truman Doctrine In 1947 President Truman pledged the USA 'to support free peoples who are resisting attempted subjugation by armed minorities or by outside pressure'. Although he did not mention the Soviet Union by name, he clearly had it in mind as the aggressor. Two particular developments indicated the willingness of the Labour government to support the USA in the growing Cold War: the Berlin Airlift and the Korean War.

The Berlin Airlift 1948–9

At the end of the Second World War, the four Allied powers divided defeated Germany into four separately occupied zones. The eastern zone, which was under Soviet control, included Berlin, which itself was divided into four sectors. The descent of the 'iron curtain' (see page 10) left West Berlin in a very vulnerable position. A hundred miles within East Germany, it was accessible from the West only by the most limited routes. When the Western powers in June 1948 introduced the new German currency (the Deutschmark), already operative in West Germany, into West Berlin, the Soviet Union retaliated by imposing a blockade. This amounted to cutting off all electricity and fuel supplies to West Berlin and closing all road and canal links to West Germany. The aim of the Soviets was to oblige the Western allies to abandon their plans for a separate German state.

The USA and Britain decided to break the siege by a massive airlift of essential supplies, using the narrow air corridors; if the Soviet Union dared to interfere with the planes, it would be an act of war. In a period of 318 days the Western allies maintained the 2.5 million population of West Berlin with 1.25 million tons of food and fuel by an average of over 600 flights per day. The prodigious effort was successful. In May 1949 the Soviet Union ordered the siege to be abandoned.

The Korean War 1950–3

This was the first open conflict of the Cold War. In 1945 Korea, after being liberated from Japanese occupation, was divided between a Communist-dominated north and a US dominated-south. In 1950, northern troops, strongly supported by Chinese Communist forces, invaded the south. (Mao Zedong had led his Chinese Communist Party to power in China in 1949.) South Korea appealed to the UN Security Council for assistance. The USA immediately proposed that a UN force be sent to aid the South Koreans. The Soviet Union had temporarily withdrawn from the Security Council in protest against its refusal to recognise Mao Zedong's People's Republic of China. This enabled the US resolution to be pushed through without the USSR being present to exercise its usual veto. Large numbers of US troops under the UN flag were dispatched to Korea, where bitter fighting causing heavy casualties, particularly on the Chinese side, ensued before a stalemate truce ended the war in 1953. From the first, Britain gave the USA substantial diplomatic and military support. British casualties were 1788 servicemen killed or missing, and 2498 wounded.

Labour and Europe

After 1945 there was a significant movement among the war-weary Western European nations to avoid future conflict by agreeing on mutual co-operation and the establishing of some form of economic and political organisation to link them. This culminated in 1951 with the acceptance of the Schuman Plan. First introduced by **Robert Schuman** in 1950, this was a scheme for the European nations to pool their most productive resources – coal and steel – in a European Coal and Steel Community (ECSC). Britain deliberately refrained from being involved in this. Not having experienced hostile occupation in wartime and now a nuclear power (see page 14), it was not convinced of the need for a formal European union as a means of preserving peace. Ernest Bevin, believing that Britain's future could best be guaranteed by developing its ties with the USA and the Commonwealth, chose not to attend the preliminary talks and so did not join **the Six** in the signing of the Treaty of Paris in April 1951 which formally set up the ECSC.

When Clement Attlee was asked in the House of Commons in 1950 why his government was not considering joining the Schuman Plan, he replied unequivocally: 'We are not prepared to accept the principle that the most vital economic forces of this country should be handed over to an authority that is utterly undemocratic and is responsible to nobody.' Interestingly, the Conservatives at this time fully shared the Labour government's view on Europe. Harold Macmillan, a Conservative politician, directly echoed the view of Attlee and the trade unions when he declared, also in 1950, that Britain was not prepared to take risks with the British economy by subjecting it to the control of a foreign organisation: 'We will allow no **supranational** authority to put large masses of our people out of work in Durham, in the Midlands, in South Wales and in Scotland.'

Labour and Indian independence 1947

In 1942, Mohandas Gandhi inaugurated the 'Quit India' movement, which openly agitated against British rule. The local police and army remained largely loyal and British control was maintained, although only through increased political repression. The Labour Party, which from its beginnings had condemned colonialism as immoral, came to power in 1945 fully committed to independence for India. The problem was when and how this could be best arranged. The Muslim League, led by Mohammed Jinnah, was increasingly suspicious of the Hindus, represented by the Congress Party and its leader Pandit Nehru. A sizeable Sikh minority was equally apprehensive of being swamped in an independent India.

Eager now to settle 'the Indian problem', the government dispatched Earl Mountbatten as special envoy to negotiate Britain's final withdrawal. After much haggling, the Hindu Congress and Muslim League agreed to the Mountbatten proposals for partition:

- The subcontinent was to be divided into two distinct states: India, overwhelmingly Hindu, and Pakistan and East Pakistan, predominantly Muslim.
- The date for the formal end of British rule was brought forward from 1948 to 1947.

KEY FIGURE

**Robert Schuman
(1886–1963)**
Luxembourg-born, French statesman.

KEY TERMS

The Six France, Germany, Italy and the Benelux countries (Belgium, the Netherlands, Luxembourg).

Supranational
An organisation having power over its individual member states.

Considering the scale of the problem, this compromise was doubtless the best solution that could be arrived at, but how far it was from being a lasting one was soon revealed by the tragedy that ensued. In the same week in which the transfer of power from Britain became law, civil war broke out. Muslim–Hindu–Sikh passions spilled over into desperate acts of mutual violence.

Whatever the arguments about its timing, the granting of independence was hugely significant. It marked the point at which Britain began to dismantle its empire and set in train a process of **decolonisation** that all subsequent governments would follow.

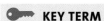 **KEY TERM**

Decolonisation
The granting of independence by Britain to the majority of its colonies and dependencies.

Britain's independent nuclear deterrent

Ernest Bevin had claimed that if Britain wished to maintain parity with the USA as a world power, it had to have its own nuclear weapon. Referring to the atom bomb, Bevin declared: 'We've got to have it here, whatever it costs, and it's got to have a bloody Union Jack on it.' Attlee fully accepted his foreign secretary's reasoning. In January 1947, he told a secret Cabinet sub-committee that Britain could not allow the USA to have a nuclear monopoly and was, therefore, embarking on a programme for the construction of its own bomb. The research programme was begun in 1947, although this information was not revealed to Parliament or the people at the time of the decision. Britain's first atomic bomb was detonated in 1952 and its hydrogen bomb in 1957.

The adoption of a nuclear weapons programme outraged the Labour left, who were offended both by the decision itself and by the way it had been arrived at in secret with no opportunity given to Labour MPs or party members to discuss the issue. The question of whether the possession of an independent nuclear deterrent was morally defensible or strategically necessary, quite apart from whether Britain could afford it, was to cause deep dissension in the Labour Party for generations.

Summary diagram: Foreign affairs

United Nations
- Britain one of the 'big five' members of the UN Security Council
- Bevin sided with USA against Soviet Union in Cold War

Europe
Government uninterested in joining European supranational body

Left–right internal party rivalry over government policy
- Pro-Americanism
- Decision to develop atomic weapons
- Support of Truman Doctrine

India
Labour fulfilled its pledge to grant Indian independence

Government proactive over:
- Berlin Airlift 1948–9. RAF joined USAAF in supplying Berlin
- Korean War 1950–3. British troops fought as part of UN forces

Independent deterrent
Britain became a nuclear power

Labour's defeat 1951

▶ *What caused Labour to lose the 1951 election?*

In 1951, forced by its financial difficulties to make savings in public expenditure, Attlee's government had imposed charges on medical prescriptions. Aneurin Bevan, the designer of the NHS (see page 5), led a number of ministers in resigning from the Cabinet in protest. Those who followed him in this became known as Bevanites. Their rebellion encouraged other Labour MPs and members of the party to voice their doubts over the direction the government had taken over economic and foreign policy. Such divisions stimulated the Conservatives and gave them ammunition to fight the 1951 election campaign. In the election itself the Conservatives gained a narrow victory.

Table 1.1 Election results in 1951

Party	Votes	Seats	Percentage of vote
Conservative	13,717,538	321	48.0
Labour	13,948,605	295	48.8
Liberal	730,556	6	2.5
Others	198,969	3	0.7

Reasons for Labour's 1951 defeat

While the Bevanite revolt certainly contributed to Labour's problems in 1951, there were a whole set of factors that cumulatively explain the election defeat:

- Attlee's government was worn down by heavy economic and financial difficulties.
- Collectively and individually, the government was exhausted after six troubled years in office.
- A number of its ministers, for example, Attlee himself and Ernest Bevin, had been working continuously in office since 1940.
- Serious divisions had developed between the right and left of the party over economic, welfare and foreign policies.
- There was resentment among some trade unions at Labour's slowness in responding to workers' demands.
- The shrinking in the 1950 election of its large majority made governing difficult and damaged party morale.
- Labour found it difficult to shake off its image as party of rationing and high taxation.
- In their call for the austerity that they claimed the times demanded, leading ministers such as the ascetic Stafford Cripps as chancellor of the exchequer did not present an attractive picture to the electorate.
- Britain's entry into the Korean War in 1950 (see page 12) made Labour's left wing unhappy; it argued that although technically British forces fought as part of a UN force, in reality the Labour government was sheepishly following the USA into a Cold War engagement.

KEY FIGURE

**Lord Woolton
(1883–1964)**

Minister of food in Churchill's wartime government. Minister of reconstruction 1943–5. Conservative Party chairman 1946–55.

Conservative strengths

There were, of course, more positive aspects to the victory of the Conservatives. Their heavy and unexpected defeat in 1945 had left them shell-shocked. However, by the late 1940s their fortunes had begun to improve. Much of this was due to the reorganisation of the party undertaken by **Lord Woolton**, the Conservative Party chairman. It was also at this time that younger Tory MPs, such as R.A. Butler, began to bring new ideas and confidence to the party. The nationalisation issue gave them a cause round which they could rally and on which they could attack the government. Conservative advantages in 1951 can be listed as:

- The Conservatives had begun to recover from the shock of the party's defeat in 1945.
- The 1950 election saw an influx of bright young Conservative MPs eager for battle against a tiring government.
- Under the direction of the dynamic Lord Woolton, 'a cheerful cove' as a colleague put it, the Conservative Party had reformed its finances and constituency organisation and was much better positioned to fight for seats and votes than in 1945.
- The government's nationalisation of iron and steel provided an easy target for opposition attacks.
- Some of the electorate were impressed by the Conservatives' projection of themselves as upholders of liberty and individualism against the deadening hand of state centralisation and collectivism.

The explanation for Attlee's losing office in 1951 is not so much Labour's decline as the Conservatives' recovery. Yet they only just squeezed into power. What benefited them was the Liberal Party's decision to put up only 109 candidates, a drop of 366 compared with 1950. The nearly 2 million ex-Liberal votes that became available went largely to the Conservatives.

The election figures for 1951 reveal one of the oddest aspects of British electoral politics. It is possible for a party to poll more votes than its opponents yet still be defeated. After six years of government Labour had in fact more than held its share of the vote. Remarkably, the 1951 election saw Labour gain the highest aggregate vote ever achieved by any party up to that point. It outnumbered the Conservatives by a quarter of a million and had nearly one per cent more of the vote. The ratio of votes to seats was as follows:

- Labour: 47,283:1
- Conservative: 42,733:1
- Liberal: 121,759:1

It was clearly not the case that Labour had been thrown out of office by a disillusioned electorate. It was more a matter on this occasion of Labour's being the victim, not the beneficiary, of the imbalance of the British electoral system.

Summary diagram: Labour's defeat 1951

Reasons for Labour's defeat	Conservative recovery
• Attlee's government was worn down by burdens • Ministers exhausted after six years in office • Trade unions' disillusion with Labour's economic policies • Tight majority after 1950 election made governing difficult • Labour gained reputation as party of rationing and taxation • Austerity measures were not popular • Left vs right internal divisions over foreign policy and NHS	• The 1950 election saw an influx of fresh and eager Conservative MPs • Conservative Party had reformed its finances and organisation • Its crusade against iron and steel nationalisation had galvanised the party • Electorate impressed by the Conservatives' resistance to state control

1951 Result a close-run thing – Labour gained more votes than Conservatives

5 The legacy of the Labour governments 1945–51

▶ *What was the legacy of the Labour governments?*

There is little doubt that the period 1945 and 1951 had been a momentous one:

- Labour had created the welfare state.
- Labour had carried into peacetime the notion of state-directed planning, which had always been one of its socialist objectives.
- In doing so, Labour had established Keynesianism as the basic British approach to economic planning (see page 6).

In its six years of government, the Labour Party had laid down the policies that were followed in all essentials by successive Conservative and Labour administrations during the next 35 years. Until Margaret Thatcher came into power in 1979 and deliberately challenged this consensus (see page 118), there was a broad level of agreement on what the major domestic and foreign issues were and how they were to be handled.

Conservative and Labour strategies were both founded on:

- economic policies based on Keynesian principles of public expenditure and state direction
- welfare policies based on the implementation of the Beveridge Report
- foreign policies based on a pro-American, anti-Soviet stance
- imperial policies based on the principle of independence for Britain's former colonies.

R.A. Butler, a leading Conservative, put the Labour reforms into historical perspective by describing them as 'the greatest social revolution in our history'. What gives particular significance to Butler's words is that the Conservative Party came in all major respects to accept that revolution. The distinctive characteristic of the policies followed by Conservative governments from 1951 was how closely they coincided with those introduced by the Attlee governments. In the words of a modern historian, Dilwyn Porter, 'Attlee's patriotic socialists gave way to Churchill's social patriots'. Just as Labour had moved to the right by accepting capitalism and the mixed economy, so the Conservatives moved to the left by accepting Keynesianism and the managed economy. While in opposition the Conservatives had opposed every nationalisation measure and many of the welfare proposals. Yet, in government themselves after 1951, they fully denationalised only one industry, steel, and built on the welfare programme which they had inherited. Labour could justly claim that it had converted the Conservative Party to the welfare state. This was perhaps one of Attlee's most enduring legacies.

Summary diagram: The legacy of the Labour governments 1945–51

Created the welfare state	**Shaped UK's foreign policy**
by implementing Beveridge Report	by adopting a pro-American, anti-Soviet approach

Established the notion of state-directed economic and social planning	**Introduced the principle of independence for Britain's colonies**
by implementing Keynesianism	by granting independence to India

Chapter summary

Possessed of a huge majority after 1945, Attlee's government set about establishing the welfare state and embarking on a nationalisation programme. These reforms were undertaken against a backdrop of chronic financial problems. Heavily in debt at the end of the Second World War and burdened with the cost of an extensive defence programme, which included the development of Britain's own atomic weapons, Attlee's administration resorted to increased taxes at home and borrowing from abroad. Yet Britain's dollar gap continued to widen. The result was two major sterling crises, which led to huge losses in the government's financial reserves. The crisis of 1949 was so severe that it caused the government to devalue the pound.

To the anger of the left of the party, Bevin followed an essentially pro-US, anti-Soviet policy which included the creation of NATO, the Berlin Airlift and the Korean War. Elsewhere, Britain gained credit for granting Indian independence but showed a less progressive attitude by declining to join Europe in the ECSC. The Labour government's financial and political problems collectively led to its defeat in the 1951 election, but not before it had established, in the face of criticism from both left and right, the main lines of domestic and foreign policy that all subsequent governments were to follow.

 Refresher questions

Use these questions to remind yourself of the key material covered in this chapter.

1 How had the Beveridge Report prepared the ground for Labour's introduction of the welfare state?

2 What were the main features of the welfare state, as introduced under Attlee?

3 According to Keynes, what role should government play in the economy?

4 How did Labour attempt to deal with the financial problems it confronted?

5 What did Labour achieve during its six years of office 1945–51?

6 Why did the Labour government commit Britain to the support of the USA in the Berlin Airlift and the Korean War?

7 What benefits did Britain derive from Marshall Aid?

8 What was the economic and social legacy of the Labour governments (1945–51)?

9 What political legacy did the Labour governments (1945–51) leave?

10 In what sense did the Attlee governments lay the basis of consensus politics in Britain?

CHAPTER 2

The Conservatives in office 1951–64

Having gained a marginal victory over Labour in 1951, the Conservatives went on to govern for the next thirteen years. During that time they continued in all major respects the policies begun by the previous government. This chapter considers how the Conservative governments of 1951–64 dealt with the issues and policies that they inherited from Labour, and examines why they remained politically dominant during this period. The major themes covered are:

★ The Churchill and Eden governments 1951–7
★ Macmillan's government 1957–63
★ Britain's relations with Europe
★ The Conservatives' last years 1963–4
★ The Labour Party 1951–64

The key debate on *page 28* of this chapter asks the question: How unpopular was Eden's Suez venture?

Key dates

1951	Conservative election victory	1960	Macmillan's 'wind of change' speech
1952	UK's first atomic bomb tested		Labour Party adopted unilateralism
1953	End of Korean War	1962	Commonwealth Immigration Act
1956	Suez affair		Cuban Missile Crisis
1957	UK's first hydrogen bomb tested	1963	Britain's application to join EEC vetoed by France
	Homicide Act		
	Rent Act		Profumo affair
1958	Life peerages introduced		Macmillan retired as prime minister
1959	Conservatives won general election	1963–4	Douglas-Home Conservative prime minister
	Britain became founding member of EFTA		

The Churchill and Eden governments 1951–7

▶ *What key developments took place under the Conservatives 1951–7?*

During the thirteen years the Conservatives were in power after 1951, there were four leaders who held office as prime minister (see Table 2.1).

Table 2.1 Conservative prime ministers 1951–64

Years in office	Prime minister
1951–5	Winston Churchill
1955–7	Anthony Eden
1957–63	Harold Macmillan
1963–4	Alec Douglas Home

Churchill's government 1951–5

Winston Churchill was 77 years old when he became prime minister for the second time. He regarded his return to office in 1951 as a belated thank you from the British people for his wartime leadership. He was now too old and frail to be much more than a figurehead. Indeed, for some months in 1953 he was out of action altogether following a stroke, although this did not become public knowledge. But he did not need to do much; he was sustained by his past reputation as a statesman. Yet his period in government between 1951 and 1955 witnessed a number of important developments.

Developments 1951–5

- Rationing was ended.
- The steel industry was denationalised.
- The Conservative Party committed itself to building 300,000 houses a year.
- The government continued with Keynesian policies.
- The accession of Queen Elizabeth II (aged 25) in 1952 ushered in a new 'Elizabethan age'.
- Britain detonated its first atomic bomb in 1952.
- The Korean War ended in 1953 (see page 12).

'Butskellism'

With hindsight, it can be seen that the key figure in Churchill's government of 1951–5 was not the prime minister but R.A. Butler, his chancellor of the exchequer.

Although Butler never became prime minister or Conservative leader, he held all the other major offices of state (chancellor of the exchequer 1951–5; home secretary 1957–62; foreign secretary 1962–4), and was a formative influence in the development of modern Conservatism, pushing the party in a progressive direction. As minister of education in Churchill's wartime coalition, Butler had been responsible for the Education Act of 1944 (see page 4). Arguably, this was to remain his greatest achievement; it indicated his concern for social issues, something that the Conservatives were to adopt as one of the planks in their political platform.

After his party's heavy defeat in 1945, Butler went on to play a central role in restoring Conservative morale during the Attlee years. He was a leading light among a group of Conservatives who had begun to study ways in which they could modernise their party's attitude and policies so as to prevent the Labour opposition, claiming a monopoly of progressive thinking. An interesting product of this was the presentation in 1947 of a document known as the Industrial Charter, in which Butler and his colleagues accepted that Britain should operate a **mixed economy** in which the trade unions would have a legitimate and respected role. It was Butler who set the pattern of economic policy that was followed throughout the period of Conservative government to 1964. His policies between 1951 and 1955 showed that he had accepted the new form of Keynesian economics adopted by the preceding Labour government (see page 6). He continued Labour's main aims of:

- trying to maintain full employment while at the same time achieving economic growth
- expanding the welfare state
- keeping to Britain's heavily committed military defence programme (which included the costly Korean War 1950–3)
- developing a nuclear weapons programme.

Butler acknowledged that the deflationary policies of the Labour government before 1951 had had beneficial effects in the short term (see page 8). The cost of British goods had dropped and exports had picked up. There was also a major uplift in the international economy in the early 1950s, largely as a result of the Marshall Plan (see page 9), which led to increased demand for British products. Yet Butler was faced, as Labour had been, with the hard fact that Britain was heavily in debt, a consequence of its wartime borrowing and continuing defence commitments. All this had produced a severe and chronic balance of payments deficit. A strong criticism made at the time and voiced by later observers was that, after 1945, British governments, Labour and Conservative, over-reached themselves. They tried to rebuild a modern competitive industrial economy but hampered themselves by taking on the huge costs involved in running a welfare state and maintaining an extensive defence programme.

Butler's ideas were seen to be so close to those of the Labour Party that his name was used to coin a particular term: 'Butskellism'. The word, first used in 1954 by the journal *The Economist*, joined together the names of Butler, seen

KEY TERM

Mixed economy A system in which the private and public sectors of the economy both operate.

as representing the Conservative left, and **Hugh Gaitskell**, regarded as a key figure on the Labour right. It suggested that the left and right wings of the two parties met in the middle to form a consensus on matters such as finance, the economy and the welfare state.

There have been suggestions that there was insufficient common ground between Butler and Gaitskell for the word to be more than a clever but inaccurate piece of terminology. However, although it is true that there were differences between Butler and Gaitskell over detail, particularly in financial matters (Gaitskell favoured high direct taxation and greater government direction, while Butler believed in economic control through the use of **interest rates**), the two men did share a noticeably similar approach in a number of key areas. Kenneth Morgan (2001), a leading authority on British political history, suggests that 'Butskellism' existed as 'a state of mind': 'It implied a coherent attempt to maintain a social consensus and to try to "set the people free" through greater liberalization, lower [indirect] taxation and decontrol, without dismantling the popular welfare and industrial fabric of the Attlee years.' What is clear is that all the succeeding administrations, Labour and Conservative, tried to govern from the centre, believing that that was the position the bulk of the electorate would support.

Eden's government 1955–7

Anthony Eden had long been regarded as the heir-apparent to Churchill as Conservative leader. However, he had had to wait far longer than he had expected since Churchill did not finally retire until 1955. The election that Eden called soon after becoming prime minister in 1955 produced an increased Conservative majority. This was to prove the only real success of his short administration.

It was Eden's fate to have lived the greater part of his political life in the shadow of Winston Churchill, the man he admired and whom he was destined to succeed, but not until 1955 when he himself was ageing and past his best. It is true that Eden had held the prestigious office of foreign secretary for ten years under Churchill. However, given that throughout that time Churchill had made foreign affairs his particular area of interest, Eden's role as foreign secretary was reduced to that of the ever-present loyal confidant and background figure.

Having had to wait so long, by the time he reached the highest office in 1955 Eden was a man in a hurry. Irritated by criticism in the Tory press that his uninspiring domestic policies lacked '**the smack of firm government**', he was determined to silence criticism by achieving success in foreign affairs, in which he felt he had a special expertise. This drew him into the ill-fated Suez affair, the event which overshadowed his years as prime minister and destroyed his reputation as a statesman.

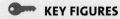

KEY FIGURES

Hugh Gaitskell (1906–63)
MP 1945–63. Minister of fuel 1947–50. Chancellor of the exchequer 1950–1. Leader of the Labour Party 1955–63.

Anthony Eden (1897–1977)
Secretary for war 1940. Foreign secretary 1940–5, 1951–5. Prime minister 1955–7.

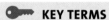

KEY TERMS

Interest rates
A mechanism for raising or lowering the cost of borrowing money by adjusting the amount of interest charged on financial loans.

The smack of firm government Eden had a habit, when emphasising a point, of smacking the palm of one hand with the back of the other. It was this image that the press used to mock his indecision.

The Suez affair 1956

Aswan Dam Intended to modernise Egypt by providing a huge supply of hydroelectric power.

Soviet bloc The satellite countries of Eastern Europe under the domination of the USSR, for example, Poland, Hungary and Czechoslovakia.

French Algeria A French colony, the majority of whose indigenous Arab population supported the Algerian independence movement. French forces became involved in a bitter struggle (1954–62) against Algerian nationalists.

Veto Each individual member of the UN Security Council had the right to block the collective decisions of the others.

Israelis The people of Israel, which became a sovereign state in 1948, taking most of Palestine.

Colonel Nasser, the president of Egypt since 1952, had at first been on good terms with the West. He had been promised US and British loans for the construction of the **Aswan Dam** on the upper Nile river, a project on which he had staked his own and his country's future. However, when the USA learned that Nasser had also approached the **Soviet bloc** countries for aid, it withdrew its original offer. In July 1956 Nasser, in desperation, announced the nationalisation of the Suez Canal as a means of raising the necessary finance. Foreign ships would have to pay to pass through what was now an Egyptian waterway.

Eden declared that such a man as Nasser could not be allowed 'to leave his thumb on Britain's windpipe', a reference to the threat to the essential oil supplies that came to Britain from the Middle East through the Canal. He began to plan ways to bring Nasser down. The French, long resentful of Egypt's support of Arab nationalists in **French Algeria**, were very willing to join the British in anti-Nasser moves. Eden also hoped that the Americans would favour such a policy; he had been led to believe that the USA would give at least moral backing to Anglo-French attempts to free the Canal. The Americans did, indeed, join Britain and France in seeking to apply pressure to Egypt by the creation of a Canal Users' Association.

Nasser, however, despite the international line-up against him, refused to budge. Britain and France then referred the issue to the UN Security Council. This proved fruitless, since the Soviet Union used its **veto** to block proposals in the Council to have Egypt condemned internationally. To Eden, all this confirmed his belief that only force could shift Nasser. Eden began secret discussions with the French and the **Israelis**, who were eager to launch a major strike against Egypt, which had become a major base for terror attacks on Israel. British–French–Israeli plans were prepared for a combined military invasion of Egypt. The strategy, finalised in mid-October 1956, was that the Israelis would attack Egypt across Sinai. Britain and France, after allowing sufficient time for the Israelis to reach the Canal, would then mount a joint assault on the Canal region from the north, under the pretence of forcing Egypt and Israel to observe a ceasefire. The plan was accepted by Eden's Cabinet. On 29 October 1956, the Israelis duly attacked across the Gaza Strip; on 30 October the Anglo-French ultimatum was delivered and on the following day the two European allies began their invasion of Egypt.

The UN immediately entered into an emergency debate in which the Americans, infuriated by Eden's having totally ignored them, led the condemnation of Israel and its two allies. Over the special telephone hotline that linked the US president and British prime minister, Eisenhower swore at Eden in four-letter expletives. In a particular irony, Britain, deprived of US backing, used its veto for the first time to defeat a UN resolution demanding an immediate ceasefire.

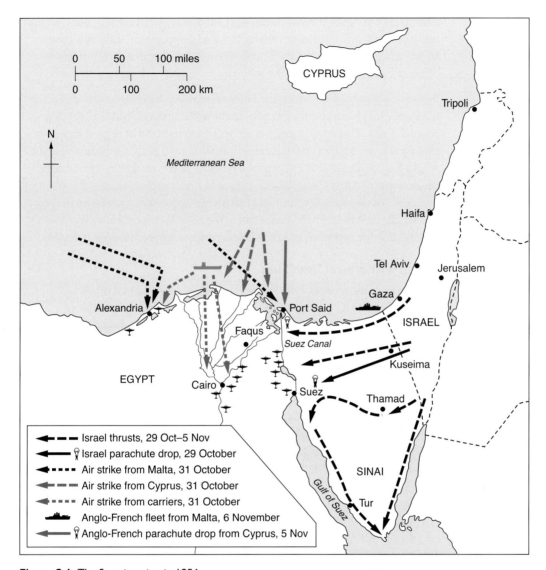

Figure 2.1 The Suez invasion in 1956.

Soviet involvement

Besides resentment at not being informed of Britain's plans, what angered the Americans was that in the Cold War atmosphere of the day, Eden's actions threatened to allow the Soviet Union to seize the initiative. As it happened, the USSR had been initially distracted by its own problems arising from the Hungarian crisis, which coincided with the Egyptian affair. After Stalin's death in 1953, the Soviet Union appeared to allow greater freedom to its **satellites**. However, when, in October 1956, Hungary pushed too hard for independence, the new Soviet leader, Nikita Khrushchev, sent in tanks to occupy Budapest, the Hungarian capital. The Hungarians made desperate appeals for Western

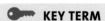 **KEY TERM**

Satellites Smaller states that are dependent on a larger state for economic, diplomatic and military assistance, often in alliance – in this case, the Eastern European states under Soviet control.

assistance, but, while the West expressed outrage at Soviet actions, intervention was not seriously considered. The military and geographical difficulties were simply too great. Moreover, the British–French–Israeli attack on Egypt made it difficult for the West to adopt the moral high ground over matters of invasion.

By the first week of November, the Hungarian rising had been crushed and the USA's refusal to accept the legitimacy of the allied invasion had become clear beyond doubt. This encouraged the Soviet Union to make its biggest move yet over Egypt. On 5 November it issued a formal note to Britain. Condemning the Anglo-French invasion of Egypt as the bullying of the weaker by the stronger, the note warned that the USSR was prepared to use rockets against the Western invaders: 'We are fully determined to crush the aggressors and restore peace in the Middle East through the use of force. We hope at this critical moment you will display due prudence and draw the corresponding conclusions from this.'

British withdrawal from Suez

The day after the receipt of the Soviet note, Eden gave way and Britain accepted the UN demand for disengagement. But while the possibility of Soviet intervention undoubtedly helped concentrate Eden's mind, the still more pressing reasons for his ordering a withdrawal from Suez were the following:

- the strength of opposition among the British people; Gaitskell and Bevan made withering attacks on what they described as Eden's 'mad venture'
- the fury of Eisenhower and the Americans at not being consulted
- Britain's failure to gain international backing
- condemnation of Britain at the UN
- the reluctance of all but a few of the Commonwealth countries to support Britain
- a catastrophic fall in Britain's currency reserves caused by large withdrawals of deposits by international investors. Britain faced the threat of economic collapse.

Eden's personal role

Historians, reflecting on the Suez crisis, have made much of the role played personally by Anthony Eden. It has been suggested that the crisis took the form it did largely because of his particular perception of the problem and how it might be solved. Eden had a deep distaste for Nasser, whom he saw in the mould of the **dictators** of the 1930s, with whom he had dealt as foreign secretary between 1935 and 1938. This led him to put the worst construction on the Egyptian leader's actions. Anxious for the maintenance of essential oil supplies, Eden suspected that beneath Nasser's campaign to modernise Egypt lay an essentially anti-British motive. He concluded that in the end it might be that Nasser would have to be stopped by military force. Mistaking the initial Western disapproval of the Egyptian seizure of the Canal as implying support for any moves he might initiate, Eden had colluded with France and Israel for a pretext to invade Egypt and topple Nasser.

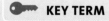 **KEY TERM**

Dictators Chiefly Adolf Hitler (German leader 1933–45) and Benito Mussolini (Italian leader 1922–43).

Already on dangerous ground, Eden did not help his cause by the manner and style in which he acted. Tetchy and short-tempered, he did not try to hide his distaste for those who disagreed with him. This mattered especially in his dealings with the USA, the ally that the British government most needed at this critical juncture. Eden's undisguised annoyance with Eisenhower was hardly likely to win the Americans over to his point of view. A particular blindness of Eden's was his failure to appreciate that with a presidential election imminent in the USA, the US government was simply not prepared to become embroiled in a costly, military venture that recalled old-style **imperialism**.

It has also to be said that Eden's chronic poor health, which deteriorated further during the crisis, weakened his judgement. The strain of Suez wore him out. J.P. Mallalieu, a Labour MP, gave a striking description of the physical and mental state to which Eden had been reduced (see Source A).

SOURCE A

From Paul Johnson, *The Suez War*, MacGibbon & Kee, 1957, p. 126.

The Prime Minister sprawled on the front bench, head thrown back and mouth agape. His eyes, inflamed with sleeplessness, stared into vacancies beyond the roof except when they switched with meaningless intensity to the face of the clock, probed it for a few seconds, then rose again in vacancy. His hands twitched at his horn-rimmed spectacles or mopped themselves in a handkerchief, but were never still. The face was grey except where black-ringed caverns surrounded the dying embers of his eyes. The whole personality, if not prostrated seemed completely withdrawn … the overwhelming burden of taking on his own account, decisions which have come near to breaking the Anglo-American alliance and the Commonwealth have now made him incapable of distinguishing between success or failure as it has made him incapable of distinguishing between truth and lies.

Eden's wife, Clarissa, recorded that during the weeks of the crisis it felt as if the Suez Canal was flowing furiously through her drawing room. Within weeks of the crisis Eden stepped down as prime minister. The official reason was ill-health and it was certainly true that he was seriously unwell, but the Suez disaster had shattered his standing at home and abroad. Even if he had been fully fit, he could not have carried on as head of government.

Significance of the Suez affair for Britain

It is important to note that Britain was not defeated militarily in Egypt. Indeed, British forces were withdrawn from Suez when they were on the verge of successfully completing their mission. That was why the Israelis were so bitter with the British for leaving the job half done. The truth was that Britain's withdrawal was a failure not of military resolve but of political will. Fearing the consequences of being internationally isolated, Eden's nerve broke and he accepted that Britain could no longer continue with a policy that the world

KEY TERM

Imperialism
The nineteenth-century takeover by separate European powers, such as Britain and France, of many parts of Africa and Asia.

What image of the strain Eden was under is presented in Source A?

condemned. It was an admission that in the post-war world Britain could not act alone. The realisation of this led a number of people in both major political parties to consider whether Britain should consider closer union with Europe (see page 50).

The Suez crisis was a landmark in Britain's foreign policy. In attacking Egypt, Britain had attempted to act independently of NATO and the USA, without consulting the Commonwealth, and in disregard of the UN. The international and domestic protests that the Suez venture aroused meant that it was the last occasion Britain would attempt such independent action. While there would be occasions in the future when Britain would use armed force unilaterally, as for example over the Falklands (see page 122), this would only be when it considered that its own sovereign territory had been occupied by a hostile power.

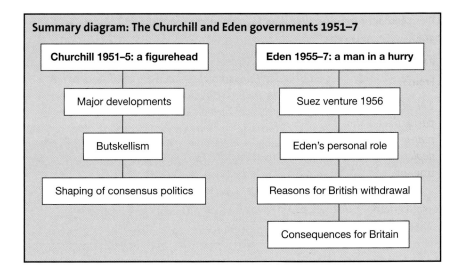

Summary diagram: The Churchill and Eden governments 1951–7

- **Churchill 1951–5: a figurehead**
  - Major developments
  - Butskellism
  - Shaping of consensus politics

- **Eden 1955–7: a man in a hurry**
  - Suez venture 1956
  - Eden's personal role
  - Reasons for British withdrawal
  - Consequences for Britain

② Key debate

▶ *How unpopular was Eden's Suez venture?*

So vociferous was the anti-war campaign that it is easy to forget that Eden may well have had majority support among the British people. This has led writers then and since to debate the key question, 'How unpopular was Eden's Suez venture?'

The tone was set in a sense by the anti-war rally of 4 November 1956 in London's Trafalgar Square, at which the principal speaker was Aneurin Bevan. Addressing the 30,000 protesters in passionate terms, Bevan accused the government of blackening the name of Britain: 'They have offended against every principle of decency and there is only one way in which they can even begin to restore their tarnished reputation and that is to get out! Get out! Get out!' Powerful rhetoric though this was, it did not necessarily reflect public opinion. British historian Barry Turner later wrote about the situation.

EXTRACT 1

From Barry Turner, *Suez 1956*, Hodder & Stoughton, 2006, p. 354.

The public reaction to press comment highlighted the divisions within the country. But there was no doubt that Eden still commanded strong support from a sizable minority, maybe even a majority, of voters who thought that it was about time that the upset Arabs should be taught a lesson. The Observer *and* Guardian *lost readers; so too did the* News Chronicle, *a liberal newspaper that was soon to fold as a result of falling circulation.*

The Conservative novelist and essayist, A.N. Wilson, suggested that those who remained silent at the time may have been for Eden rather than against him.

EXTRACT 2

From A.N. Wilson, *Our Times*, Hutchinson, 2008, p. 66.

The bulk of the press, the Labour Party and that equally influential left-leaning party, the London dinner party, were all against Suez together with the rent-a-mob of poets, dons, clergy and ankle-socked female graduates who deplored British action, but they did not necessarily constitute the majority of unexpressed public opinion.

It was certainly true that the left-wing press assumed that the British people were overwhelmingly against Britain's attack, yet Eden himself was able to claim that the correspondence he received swung from eight to one against his Egyptian intervention to four to one in favour of it by the time of the ceasefire. However, Robert Blake, the leading analyst of the Conservative Party, while accepting that it was possible to exaggerate the degree of opposition to Eden, cautioned that neither should the degree of support be overstated.

EXTRACT 3

From Robert Blake, *The Conservative Party from Peel to Major*, Arrow Books, 1998, p. 279.

The 'nation' as far as judgement can be made about that intangible quality, felt bewildered rather than humiliated. It is not true, as sometimes said, that public opinion was strongly pro-Suez, but it was not against. Polls on 11 November and 2 December 1956 recorded slightly over 50 per cent in favour of Eden's policy. The moral issue cut little ice. Gaitskell, Attlee's successor, did himself harm by pressing it.

A balanced perspective of the question was offered by the left-leaning historian Dilwyn Porter.

EXTRACT 4

From Dilwyn Porter, *From Blitz to Blair*, Phoenix, 1997, p. 115.

For some British people [the Suez affair] was a traumatic experience, mercifully short lived, which challenged widely held assumptions about the nation to which they belonged. Public opinion, though confused, had rallied to Eden at the height of the crisis, responding not just to headlines of the 'EDEN GETS TOUGH' and IT'S GREAT BRITAIN AGAIN!' variety, but to deeply rooted patriotic instincts and a sense of Britain's rightful place in the world.

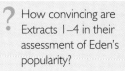

? How convincing are Extracts 1–4 in their assessment of Eden's popularity?

 ## 3 Macmillan's government 1957–63

▶ *In what sense did Macmillan follow 'a middle way?'*

Eden was followed as prime minister not by R.A. Butler, who, until Suez, had been generally regarded as the likely successor, but by Harold Macmillan. Although an outstanding figure in the Conservative Party, Butler had a diffident and detached manner that made him reluctant to engage in the in-fighting that party politics requires. Nor had he impressed when he had stood in for Eden during the Suez crisis. Macmillan, in contrast, had a much sharper political sense. Although he had firmly supported Eden over Suez, he came out of the escapade relatively unscathed. As chancellor of the exchequer, he made a rallying call to the Cabinet on 3 January 1957. Admitting that the military operation had swollen Britain's debts by £564 million, he told his colleagues that they must learn lessons from Suez but not be overwhelmed by it: 'The Suez operation has been a tactical defeat. It is our task to ensure that, like the retreat from **Mons and Dunkirk**, it should prove the prelude to strategic victory.'

 **KEY TERM**

Mons and Dunkirk
Occasions in the First and Second World Wars when British forces recovered from initial defeats to win the final military struggle.

Macmillan's rousing speech undoubtedly helped his bid for leadership. A week later he became prime minister. At this time the Conservative Party obtained opinions from MPs and party workers as to who should be appointed prime minister. It was not a democratic system and both Macmillan and his successor in 1963, Sir Alec Douglas Home (see page 55), 'emerged' as premiers as a result of this informal and secretive system.

In forming his first Cabinet in 1957, Macmillan made Butler his home secretary. This proved an important move. At the Home Office, Butler took a basically liberal approach towards legal and social issues, placing the emphasis in penal matters on reform rather than punishment. A significant example was the introduction of the Homicide Act in 1957, which effectively ended the death

Harold Macmillan

1894	Born into the Macmillan publishing family
1924	Elected as Conservative MP
1938	Published *The Middle Way*
1940–2	Minister of supply
1942–5	Minister with special responsibility for the war in North Africa
1951–4	Minister for housing and local government
1954–5	Minister of defence
1955	Foreign secretary
1955–7	Chancellor of the exchequer
1957–63	Prime minister and leader of the Conservative Party
1986	Died

Macmillan's appearance was that of a typical English gentleman. Yet by birth he was half Scottish, half American. He had served gallantly in the First World War, an experience which gave him a particular respect for the working classes. This was deepened by his witnessing, as MP for a Durham constituency, the grim effects of the depression in the north-east of England. He expressed his unorthodox Conservatism in 1938 in his book, *The Middle Way*, which may be regarded as an early appeal for consensus politics. He argued for the acceptance of Keynesianism and pressed the case

for extending state direction of a broad range of services. Having held key posts in Churchill's governments, he became prime minister in 1957. Although he was chancellor of the exchequer at the time of the Suez affair in 1956, Macmillan was not generally regarded as being involved in the debacle. This left him well placed to heal the wounds in the party. He was the first prime minister to commit Britain to entering what eventually became the European Union and was an outspoken supporter of independence for African colonies. He proved himself a keen 'Cold Warrior' by supporting the USA in its conflicts with the Soviet Union, notably in 1962 when he stood by President Kennedy during the **Cuban Missile Crisis**.

Despite his seemingly relaxed style, Macmillan worked extremely hard and could be ruthless on occasion: in 1962 in the '**Night of the Long Knives**' he dismissed half his Cabinet. Despite considerable unhappiness in his private life, he maintained an 'unflappable' air in public. He took particular delight in the satirists' portrayal of him as 'Supermac', originally intended as an ironic reference to his government's uncertain economic performance. His own comment on this was famously that under Conservatism Britain had 'never had it so good'.

penalty except for certain rare categories of murder. Butler's liberal stance as home secretary hinted strongly that the Conservative Party under Macmillan was prepared to modify its traditional social attitudes. Its opponents would find it harder to dismiss it simply as a party of reactionaries. Butler's liberal attitude was one on which subsequent home secretaries, such as Labour's Roy Jenkins, would build (see page 72), providing another example of the consensus that applied to so many areas of British politics and government in the second half of the twentieth century.

Conservative economic policy 1957–64

Although Britain had picked up economically in the Churchill and Eden years, allowing the ending of rationing, its recovery was not as pronounced as had been hoped. Compared with developments in Europe and the USA, the British economy appeared sluggish. Nevertheless, Macmillan's chancellors of the exchequer after 1957 made no serious attempt to change Britain's economic and financial strategies. They continued Butler's main lines of policy:

 KEY TERMS

Cuban Missile Crisis
In October 1962 the USA, having discovered that Soviet nuclear missiles were being installed on the island of Cuba, ordered their removal. After days of acute tension, the USSR gave way and ordered their dismantling and withdrawal.

Night of the Long Knives
A deliberate overdramatic phrase used by the press to compare Macmillan's Cabinet reshuffle with an episode in Nazi Germany in 1934 in which Hitler had massacred a number of his leading supporters.

- to operate a mixed economy
- to follow a loose form of Keynesianism.

The aim of these policies was to avoid the extremes of inflation and deflation by a series of adjustments to meet particular problems as they came along. If inflation (seen in Britain, in the second half of the twentieth century, as the major threat to economic stability) rose too quickly, measures to slow it down were introduced. These invariably involved raising interest rates to discourage borrowing and increasing import controls to limit purchases from abroad, with the aim of reducing the trade gap. The annual budgets were an important part of

Macmillan's chancellors of the exchequer

- Peter Thorneycroft 1957–8
- Derick Heathcote-Amory 1958–60
- Selwyn Lloyd 1960–2
- Reginald Maudling 1962–4

SOURCE B

? Why, despite its mocking intention, did the cartoon in Source B become one of Macmillan's favourites?

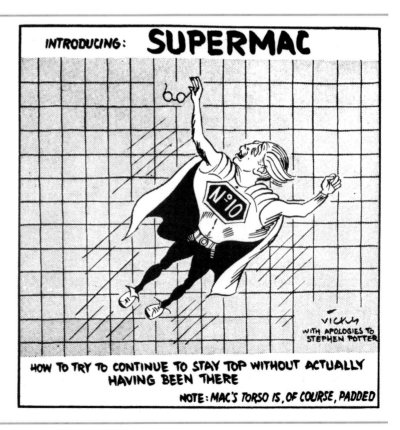

'Introducing Supermac', published in the *Evening Standard* newspaper, 6 November 1958. Macmillan as Superman, the popular comic-book hero for whom nothing was impossible. Macmillan became the butt of the political and social satirists who flourished in the late 1950s and 1960s in the press and in the theatre, and in particular in the BBC programme *That Was The Week That Was*.

the mechanism. As a check on overspending or too rapid a rise in wages, taxes might be increased. Treasury officials spoke of such moves as preventing the economy from 'overheating'.

Alternatively, if there was a fall in demand for goods, which meant difficulties for manufacturers and retailers, the chancellor of the exchequer of the day might introduce 'a give-away' budget in which taxes and interest rates were lowered. It was hoped that this Keynesian approach would encourage more spending and thus result in a demand-led recovery.

Budget politics

A common criticism from both parties when in opposition was that budgets were too often used as short-term measures to buy votes in general elections. An interesting illustration of vote-catching were the Conservative budgets of the late 1950s and early 1960s. In his 1959 budget, Derick Heathcoat-Amory made an effort to boost support for the government in the forthcoming election by introducing a range of tax cuts. This was at a time when the prevailing high inflation suggested that financial restraint would have been more appropriate. The result was increased consumer spending, which led to still higher inflation and a wider trade gap. Faced with this, Heathcoat-Amory changed direction and adopted deflationary measures which included tax and interest-rate rises, cuts in public spending, and an attempt to put a limit on wage increases.

Successive Conservative chancellors continued with these restrictive measures until the 1964 election loomed. To regain lost popularity, Macmillan's government in 1963 returned to an expansionist budgetary policy; taxes and interests rates were again lowered. The consequence was another boom in consumer spending. Since the sudden demand for goods could not be met from British stocks there was a sharp increase in the import of foreign manufactures. The net result was that by the end of 1964 Britain had a balance of payments deficit of over £800 million.

'Stop–go'

According to some observers, such events showed that Britain lacked a genuine economic strategy. The series of adjustments made by governments did not really add up to an integrated plan. Policy lagged behind events; it did not direct them. This is what led to the coining of the terms 'stop–go' and 'stagflation' to denote the failure of governments to develop policies that encouraged a consistently performing economy. The 'stop' part of the term described the situation arising when consumption and prices rose too quickly, which the government responded to by putting on the 'brake' through increased taxation and raised interest rates, thus making it more difficult to borrow money. The 'go' part referred to the situation where production and exports declined, prompting the government to press the 'accelerator' by cutting taxes and lowering interest rates, thus making it easier to borrow money.

GDP Gross domestic product: the annual total value of goods produced and services provided.

R&D Research and development in the economic sphere.

Table 2.2 GDP growth rate 1951–64

State	Percentage growth
Italy	5.6
West Germany	5.1
France	4.3
UK	2.3

Table 2.3 Relative percentage of R&D spent on defence 1963–4

State	R&D percentage
Japan	0.9
Netherlands	1.9
Italy	2.6
West Germany	10.8
France	26.2
UK	34.5
USA	40.6

❓ According to Source C, what are Macmillan's main concerns about the British economy?

Stagflation

'Stagflation' was a compound word of stagnation and inflation. It referred to the situation in which industry declined but inflation still persisted, with the result that the economy suffered the worst of both worlds. All this pointed to the difficulty of managing a modern economy, which is always vulnerable to the play of unforeseeable circumstances. When Harold Macmillan was asked by a reporter what he regarded as the most difficult feature of government planning, he replied 'events, dear boy, events'.

Britain's industrial growth rate

Britain's economic record cannot be taken in isolation. A principal worry was that Britain was performing poorly in comparison with its chief international competitors. Its **GDP** growth rate was the lowest in Western Europe.

The figures did not mean that Britain was less productive or less efficient than those other countries in Table 2.2. The major reason for Britain's relatively weak performance was heavy defence expenditure. It still maintained costly military and naval bases around the world and it ran an expensive nuclear arms development programme. None of the other countries listed in the table carried the burdens that Britain did. By 1964, the final year of the Conservative government, Britain was spending £1.7 billion on defence, ten per cent of its GDP. Compared with its major industrial competitors, Britain was committing an extraordinary proportion of its **R&D** investment to defence. Only the USA spent more.

Living standards under the Conservatives: consumerism

In July 1957, Harold Macmillan memorably stated that the British people had 'never had it so good'. Although the assertion was challenged by his opponents, it has come to be regarded as a representative description of the achievements of the Conservative governments between 1951 and 1964. What has sometimes been overlooked is that in the speech Macmillan also sounded a note of warning:

SOURCE C

From Macmillan's speech in July 1957, quoted in D. Kavanagh and P. Morris, *Consensus Politics from Attlee to Thatcher*, Oxford University Press, 1989, p. 40.

Let's be frank about it: most of our people have never had it so good. Go around the country, go to the industrial towns, go to the farms, and you will see a state of prosperity, such as we have never seen in my lifetime – nor indeed in the history of the country. [However] what is beginning to worry some of us is 'Is it too good to be true?' or perhaps I should say 'Is it too good to last?' For midst all this prosperity, there is one problem that has troubled us – in one way or another since the war. It's the problem of rising prices. Our constant concern today is – can prices be steadied while at the same time we maintain full employment in the expanding economy? Can we control inflation? This is the problem of our time.

Wages

Despite periods of serious hardship for some of the population in Britain under the Conservatives, the broad picture was one of a continuous rise in living standards. The various financial problems that confronted the nation did not prevent the great majority of the population from gaining in material prosperity. This is an area where figures speak loudest. Wages rose ahead of prices. One example of the overall improvement in working people's income is that the average weekly wage of the adult male worker more than doubled from £8 and 6 shillings (£8.30) in 1951 to £18 and 7 shillings (£18.35) in 1964. It was not simply that wages increased in overall amount. The key fact was a growth in **real wages**; income kept ahead of prices. People were able to buy more with their money. This meant that although inflation continued to climb throughout the period it never overtook the increase in real wages.

Financial credit (hire purchase)

Another vital factor in the raising of living standards was the greater availability of credit, a facility provided by banks and finance companies that enabled people to borrow much larger sums of money than they could obtain by saving. With loan repayment spread out over a number of years on 'easy terms', usually a relatively small amount each month, people were able to buy items they previously could not have afforded. Access to credit (also known as 'hire purchase') enabled consumers to buy an unprecedented range of manufactured goods. A consumer boom began. In the period 1950–65 the sales of private cars nearly quadrupled from 1.5 million to 5.5 million. In addition, foreign holidays, clothing and **mod cons** came within the reach of ordinary people in ways that would have been impossible without the existence of credit.

Housing

Perhaps the most impressive feature of the consumer boom was the growth in house buying. Housing had been a proud claim of Attlee's government, which had built over 600,000 homes by 1951. The Conservatives tried to better the Labour record. To great acclaim at the 1950 Conservative conference, the party leaders had responded to emotional pleas from the floor by committing themselves to build 300,000 houses annually. Macmillan was instrumental in fulfilling that pledge. As housing minister between 1951 and 1954, he achieved the target of 300,000 new homes each year. Although the pace slowed considerably after that, the Conservatives' period of office between 1951 and 1964 witnessed the building of 1.7 million homes, 60 per cent of those being private dwellings.

Table 2.4 Growth in real wages 1951–64 (calculated as an average hourly rate percentage increase for each individual worker)

Period	Growth (%)
1951–5	2.2
1955–60	2.9
1960–4	4.0

 KEY TERMS

Real wages The purchasing power of earnings when set against prices. When prices are high money will buy less; when prices are low the same amount of money will buy more.

Mod cons Short for modern conveniences; for example, central heating, and household accessories such as vacuum cleaners, refrigerators and washing machines.

It was during his own administration in 1957 that Macmillan presided over the introduction of the Rent Act which, by abolishing rent control, put 6 million properties on the market. The downside of this was that rents rose considerably, making it difficult for tenants at the lower end of the scale to afford leases. But that was the trade-off Macmillan felt had to be made in order to stimulate the rented property market. What made this housing explosion possible was the relative ease with which money could be borrowed and repaid over long periods of time. Encouraged by the government, banks and building societies advanced the necessary capital in the form of mortgages that allowed increasing numbers to own their own homes. This created the conditions for what the Conservatives called a **property-owning democracy**. It was such developments that Harold Macmillan had in mind when he declared in 1957 that the British people had 'never had it so good'.

There is no doubt that Macmillan was being politically astute in calling attention to the material improvement in people's lives and implying that it was largely the result of Conservative policies. Yet although Macmillan was always an optimist on the surface, remarking on one occasion that if you weren't optimistic you might as well be dead, he did harbour fears. In the same 'never had it so good' speech of 1957 (Source C, page 35), he had been careful to warn that the prosperity could be threatened by inflation. It was his concern that the affluent times might not last that drew him towards the idea that Britain should consider joining the European Common Market (see page 50).

Unemployment

As Macmillan was well aware, despite the evident improvement in the material well-being of so many in the population, problems remained. Although the Conservatives willingly inherited the Labour Party's commitment to full employment as a basic economic aim, achieving this proved much more difficult. Table 2.5 shows that the lowest annual figure for joblessness was well over a quarter of a million in the mid-1950s, rose rapidly in the late 1950s and, after falling in the early 1960s, reached a high point in Macmillan's final year in government. The persistence of high unemployment levels cast doubt on just how realistic it was to claim that the people had 'never had it so good'.

Table 2.5 Number of workers unemployed in Britain

Year	Number	Year	Number
1951	367,000	1958	536,000
1952	468,000	1959	621,000
1953	452,000	1960	461,000
1954	387,000	1961	419,000
1955	298,000	1962	566,000
1956	297,000	1963	878,000
1957	383,000	1964	501,000

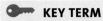

KEY TERM

Property-owning democracy A society in which people are encouraged to become homeowners, on the principle that the ownership of property is a necessary part of democracy.

Education

Controversy between the major parties over state schooling rumbled on throughout the second half of the twentieth century. The central disagreement was between those who wished to end separate three-tier schooling (see page 4) altogether and replace it with a system of comprehensive schools, and those who defended the grammar schools since they were proving successful in providing education for working-class children.

Yet, while it is true many Conservatives, particularly at local level where the fate of particular schools was being decided, strongly opposed the spread of comprehensives, the Conservative Party in its official policy came to accept that this form of schooling best fitted British needs. Edward Boyle, minister of education from 1962 to 1964, was one of the younger Conservatives under Macmillan who urged the abolition of the eleven plus exam and the provision of better education for all children. The following list shows that the Conservatives, far from being a barrier to the spread of comprehensive schools, were in office when the first purpose-built schools appeared:

- Ysgol Gyfun Llangefni in Anglesey, north Wales, 1954
- Kidbrooke School in south London, 1954
- Sandfields School in Wales, 1958
- Risinghill School in Islington, north London, 1960.

Main arguments for the comprehensive system

- Selective education meant the undervaluing of the majority of children who did not meet the artificial standard of selection imposed.
- The selection process, such as the eleven plus exam, was psychologically dubious and unreliable.
- Selection was socially divisive, since it operated a system which separated groups of children from each other.
- Under selection, the greater share of public money went to the top tier of schools, leaving the lower tiers impoverished.
- Children in the lowers tiers were liable to be regarded as failures.
- The record showed that bright pupils performed as well academically in comprehensive schools as in grammars.

Main arguments against the comprehensive system

- In practice, comprehensive schools had denied able children from disadvantaged backgrounds the chance to benefit from a specialist school education fitted to their needs.
- Since the quality of schools depended on the area in which they were situated, there was no alternative in a deprived area to a poor comprehensive now that grammar schools were being abolished.
- Wealthy parents had the choice of moving to a better area so that their children could go to a better comprehensive school. Poorer parents had no such choice. The result was not, therefore, greater educational fairness and opportunity but less. Selection by ability had been replaced by selection according to parental income.
- Most comprehensive schools streamed their pupils or put them into 'sets' according to academic attainment, thus, in practice, preserving the differentiation of children into distinct types.

The Conservatives' conversion, although grudging, was another sign of how a consensus had developed among the British political parties. A single statistic illustrated this: in the second half of the twentieth century more comprehensive schools were built under Conservatives than under Labour. One of the key developments in Boyle's time was the publication of the Robbins Report in 1963, which is best seen as an argument for extending the comprehensive principle into higher education.

> ## Main recommendations of the Robbins Report 1963
>
> - Expansion of the existing universities.
> - Emphasis to be given to scientific education.
> - The twelve existing colleges of advanced technology (CATs) to be upgraded to university status.
> - Larger grants to be provided so that no potential students would be deterred by lack of income.

Class

One of the allegations made by defenders of the grammar schools was that the advocates of a comprehensive system were not really concerned about education but were using the schools issue to fight a class war, trying to impose equality by social engineering. However, while it was still customary to regard Britain as a class-conscious if not a class-ridden society, things were changing. Class was ceasing to matter as much as it did:

- The Second World War had weakened class divisions. The national war effort and the common experience of dangers, like the **Blitz**, and hardships, like rationing, had made many people realise how artificial class divisions were. Churchill had recognised that important social shifts were occurring. He described the working-class trade unions as having become 'an estate of the realm'.
- The creation of the welfare state under Attlee and its acceptance by the Conservatives after 1951 were an acknowledgement that the well-being of the whole population was a matter of national concern.
- The growing affluence of Britain in the 1950 and 1960s, the spread of wealth across a much broader section of the population and the consequent rise in living standards all had the effect of blurring class distinctions.

Here it is important to stress that the term 'class' does not have a fixed meaning. As Arthur Marwick, one of Britain's distinguished social historians, writing in the early 2000s, pointed out, class does not belong in 'the same category as the facts of geography, demography and economics'. The term class should not be given the rigid meaning that **Marx** gave it: 'Classes', Marwick said, 'evolve and change as circumstances change'. This does not prevent our using the word in a descriptive sense; class can be helpfully applied to broad groups

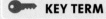

KEY TERM

Blitz The German aerial bombing of London and other British cities, which was at its most intense between September 1940 and May 1941.

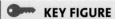

KEY FIGURE

Karl Marx (1818–83)
Influential German revolutionary who taught that all history was determined by class war, which would climax with the final victory of the workers (the proletariat) over the capitalists (the bourgeoisie).

which experience common social and economic change. Most people in mid-twentieth-century Britain would have accepted that there were three major social groups or classes:

- upper classes, drawn from the traditional landed aristocracy and gentry
- middle classes, who worked in trade or the professions
- working classes, who worked for wages in industry or on the land.

These were not exact definitions, of course; there were grades within each class, particularly the middle class. It was also increasingly possible to move from one class to another. It was this mobility that became evident in the Macmillan years.

The Establishment

Another category that deserves mention was 'the Establishment'. This term, which came into common use in the 1960s, referred not to a specific social class but to those individuals or groups whose wealth, political, educational or religious connections, intellectual status or control of the media gave them the means to influence government policy and shape public opinion and attitudes. Collectively, they could be said to form an elite which was all the more powerful because it was not precisely defined and, therefore, could not easily be held to account. Elections and changes of government might alter some of the personnel belonging to the Establishment, but did not change its character as a body that was independent of direct political control. An appropriate colloquial definition for the Establishment might be the 'old boy network' (see page 56).

Social mobility

An important claim made by R.A. Butler was that modern Conservatism, far from perpetuating class differences in Britain, was actually ending them: 'We have developed instead an *affluent*, open and democratic *society*, in which the class escalators are continually moving and in which people are divided not so much between "haves" and "have-nots" as between "haves" and "have-mores".' The speech in 1960 in which he used those words clearly complemented Macmillan's 'never had it so good' speech three years earlier. Between them, the two speakers had defined the aim of the Conservative government as being the development of a socially mobile society which left its individual members free through their own efforts to enjoy the fruits of the nation's increasing wealth.

The key to the social shift and the blurring of class divisions was the availability of financial credit (see page 35). In a pre-credit age, only the rich had been able to afford to buy ostentatiously. But, now that borrowing and purchasing on credit were possible for nearly everybody, having possessions was no longer a clear guide to social status. Since people on a regular wage could buy things on hire purchase, there was an increase in the number of consumers and a consequent increase in production to meet their demands. Such consumerism was the great equaliser in class terms. Indeed, a process developed in which working-class incomes often exceeded lower middle-class ones. Yet it was still possible for lower middle-class people living in genteel poverty to regard themselves as in some way socially superior to, and more respectable than, car workers or plumbers who were earning much more than they were. This suggests that in Britain class was as much an attitude of mind as of possessions and wealth.

Responses to the Conservatives' social and economic policies

Critics of the Conservative economic record stressed that, although Britain had indeed become more affluent between 1951 and 1964, the gap between rich and poor had widened in that same period. Supporters of Macmillan's policies accepted the truth of this, but argued that wealth and poverty were relative terms. The material quality of life was improving for nearly everybody. Some observers compared the process to a cruise ship going through a set of locks. The first-class passengers keep their superior position in the higher decks but the less well-off in the lower decks also rise as the vessel goes up. The reality was that the great majority of those designated poor in Britain now had access to resources that their forebears could not even have imagined.

Those unimpressed by this argument faulted the Conservatives on the following points:

- The Conservative governments had not developed coherent economic policies but had simply employed 'stop–go' tactics to prevent the economy swinging too wildly between deflation and inflation.
- Apart from a wish to keep the value of the pound sterling, they had no structured financial strategy. They had used budgets and tax adjustments not in a responsible way but as a technique for buying votes at election time.
- A major error was the government's failure to invest in industrial research and development. It had shown equal misjudgement in not making efforts to improve Britain's poor employer–worker relations. The result of all these shortcomings was 'stagflation'; by the mid-1960s Britain had one of the poorest growth rates among the advanced industrial nations.

There were also moralists who argued that Macmillan's pursuit of a property-owning democracy was based not on genuine national prosperity but on heavy borrowing by government and consumers. The scale of debt which this created was economically dangerous and socially harmful since it encouraged materialism, consumerism and irresponsibility.

Changing attitudes and social tensions

As observed in the discussion of class (page 38), public attitudes towards a number of social issues were changing. Particularly notable were shifts in attitude towards women, immigration, race and young people.

Immigration and racial violence

One of the most notable features of Britain in the second half of the twentieth century was its rapid development as a multiracial society. A key stage in this occurred in 1948 with the sailing of a converted troopship, the *Empire Windrush*, from Kingston, Jamaica, to Britain. The ship carried hundreds of West Indian workers; the majority of them were young men, but there were also families and a number of older men, most of whom were Second World War veterans. They were coming to find work. The official welcome they received was a warm one. Cinema newsreels enthusiastically recorded the event and assured the newcomers that they would soon find homes and jobs.

Under existing law, the newcomers had full rights of British citizenship. This encouraged further emigration from the West Indies. The government promoted this with organised appeals for Caribbean workers to fill the vacancies, principally in the hospital and transport services, that Britain's acute post-war labour shortage had left. By the mid-1950s employers in Britain had extended their recruitment to the Asian subcontinent. Textile firms in London and the north of England eagerly took on workers from India and Pakistan.

By the late 1950s, however, disturbing reactions had begun to occur among some of the white host population. 'No coloured' notices appeared in boarding house windows and on factory gates; mutterings were heard to the effect that the newcomers were attracted to Britain as much by the generous welfare benefits as by the prospect of work. The actual number of white residents who believed such slanders may have been small, but troublemakers were able to exploit the housing shortage, which was a major problem in the poorer areas, by suggesting that it was all the fault of the immigrants. However, race relations problems have never been simply about numbers. Those who spoke of Britain being 'swamped by waves of immigrants' were grossly exaggerating. The proportion of people of non-European origin has never been more than six per cent of the overall population of Britain. Moreover, as Table 2.6 shows, in every decade of the century up to the 1970s net emigration exceeded net immigration.

The main difficulties arose over accommodation. When immigrants first arrived in Britain they tended to live in the poorer areas of cities and urban areas where the cheaper properties for buying or renting were to be found.

Table 2.6 Emigration from, and immigration into, the UK (to nearest 100,000)

Decade	Outflow	Inflow
1900–9	4,404,000	2,287,000
1910–19	3,526,000	2,224,000
1920–9	3,960,000	2,590,000
1930–9	2,273,000	2,361,000
1940–9	590,000	240,000
1950–9	1,327,000	676,000
1960–9	1,916,000	1,243,000

This was understandable and unavoidable given their limited resources. But since Britain's inner cities suffered from a severe shortage of affordable housing, there was bound to be competition between residents on low incomes and newcomers. The same problems arose in the job market. Where work was scarce, those who could not get a job tended to blame immigrants for squeezing them out of employment by taking work at lower pay rates than whites were prepared to accept.

Race riots 1958–9

Tension turned to violence in 1958 when a series of riots broke out in a number of urban areas in Britain, most notably in Nottingham, Bristol and some of the poorer London districts. There was a pattern to the trouble everywhere it happened; gangs of white youths went round harassing black residents who frequently retaliated. The most disturbing incident occurred in August 1958 in London's Notting Hill where a crowd of over 600 white males tried to batter their way into black-owned properties. Television film showed disturbing scenes of police battling to keep white and black mobs apart, while the fire services struggled to quench the blazes started by the throwing of petrol bombs.

? What ironic point is being made by the cartoonist in Source D?

SOURCE D

'They just ain't civilised – like we are ... !' The youths depicted in this cartoon wear the hairstyle, long jackets, drainpipe trousers and crêpe-rubber-soled shoes of the typical 'Teddy boy' uniform of the day. In May 1959 in the west London borough of Notting Hill, Kelso Cochrane, who came from Antigua, was stabbed to death in the street by a group of six whites. Despite witness statements being collected, no charges were brought, a situation that led many immigrants to fear that the law would not really protect them. This cartoon was published in the *Evening Standard*, 19 May 1959.

To quell the trouble, at least in the short term, severe prison sentences were imposed on the nine white ringleaders who were found guilty of inciting the disturbances. It was revealed that a number of the white rioters belonged to the **White Defence League**. Macmillan's government also set up an official inquiry under Lord Salmon to examine the underlying reasons for the outrages. The Salmon Report suggested that the chief factors were:

- sexual jealousy of young white men who resented white women going out with black men
- the anger of white people at the willingness of black people to work for low wages
- bitterness at the rise in rents that white people believed were a result of the readiness of black people to live in cramped conditions and, therefore, pay higher collective rents than individual white people could afford
- white **Teddy boys** who used violence against immigrants to become 'local heroes' to whites fearful of the growing number of black residents.

The Salmon Report approached the riots very much as a law-and-order issue. It put the problem down to white reaction to increased immigration and made no overt reference to the racism or discrimination suffered by immigrants. The government then acted in the same spirit as the Report. Interpreting the disorder as a sign that immigrant numbers had to be controlled, it introduced a **Commonwealth Immigrants Act** in 1962. This proved a highly controversial measure and was condemned in many quarters as being racist since it placed restrictions on would-be entrants according to their ethnic origin. One consequence of the news that an Immigration Act was to be introduced in 1962 was a rush of immigrants into Britain in the period before its terms came into force. Between 1960 and 1962, over 230,000 **New Commonwealth** citizens entered. This, in fact, marked an immigration peak but it was such numbers that fuelled the anxieties of those who called for a complete block on entry.

In opposition, the Labour Party stoutly opposed the Act, but, when in office itself, it introduced a second Commonwealth Immigrants Act in 1968. Both major parties had concluded that limitations on entry into Britain were necessary in the interests of good race relations. To make that point, the Labour governments introduced Race Relations Acts in 1965 and 1968 (see page 110).

Table 2.7 Commonwealth immigrants living in the UK

Year	Mainly from Australia, New Zealand, Canada and South Africa	Mainly from the West Indies, India, Pakistan and Bangladesh*	Total
1961	307,697	289,058	596,755
1971	528,810	765,095	1,293,905

* Formerly East Pakistan.

KEY TERMS

White Defence League A racist organisation formed in 1957 in Notting Hill and modelled on Oswald Mosley's Union of Fascists, which had been active in the 1930s.

Teddy boys Young men of the 1950s with a strong tendency to violence when gathered in numbers; they took their name from their style of dress which recalled the fashions of Edward (Teddy) VII (king from 1901 to 1910).

Commonwealth Immigrants Act This aimed to limit immigration by creating a voucher scheme, restricting the right of entry to those who had actual jobs to go to.

New Commonwealth Bangladesh, India, Pakistan, West Indies.

A 'youth subculture'

Social disorder did not always involve race. Britain by the 1960s had seen the development of what has been termed a 'youth subculture'. This referred to the unwillingness of some young people to accept the standards and values of their elders. This could easily descend into antisocial behaviour and hooliganism, as evident in the affrays that began in 1964 between **'mods and rockers'**.

Explanations for the antisocial behaviour of the young

- The growing affluence of society enabled some young people on good wages to feel independent and ready to ignore traditional ways.
- Conversely, there were pockets of poverty which left those who did not share in the general prosperity embittered and alienated.
- The young people of the 1960s were the first generation not to have lived through the grim times of the Depression and the Second World War. Deliberately targeted by advertisers, eager to sell them fashionable clothes and pop music records, young people were encouraged to regard themselves as special and different. The concept of 'teenagers' as a special section of society was now established, providing a new type of customer for a new type of industry (see pages 110–13).
- The psychological theories of the day encouraged people, especially the young, to throw off traditional restraints and act out their feelings and desires.
- The scandals associated with some of those in the Establishment and the upper echelons of society hardly set a good example of responsible behaviour (see page 53).
- The 1960s were a boom time for satire; the regular mocking on television and in newspapers of the nation's political leaders played a part in undermining traditional notions of respect and deference.

The status of women

A further key development in British social life was the changing status of women. Measuring social change is not always easy, but in this case a convenient guide is provided by the reform measures introduced by government and Parliament. The progress of equality in the twentieth century has been described as 'playing catch-up', that is women gaining constitutional and legal rights as citizens on the same terms as men. Already by the middle of the century specific reforms had made a major breakthrough (see box on page 45).

KEY TERM

Mods and rockers Mods drove motor scooters and were rather more smartly dressed than rockers, who rode motorbikes; their prearranged fights usually took place in seaside resorts on bank holidays.

> ## Important legal reforms relating to women's status
>
> - Sex Disqualification (Removal) Act 1919: opened all the professions (except holy orders) and the universities (although not all individual colleges) to female entry.
> - Matrimonial Causes Act 1923: gave a wife the right to divorce her husband on the grounds of his adultery.
> - New English Law of Property 1926: entitled married and single women to hold and dispose of their property on the same terms as men.
> - Representation of the People Act 1928: gave all women over the age of 21 the right to vote in parliamentary and local elections.
> - British Nationality of Women Act 1948: gave British women the right to retain British nationality on marriage to a foreigner.

Important though such advances were in legal terms, they did not necessarily indicate a steady rise in women's social status. The Second World War had apparently elevated their position, since the demand for female workers made them an indispensable part of the war effort. Yet, when peace came, women were expected to give up their jobs to the returning men. Within a few months of the war's end, three-quarters of female workers had left work to return to their traditional role in the home. Married women found it especially difficult after 1945 to find employment. It was noticeable that the Labour governments of 1945–51, although broadly supportive of women's rights in principle, did not make a consistent effort to advance them. Equal pay for women was not made a government policy. Stafford Cripps let it be known that, in the austere economic climate, he expected women to behave with extra responsibility by not seeking new freedoms; he preferred them to play their traditional role as homemakers. The family was still regarded as the bedrock of society; divorce, which was permitted only on grounds of adultery, cruelty or desertion, was frowned on. Nonetheless, the rate of divorce was beginning to rise. The disruptive impact of the war and its aftermath on married couples is evident in the statistics shown in Table 2.8.

Table 2.8 Number of divorces in Britain

1939	7,012
1944	12,314
1947	60,190

The 1950s appeared to provide greater opportunities for women. The end of food rationing early in the decade meant that the dispiriting practice of queuing no longer dominated housewives' lives and the growing availability of consumer goods, such as domestic appliances, gave greater leisure time. How many women actually benefited is difficult to measure, since it depended on their particular personal and family circumstances, but the general rise in standards of living, associated with 'never had it so good' years (see page 34), created the possibilities for progress. However, the advances made in the 1950s should not be overstated. By 1960, women made up a third of the workforce, but two-thirds of the jobs they held were in low-paid secretarial work and primary school teaching. Barely one in ten of the higher posts in the legal profession, the civil service and the universities was held by a woman. The tax authorities classified women as dependants of their fathers or husbands.

Macmillan and the end of empire

It is one of the most striking examples of consensus politics in Britain that it should have been the Conservatives, traditionally regarded as the party of imperialism, who took a predominant role in the dismantling of the British Empire. Fully accepting the implications of Attlee's government decision to grant independence to India in 1947 (see page 13), the Conservative government under Harold Macmillan continued the process of abandoning the empire. Despite the protests of the right wing of the party, represented by such bodies as the **League of Empire Loyalists**, the Conservatives had come to recognise that there was in post-war Britain, and, indeed, in the world at large, a broad agreement that the age of imperialism had passed. Two world wars, fought for the right of peoples to be free, had made it no longer acceptable for any nation to impose itself on another or control the people against their will. The failure of the Suez venture in 1956 re-emphasised that point.

Colonialism, therefore, was dead or dying. Macmillan put this memorably in 1960 when he spoke of the need to recognise 'the wind of change' blowing through Africa. He meant that in the face of the growing national consciousness of the African nations, the only politically realistic and morally acceptable policy was to grant independence to those who wanted it. What gave particular significance to his words and message was that they were delivered in a speech he gave to the South African Parliament while on a tour of African countries. White-dominated South Africa was at this stage the home of **apartheid**, a social and political system that preserved white minority rule.

KEY TERMS

League of Empire Loyalists Formed in 1954 as a pressure group to agitate against Britain's adopting a policy of decolonisation.

Apartheid In theory, the notion of separate and equal development for different racial groups in South Africa; in practice, the subjection of the majority black and Cape-coloured races to minority white rule.

According to Macmillan in Source E, how is the wind of change influencing the African continent?

SOURCE E

From Harold Macmillan's speech to the South African Parliament, 3 February 1960, quoted in Frank Myers, *Rhetoric & Public Affairs*, Michigan University Press, 2000, p. 555.

The wind of change is blowing through this continent. Whether we like it or not, this growth of national consciousness is a political fact. As a fellow member of the Commonwealth it is our earnest desire to give South Africa our support and encouragement, but I hope you won't mind my saying frankly that there are some aspects of your policies which make it impossible for us to do this without being false to our own deep convictions about the political destinies of free men to which in our own territories we are trying to give effect. ... As I see it, the great issue in this second half of the twentieth century is whether the uncommitted peoples of Asia and Africa will swing to the East or to the West. Will they be drawn into the Communist camp? Or will the great experiments of self-government that are now being made in Asia and Africa, especially within the Commonwealth, prove so successful, and by their example so compelling, that the balance will come down in favour of freedom and order and justice?

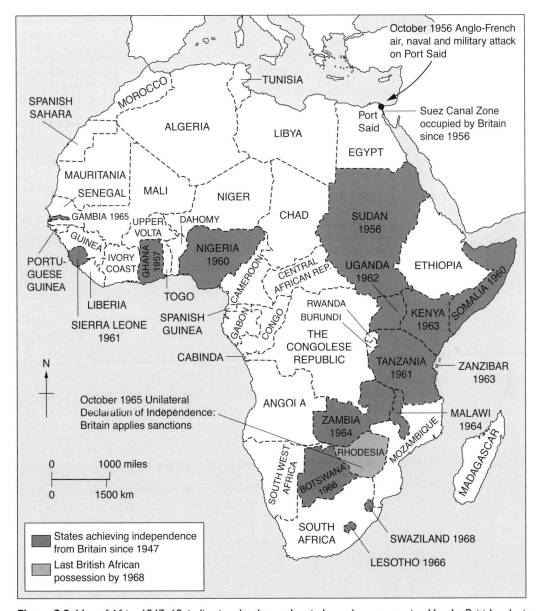

Figure 2.2 Map of Africa 1947–68, indicating the dates when independence was gained by the British colonies.

Macmillan backed his words by presiding over an extraordinary transition. Between 1957 and 1968 Britain gave independence to all its remaining colonies in Africa and the majority of those elsewhere. Despite the protest of white settlers, the British withdrawal proved, for the most part, a remarkably smooth and relatively bloodless process. There were serious exceptions, as in Kenya, where between 1952 and 1960 clashes between British forces and Kenyan nationalists resulted in the death of 13,000 native Kenyans and 100 Europeans. Yet where problems arose it was not over whether independence was to be granted but when.

The major exception to the story of peaceful transition was Southern Rhodesia. The white settler community, which held the political power, refused to accept the principles of 'majority rule' and 'one person, one vote'. It claimed that to introduce majority rule would give authority to the 'backward' black Rhodesians, who, according to the whites, were incapable of exercising it responsibly. Having failed to reach agreement with successive British governments, Ian Smith, the prime minister and leader of the white Rhodesian Front Party, declared **UDI** in 1965. For the next fifteen years Rhodesia, defying international condemnation as a white, racist, breakaway enclave, was subjected to economic sanctions, the most biting being an **embargo** on tobacco, its main export.

Eventually, the sanctions and a dispiriting civil war between black African guerrilla fighters and the white settlers in Rhodesia forced Smith to the conference table. Talks with Prime Minister Margaret Thatcher's Conservative government, which had opposed sanctions, produced a new settlement involving the acceptance of majority rule. Free elections in 1980 saw a victory for Robert Mugabe, leader of the Zimbabwe African National Union (ZANU). The new nation adopted the name Zimbabwe.

The effect on Britain of the loss of empire

A once commonly held view was that when Britain gave up its empire during the second half of the twentieth century it suffered a serious economic loss. However, the imperial balance sheet reveals that Britain as a nation had paid out more in grants and aid than it made in profits. At the end of the war in 1945, Britain, having agreed in 1940 to pay all India's war costs, found itself owing a sum of £1200 million. It was now the debtor nation. It was the same story with the colonies overall. Britain was in debt to them at the end of the war to the tune of £454 million.

Whatever profits individuals and companies might have made, Britain, overall, was a net loser financially. However, in the end, empire was abandoned not because it was making too little but because it was costing too much. Macmillan was doubtless sincere when he publicly supported the principle of colonial independence; nevertheless, the basic reason why Britain ceased to be an imperial power was because it could no longer afford to remain one. Bankrupt after the war, and heavily reliant on the USA for financial aid, Britain could not realistically continue funding the defence and economic needs of the colonies.

The loss of empire did not seriously damage British morale at home. It is difficult to see that Britain's decision to give up its colonies was regarded by the bulk of the population as other than a logical and mature thing to do. Indeed, as the Labour Party had shown over Indian independence, the abandonment of empire was seen as an act of delayed justice. Certainly, many people seemed untroubled by the loss. Historian Bernard Porter, recalling his feelings as a young man in the 1960s, has written: 'The process of losing an empire had little effect on British politics. Life in the metropolis went on much as before. The rest of us lived through it all hardly noticing it.'

KEY TERMS

UDI Unilateral Declaration of Independence.

Embargo Prohibition on sale and purchase.

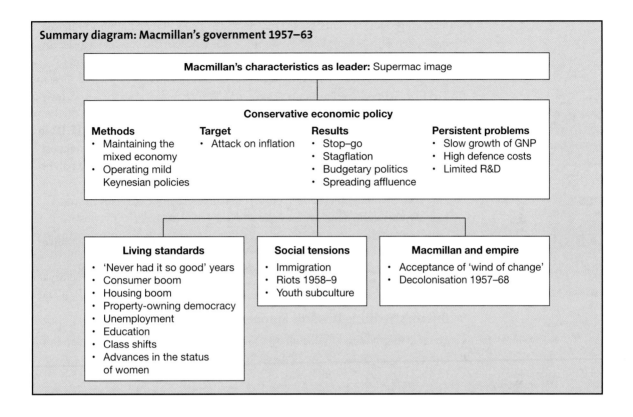

Summary diagram: Macmillan's government 1957–63

Macmillan's characteristics as leader: Supermac image

Conservative economic policy

Methods	Target	Results	Persistent problems
• Maintaining the mixed economy • Operating mild Keynesian policies	• Attack on inflation	• Stop–go • Stagflation • Budgetary politics • Spreading affluence	• Slow growth of GNP • High defence costs • Limited R&D

Living standards
- 'Never had it so good' years
- Consumer boom
- Housing boom
- Property-owning democracy
- Unemployment
- Education
- Class shifts
- Advances in the status of women

Social tensions
- Immigration
- Riots 1958–9
- Youth subculture

Macmillan and empire
- Acceptance of 'wind of change'
- Decolonisation 1957–68

 # Britain's relations with Europe

▶ *What developments led to Britain's application to join the EEC in 1963?*

After 1945 there had been a significant movement among the Western European nations towards mutual co-operation (see page 12). This culminated in 1957 with the signing of the Treaty of Rome by 'the Six', which created the European Economic Community (EEC). The treaty's key terms were as follows:

- The establishment of a **common market** and a customs union to monitor all aspects of trade between the member states.
- The adoption of a Common Agricultural Policy (CAP).
- Member states were required to operate a **protectionist** policy against all non-member nations.

The Common Agricultural Policy

CAP rested on the notion of ending rural poverty by a system by which 'poor areas' in the EEC were to be subsidised by a transfer of money from the 'rich areas'. The subsidy system, which provided the farmers with guaranteed prices

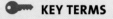 **KEY TERMS**

Common market A trading system between equal states with the minimum of regulation.

Protectionist Making non-common market goods uncompetitive by denying them entry or placing tariffs on them.

49

for their produce regardless of actual demand or cost, meant high prices for the consumer. This policy became a controversial aspect of the operation of the EEC.

The political character of the EEC

The EEC defined itself formally as an economic organisation, but it was driven as much by political considerations. This was because from the first the EEC was dominated by Germany and France. Germany's desire was to re-establish itself as a respectable and acceptable nation that had wholly thrown off its **Nazi** past. For its part, France was motivated primarily by a fear of a resurgent Germany. Far better, therefore, to control Germany within a formal organisation to which they both belonged than try to compete separately against it. As for the other four members, the Benelux countries and Italy, they judged that the post-war years offered them an opportunity to extract as many economic concessions as possible from Germany – their more powerful but guilt-ridden neighbour. This, they judged, could best be achieved within a European union organised as a **federation**.

Britain's attitude towards European union

The two main parties in post-war Britain had initially rejected the idea of joining Europe (see page 13). In the 1960s such sentiments still prevailed in the Labour Party. At the party conference in October 1962 leader Hugh Gaitskell firmly dismissed the idea of Britain's becoming a member of the EEC. He warned that, were the nation to take such a step, it would fatally undermine its standing 'as an independent European state. I make no apology for repeating it. It means the end of a thousand years of history.' Yet, already, by the time Gaitskell made his dramatic statement, the Conservative government had begun to have second thoughts about Europe and was seriously considering committing Britain to the EEC.

Britain moves towards European membership 1956–63

In the decade after the Second World War, British governments had remained convinced that Britain's economic future lay not in Europe but in its continued relationship with the USA and the Commonwealth. However, in the 1950s and 1960s the poor performance of the British economy compared to that of the EEC countries (see page 34) cast serious doubt on whether Britain could continue to remain detached. Equally disturbing for Britain was the failure of **EFTA** to match the economic success of the EEC. Set up in 1959 as a genuinely free-trade counterbalance to the protectionist EEC, EFTA was never able to match the influence of the EEC, with the result that by 1972 most EFTA members had joined the EEC.

There had also been important shifts on the wider international front. The Suez crisis (see page 24) had put a question mark against Britain's status as an independent power and raised doubts about the Anglo-American **special relationship**. Added to this was Britain's difficulty in remaining a truly

KEY TERMS

Nazi The period of National Socialist rule under Adolf Hitler, 1933–45.

Federation An organisation in which the member states surrender a significant degree of individual sovereignty for the union of states to have effective executive power.

EFTA The European Free Trade Association formed by Britain, Norway, Sweden, Austria, Portugal, Switzerland and Denmark.

Special relationship The term coined by Winston Churchill in 1946 to describe the common values that, he believed, made the USA and Britain natural allies.

independent nuclear force. Although Britain had detonated its first atom bomb in 1952 and its first hydrogen bomb in 1957, the advance of technology meant that by the late 1950s its method of delivering the weapons by bomber was outmoded. To maintain its strike power Britain had to begin buying US Polaris nuclear missiles that could be launched from submarines (see page 147).

Such developments obliged British politicians to adjust their thinking. Equally significant was the decline within the Conservative Party of the traditionally influential agricultural lobby and its replacement by the younger, **City-orientated**, managerial element, who were becoming increasingly pro-European in their sympathies. They were not moved by the notion of European unity as an ideal. Their approach was hard-headed and practical; they feared being left behind economically by their European competitors. Their view was essentially 'if you can't beat 'em, join 'em'.

It was against this background that Macmillan let it be known in 1961 that the government was now considering applying to join the EEC. This followed the advice given him in a report by Edward Heath, a keen pro-European, whom Macmillan had appointed as a minister with special responsibility for examining the implications of Britain's entering Europe. In announcing this remarkable new departure, Macmillan promised that Britain would join only on condition that Britain's existing trading agreements with the countries of the Commonwealth and EFTA would be preserved and protected. 'We must persuade the Six of the value of the Commonwealth to the Free World.' In August 1961 he spoke at length in the House of Commons, explaining why he was now convinced that Britain should apply for membership of the EEC.

KEY TERM

City-orientated Relating to the money markets in London's international financial centre, known as 'the City'.

SOURCE F

From Macmillan's speech in the House of Commons, 2 August 1961, quoted in Alistair Horne, *Macmillan 1957–1986*, Macmillan, 1989, pp. 259–60.

In this, as in most countries, there is a certain suspicion of foreigners. There is also the additional division between us and continental Europe of a wholly different development of our legal, administrative and to some extent political systems. Nevertheless, it is perhaps worth recording that in every period when the world has been in danger of tyrants or aggression, Britain has abandoned isolation.

There are, as I have said, some to whom the whole concept of our working closely in this field with other European nations is instinctively disagreeable. Others feel that our whole and sole duty lies with the Commonwealth. If I thought that our entry into Europe would injure our relations with and our influence in the Commonwealth, or be against the true interest of the Commonwealth, I would not ask the House to support this step.

I think, however, that most of us recognise that in a changing world if we are not to be left behind and to drop out of the main stream of the world's life, we must be prepared to adapt and change our methods. All through history this had been one of the main sources of our strength.

According to Source F, why is Macmillan in favour of Britain's joining the EEC?

The first French veto 1963

Macmillan's concern for the special trading privileges of the Commonwealth made Britain's readiness to negotiate with Europe appear grudging. It suggested that Britain wanted to have its cake and eat it. It was for this reason that French president, de Gaulle, used his veto to block Britain's first formal application to join the EEC, made in 1963. He explained it in Source G.

SOURCE G

From Charles de Gaulle, 'Press Conference by President de Gaulle, Paris, 14 January 1963', quoted in *WEU, Political Union of Europe*, 1964, pp. 85–9.

One might sometimes have believed that our English friends, in posing their candidature to the Common Market, were agreeing to transform themselves to the point of applying all the conditions which are accepted and practised by the Six. But the question, is whether Great Britain can now place herself like the Continent inside a tariff which is genuinely common, to renounce all Commonwealth preferences, to cease any pretence that her agriculture be privileged, and, more than that, to treat her engagements with other countries of the free trade area as null and void – that question is the whole question.

It cannot be said that it is yet resolved. Will it be so one day? Obviously only England can answer. The question is even further posed since after England other States which are, I repeat, linked to her through the free trade area, for the same reasons as Britain, would like or wish to enter the Common Market.

? According to Source G, on what grounds does de Gaulle veto Britain's application?

There was a powerful logic to de Gaulle's doubts concerning British sincerity. His rhetorical question in reaction to Macmillan's claim that 'we must persuade the Six of the value of the Commonwealth' made sound sense. How, indeed, could Britain assert such sentiments and then genuinely undertake the removal of all the preferential claims and privileges currently enjoyed by EFTA and the Commonwealth? Strong grounds for de Gaulle's scepticism had been provided in 1962 when the independent Commonwealth countries of Africa, fearing a compromising of their newly won freedom, had rejected a specially negotiated offer to become associate members of the EEC.

De Gaulle's reservations did not end with economics. More important for him were the political implications of British entry. These were spelled out by the French agricultural minister: 'At present, in the Six there are five hens and one cockerel. If you join, with other countries, there will be perhaps seven or eight hens. But there will be two cockerels. I am afraid that is not acceptable to us.'

A personal meeting between de Gaulle and Macmillan in December 1962 had done nothing to ease these fears. Indeed, the failure to reach an Anglo-French understanding on joint nuclear arms development, followed only days later by the Anglo-American agreement in which the USA agreed to supply Britain with Polaris missiles (see page 147), served to confirm de Gaulle's suspicions that Britain was the thin edge of a large US wedge about to be thrust into Europe.

De Gaulle saw the EEC as a counterbalance to American power and did not want British membership undermining this.

Having been rejected by France, largely at the personal insistence of de Gaulle, Britain's only recourse was to wait until he was no longer the French leader and then apply again. It seemed to some that Britain had assumed the role of beggar, pleading to be allowed to join the feast. It was a humiliating position and can be seen as damaging Britain's relations with Europe from that point on. When Britain was eventually accepted into Europe it was not on British terms.

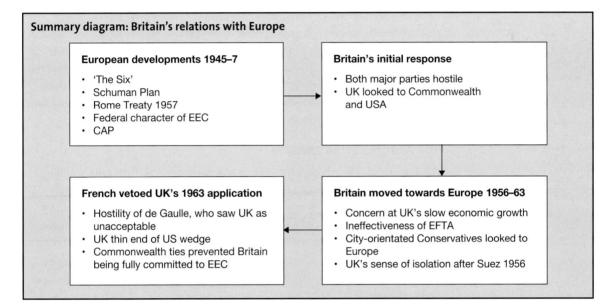

Summary diagram: Britain's relations with Europe

European developments 1945–7
- 'The Six'
- Schuman Plan
- Rome Treaty 1957
- Federal character of EEC
- CAP

Britain's initial response
- Both major parties hostile
- UK looked to Commonwealth and USA

French vetoed UK's 1963 application
- Hostility of de Gaulle, who saw UK as unacceptable
- UK thin end of US wedge
- Commonwealth ties prevented Britain being fully committed to EEC

Britain moved towards Europe 1956–63
- Concern at UK's slow economic growth
- Ineffectiveness of EFTA
- City-orientated Conservatives looked to Europe
- UK's sense of isolation after Suez 1956

 # The Conservatives' last years 1963–4

▶ *What factors weakened the Conservative governments in their last years?*

Macmillan was unlucky in that the final years of his premiership were marred by scandals which, while seldom the direct fault of the government, reflected badly upon it.

Scandals

- The Vassall inquiry 1963. The government was obliged to appoint an official investigation into the case of John Vassall, a civil servant in the admiralty, who had been caught spying for the Soviet Union in 1962. There were rumours that senior admiralty figures had tried to protect him. The inquiry found no clear evidence of this, but the talk of cover-ups suggested that the government was not in control of its departments.

- In January 1963 it was revealed that Kim Philby, a senior official in the foreign office, had for decades been passing information to the USSR as well as recruiting agents and running a spy network. Not waiting to be arrested, Philby fled to Moscow where he remained until his death in 1988. Macmillan's government took the brunt of the blame for the security services having failed for so long to spot a traitor in the heart of the Establishment.

- The Argyll divorce case. In 1963 a lurid court case, in which the Duke of Argyll sued his wife, Margaret, for divorce on the grounds of adultery, provided the public with a host of salacious details, including a list of men with whom, at various times in various numbers, the duchess had had group sex. The list was said to include two (unidentified) government ministers, one of whom allegedly appeared in a pornographic photo that was shown in court. In granting the divorce, the judge said it was beyond doubt that the duchess had engaged in 'disgusting sexual practices'.

The Profumo affair 1963

All these incidents troubled Macmillan and his government, but the scandal that gave them the most concern was the Profumo affair. In March 1963 the behaviour of Macmillan's minister for war, John Profumo, became headline news. It was revealed that Profumo had had a liaison with Christine Keeler, a model, who was having an affair with a member of the Soviet embassy. The risk to national security was obvious and was eagerly seized on by the media. In March 1963, Profumo solemnly declared in the House of Commons that there was no truth in the rumours that he had had improper relations with Miss Keeler, only to have to admit three months later that he had lied to Parliament. He resigned his position but his disgrace spread far beyond him, implicating the government and Conservative Party.

Details emerged that Profumo had first met Christine Keeler at Cliveden, a famous country house in Buckinghamshire used as a high-class brothel by Dr Stephen Ward, an osteopath who used his contacts to procure girls for upper-class men. Since Ward, as a popular doctor, had many Conservatives on his books, the party was damaged by association even though most of those he treated were genuine patients. Ward was subsequently put on trial, charged with living off immoral earnings. Fearing that the court case was going heavily against him, he killed himself. At another trial not connected with Ward's, Christine Keeler was found guilty of perjury and sentenced to nine months' imprisonment.

The impact of the Profumo affair

The scandal did not in itself bring down the government, but Macmillan's readiness to believe Profumo's original denial of impropriety suggested that the prime minister was losing his political grip. Macmillan said wearily that it was a sorry state of affairs that he should be criticised for believing the word of a friend and colleague who had personally assured him that there was no truth in the rumours.

It was not merely the tabloids that kept the issue before their readers. *The Times* weighed in with a portentous leader headed 'It *is* a moral issue' in which it argued that the scandal was about more than a minister lying in Parliament, serious though that was. The affair had invaded the public sphere and could not be dismissed simply as an individual indiscretion; it reflected on the character of British public institutions and government. *The Times* caught the prevailing response of most people; while neither the prime minister nor the government was directly to blame for the failings of one minister, the Profumo affair seemed somehow to emphasise that, after twelve years in office, the Conservative Party had weakened its claim to lead the nation. There was a feeling that Macmillan and the government he led had become faintly ridiculous and outmoded.

The struggle to succeed Macmillan 1963

When Macmillan, weary and unwell after six years in office and damaged by the Profumo affair, announced his intention of resigning, he asked for the party to follow the 'customary processes' in choosing a new leader. This meant asking the Cabinet and the MPs to find out whom the majority would accept. At the time, most of the press thought it was a straight fight between R.A. Butler and **Lord Hailsham**, a contender with the right aristocratic connections to appeal to old-fashioned members of the party, but who had a somewhat abrasive manner.

Butler seemed to be well placed to become premier. His work as home secretary and then foreign secretary under Macmillan appeared to have been highly successful. In 1962 he had been one of the few leading Cabinet members to survive the 'Night of the Long Knives' (see page 31), Macmillan's Cabinet reshuffle, in which he elevated a number of younger Conservatives and demoted some of the established ones. Macmillan then raised him to the position of deputy prime minister. However, in 1963 Butler once again did little to push his leadership claims at the critical moment despite his appearing to be in a strong position. There was also the fact that, although Macmillan admired Butler's abilities, he disliked him as a person and did not wish to see him become prime minister.

Douglas-Home succeeds Macmillan

To everybody's surprise outside the party and many within it, a late runner then entered the race: **Lord Home**, Macmillan's foreign secretary. To make himself eligible, since convention required the prime minister to be a member of the House of Commons, he renounced his peerage to become plain Sir Alec

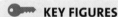

KEY FIGURES

Lord Hailsham (1907–2001)
MP 1938–50 and 1963–70. Leader of the House of Lords 1960–63. Minister for sport 1962–4. Minister of education 1964.

Lord Home (1903–95)
MP 1931–45, 1950–1 and 1963–74. Secretary for Commonwealth relations 1955–60. Leader of the House of Lords 1957–60. Foreign secretary 1960–3, 1970–4. Prime minister 1963–4.

Douglas-Home. Hailsham did the same, reverting to his family name, Quintin Hogg. Their ability to do this had a certain irony, since the right to give up their titles existed only because of the work of the Labour radical, Tony Benn (see page 152). He had successfully campaigned for a Peerage Act, which became law in 1963, allowing him to renounce his hereditary peerage, drop his title of Lord Stansgate and remain in the House of Commons.

Macmillan deliberately kept the party waiting before announcing the date of his resignation, thereby giving Douglas-Home time to press his candidacy. Eventually, from his hospital bed where he was being treated for prostate problems, Macmillan sent his letter of resignation to the Queen, in which he included a recommendation that Douglas-Home be invited to be the next prime minister. The Queen acted on the advice and on 16 October 1963 Douglas-Home duly became prime minister. He was to hold the office for one day short of a calendar year.

There is little doubt that it was Macmillan's support as retiring prime minister that won the day for Douglas-Home. It made the consultations Macmillan had asked the party to engage in little more than a charade. It had always been Macmillan's intention to block Butler; the only question was whom did he support. He had initially backed Hailsham but then switched to Home, judging that on balance he was a safer choice. There was considerable resentment among some party members that Butler had been ignored for a third time. Enoch Powell (see page 110) and **Iain Macleod** declared that they would not serve under Home, whose leadership, they believed, would give the electorate the wrong image of Conservatism.

The manner in which Macmillan and the party dignitaries were able to nominate Douglas-Home as his successor indicated that class and the 'old boy network' were still a force (see page 39). Nine of those most closely involved in the manoeuvrings that saw Home emerge as leader were old **Etonians**. However, it is significant that this proved to be the last time the party would employ such a dated process. Following its defeat in the 1964 general election, the party adopted an open democratic system involving the balloting of Conservative MPs. In 1965 Edward Heath became the first Conservative leader to be elected under the new arrangements.

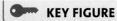

KEY FIGURE

Iain Macleod (1913–70)
Minister of health 1952–5. Minister of labour 1955–9. Colonial secretary 1959–61. Chancellor of the exchequer 1970. An eloquent parliamentary speaker, he was disliked by the Conservative right for his progressive views on social issues and decolonisation.

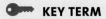

KEY TERM

Etonians 'Old boys' of Eton, one of Britain's most prestigious public schools, which traditionally provided a high number of Britain's government ministers and statesmen.

Summary diagram: The Conservatives' last years 1963–4

Weakening factors	Power struggle over succession
• Macmillan and the government rocked by scandals 1963 • Government embarrassed by French rejection of UK's EEC application • Prime minister and government mocked by satirists	• Ailing Macmillan announced his intention to retire 1963 • Hailsham, Butler, Douglas-Home rival candidates to the premiership • Antiquated system of selecting leader saw Douglas-Home 'emerge' as new prime minister • Result largely a matter of Macmillan's backing Douglas-Home • Whole matter seen as ridiculous by many in the population • Last time such a system would be used

---

 # The Labour Party 1951–64

▶ *What problems did the Labour Party experience in opposition?*

In British politics, disputes within parties are often more lively and more intense than those between parties. One explanation for the Conservatives' remaining in office for so long after 1951 was the condition of the Labour Party, which for much of that period remained disunited. This was despite having in Hugh Gaitskell, who succeeded Attlee in 1955, a leader who was one of the most gifted politicians of the day. Possessed of a sharp analytical mind, he was also blessed with a perfect voice for public speaking and he used its tone and cadences to great effect. Arguably, the most impressive example of his oratory and his greatest parliamentary performance was in 1956 when, with controlled fury, he forensically shredded and destroyed Eden's attempt to justify the British occupation of the Suez Canal zone. However, the fates conspired against Gaitskell. His untimely death in January 1963 at the young age for a party leader of 57, meant that he never became prime minister, a role for which his abilities appeared to make him especially fitted.

Labour's internal disputes

Gaitskell's greatest political misfortune was that he became leader of the Labour Party when it was going through one of its most disruptive periods. Despite its creative years in office between 1945 and 1951, the Labour Party had yet to decide exactly what type of party it was and what its aims were. The identity problem was to trouble it throughout its existence up to 2007. Notwithstanding its remarkable achievement in introducing the welfare state, many of the party regarded this as simply the first step in the march towards a truly socialist Britain. The left of the party argued for a much greater commitment to state control and direction of the economy and society. It had chafed under Attlee's leadership, believing that he should have led the party along a more radical path.

The **Bevanites** represented this strand of thought. They wanted the large trade unions, which, they believed, spoke for the working class and were led by committed left wingers, to have the major voice in the shaping of party policy. A key issue was Britain's independent nuclear deterrent. Many of the left were **unilateralists**. For some this was simply patriotism; they did not want Britain to burden itself with the expense of nuclear arms production which diverted resources away from providing for the needy. For others, there was an ulterior motive. They were anxious that the Soviet Union should not fall too far behind in the arms race with the West. The **CND** movement, for example, although not formally committed to a particular political standpoint, attracted those who were anti-American and pro-Soviet.

As party leader, Gaitskell resisted both trade union domination and the left's drive towards unilateralism. A representative of the moderate centre-right of the party, Gaitskell believed that his victory over Bevan in the 1955 leadership contest had given him the authority to steer the party away from policies that would alienate it from the electorate. He became even more convinced of this by the outcome of the 1959 general election.

The 1959 general election

Before the election, it had been widely held that Labour had a strong chance of winning. The election was the first to be held since the Suez crisis, providing voters with a chance to punish the Conservative government for its involvement. There was also a feeling that the budgetary policies followed by the government might count against it. However, opinion polls and the election itself showed that these factors had been exaggerated. In fact, the election came at a bad moment for Labour. It was another of Gaitskell's misfortunes that his time as Labour Party leader coincided with a period of economic recovery which, while it was not entirely due to the policies of Macmillan's government, was skilfully presented in Conservative propaganda as if it were. Macmillan's famous reference in 1957 to the British people's never having had it so good was a clever piece of populism (see page 34) and was equally effectively used by the government in the election campaign in the form of the slogan 'Life is better with the Conservatives. Don't let Labour ruin it.'

In an attempt to counter the impact of the slogan, Labour's campaign team tried to woo the voters with a scheme that promised a substantial increase in state pensions without an accompanying rise in taxation. However, the scheme was too hurriedly drafted and raised questions about how it would be financed that embarrassed rather than helped the Labour candidates in their campaigning. To the opposition's list of electoral handicaps should be added its

KEY TERMS

Bevanites Followers of Aneurin Bevan, a hero of the left. Bevan was not always as radical as his followers. At the 1957 Labour Party conference, he rejected unilateralism as an 'emotional spasm'.

Unilateralists Those who believed that Britain should give up its atomic weapons without waiting for a multilateral agreement between the nuclear powers to do so.

CND Campaign for Nuclear Disarmament. Founded in 1958 to agitate for unilateral nuclear disarmament.

attitude towards the European issue. In 1962 Gaitskell had followed Attlee in publicly declaring that the Labour Party was against Britain's joining the EEC (see page 50). Although it would later change its position on this, Labour at this stage hardly appeared progressive and forward looking. This point was made by a significant number of Gaitskell's party who suggested that he had adopted the wrong stance. The party's evident internal disagreements were certainly not a vote winner.

Table 2.9 Results of the 1959 general election

Party	Votes	Seats	Percentage of vote
Conservative	13,749,830	365	49.4
Labour	12,215,538	258	43.8
Liberal	1,638,571	6	5.9
Others	255,302	1	0.9

The election results showed that the Conservatives had gained 21 seats, while Labour had lost 19, the net effect being that the government had increased its overall Commons majority from 58 to 100. Labour had clearly failed to impress the electorate.

Reasons for Labour's defeat in 1959

The party was damaged by:

- disagreements over the true character of the party
- divisions over how far the party should push for socialist policies, such as nationalisation
- splits over the issue of unilateralism
- uncertainty over whether Britain should join the Common Market.

In the election campaign itself Labour was:

- outmanoeuvred by the Conservatives who claimed to be leading Britain towards prosperity
- handicapped by the public perception that Labour's plans would result in higher taxes.

Labour's reaction to its defeat

Anger over a third consecutive election defeat produced recriminations within the Labour Party. Gaitskell accused the left of weakening the movement by their demands for unilateralism. The left replied by attacking him over his betrayal of party principle by dropping nationalisation as a primary goal. Some on the right of the party rallied to Gaitskell's defence by forming the **CDS**. This group argued vigorously that it was undemocratic and improper for the left to use their influence with the leaders of the large trade unions such as the Transport and General Workers' Union to impose their extreme views on the Labour Party, the majority of whose members were moderates.

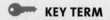 **KEY TERM**

CDS Campaign for Democratic Socialism. Made up of Labour supporters who wanted the party to distance itself from the trade unions, nationalisation and unilateralism; a number of CDS members went on to break from Labour in 1981 and form a new political party, the Social Democratic Party.

SOURCE H

'And may I say to Hon. Members opposite me … .' A cartoon from the *Evening Standard*, 5 March 1960 (showing Macmillan sitting on the left and Gaitskell standing on the right).

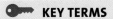

? In Source H, what is the cartoonist trying to convey in the caption and the depiction of Gaitskell's physical position?

🔑 KEY TERMS

Block vote Labour Party procedures allowed individual trade union leaders to cast their conference votes on behalf of all the members of their union, which could number millions.

Fellow travellers Secret Communists and Soviet sympathisers.

Attempts by the left to undermine Gaitskell and impose unilateralism on Labour came to a dramatic climax at the 1960 party conference. Able to rely on the **block vote** of the major unions, the unilateralists forced their policy on the party. Gaitskell, in his speech as leader, appealed to the delegates, some of whom tried to shout him down, not to give in to the demands of the **'fellow travellers'** in the party. He declared with great emotion that for the Labour Party to ignore the views of the electorate by adopting a unilateralist position was political suicide. Gaitskell promised: 'We will fight, and fight, and fight again to save the party that we love.'

Although he lost the vote in 1960, Gaitskell may be said to have won the argument, since a year later the conference agreed to drop unilateralism as party policy. It is notable that Gaitskell's argument in 1960 was essentially the one repeated 25 years later by Neil Kinnock when he turned on the 'loony left' and berated it for its lack of common sense and realism (see page 153).

Summary diagram: The Labour Party 1951–64

Problem of party unity

- Gaitskell succeeded Attlee after defeating Bevan for leadership
- Gaitskell led the party from a centre-right position

Opposed internally

- Bevanite left
- Unilateralists and CND

Why Labour lost 1959 election

- Weakened by internal divisions
- Disadvantaged by UK's rising prosperity
- Mounted a poor election campaign

Election defeat intensified internal wrangles

- 1960 Conference saw victory of left
- Trade union block vote forced unilateralism as official policy
- Gaitskell's 'fight and fight and fight again' speech rallied party
- 1961 Conference rejected unilateralism

Chapter summary

The Conservative governments of Churchill and Eden, in a form of consensus politics known as Butskellism, continued essentially the same economic, welfare and foreign affairs programme as Labour's before 1951. The outstanding episode in Eden's term of office was the Suez crisis of 1956, which marked the end of Britain as an imperial power. It was during the 1950s that such developments as class shifts, immigration, and the changing position and status of women and young people became notable aspects of British society.

Eden's successor, Macmillan, led an administration that had many financial problems, but which nevertheless presided over a period of economic growth which brought unprecedentedly high standards of living for the mass of the population. However, doubts about the relative strength of Britain's economy led Macmillan's government to request entry into the EEC in 1963, only for France to veto the application. After thirteen years in office, the Conservatives' reputation suffered from a series of public scandals that reflected badly on Macmillan even though he personally was not involved. He stood down in 1963, to be succeeded by Douglas-Home, the last unelected Conservative leader. Labour's failure to be a more effective opposition in this period was largely explained by its internal disputes over unilateralism, nationalisation, Europe and the role of the trade unions.

Refresher questions

Use these questions to remind yourself of the key material covered in this chapter.

1 Why was Eden's premiership so short lived?

2 How did Britain become entangled in the Suez venture?

3 Why did Eden call off the Suez campaign?

4 What were the consequences for Britain of the Suez venture?

5 What economic policies did the Conservative government follow under Macmillan?

6 How justified was Macmillan's claim that under the Conservatives the British people had 'never had it so good'?

7 Why was there increased social mobility in the Macmillan years?

8 In what ways did immigration increase social tension?

9 What policy did Macmillan's government follow towards Britain's remaining colonies?

10 What led Britain eventually to consider joining the EEC?

11 Why did France block Britain's entry into the EEC in 1963?

12 What was the importance of the Profumo affair of 1963?

13 Why was Douglas-Home the winner in the Conservative Party leadership contest in 1963?

14 What factors prevented the Labour Party from being a fully effective opposition to the Conservative governments 1959–64?

15 What issues divided the Labour Party between 1959 and 1964?

 Question practice

ESSAY QUESTIONS

1 'The Suez crisis of 1956 was a result of Eden's misunderstanding of Nasser's motives.' Explain why you agree or disagree with this view.

2 To what extent was the rise in standards of living in Britain in the 1960s the result of government policies?

3 'It was the weakness of its own economy that led Britain to apply to join the EEC in 1963.' Assess the validity of this view.

4 How far do you agree that the ability of the Conservatives to remain in office between 1951 and 1964 was because of the Labour Party's weakness?

SOURCE ANALYSIS QUESTIONS

1 With reference to Sources 1 and 2, and your understanding of the historical context, which of these two sources is more valuable in explaining why France vetoed Britain's application to join the EEC in 1963?

2 With reference to Sources 1, 2 and 3 (page 64), and your understanding of the historical context, assess the value of these sources to a historian studying the difficulties that confronted Macmillan's government in framing a policy towards the EEC between 1960 and 1963.

SOURCE 1

From Macmillan's speech in the House of Commons, 2 August 1961, quoted in Alistair Horne, *Macmillan 1957–1986*, Macmillan, 1989, pp. 259–60.

In this, as in most countries, there is a certain suspicion of foreigners. There is also the additional division between us and continental Europe of a wholly different development of our legal, administrative and to some extent political systems. Nevertheless, it is perhaps worth recording that in every period when the world has been in danger of tyrants or aggression, Britain has abandoned isolation.

There are, as I have said, some to whom the whole concept of our working closely in this field with other European nations is instinctively disagreeable. Others feel that our whole and sole duty lies with the Commonwealth. If I thought that our entry into Europe would injure our relations with and our influence in the Commonwealth, or be against the true interest of the Commonwealth, I would not ask the House to support this step.

I think, however, that most of us recognise that in a changing world if we are not to be left behind and to drop out of the main stream of the world's life, we must be prepared to adapt and change our methods. All through history this had been one of the main sources of our strength.

SOURCE 2

From Charles de Gaulle, 'Press Conference by President de Gaulle, Paris, 14 January 1963', quoted in *WEU, Political Union of Europe*, 1964, pp. 85–9.

One might sometimes have believed that our English friends, in posing their candidature to the Common Market, were agreeing to transform themselves to the point of applying all the conditions which are accepted and practised by the Six. But the question, is whether Great Britain can now place herself, like the Continent, inside a tariff which is genuinely common, to renounce all Commonwealth preferences, to cease any pretence that her agriculture be privileged, and, more than that, to treat her engagements with other countries of the free trade area as null and void – that question is the whole question.

It cannot be said that it is yet resolved. Will it be so one day? Obviously only England can answer. The question is even further posed since after England other States which are, I repeat, linked to her through the free trade area, for the same reasons as Britain, would like or wish to enter the Common Market.

SOURCE 3

From Cabinet Minutes, 13 July 1960. PRO CAB 128/34, quoted in Andrew Boxer, *The Conservative Governments 1951–1964*, Longman, 1996, p. 119.

The Chancellor of the Exchequer (Derick Heatcoat-Amory) [said that] a decision to join the Community would be essentially a political act with economic consequences, rather than an economic act with political consequences. The arguments for joining the Community were strong. If we remained outside it, our political influence in Europe and the rest of the world was likely to decline. By joining it we should not only avoid tariff discrimination by its members against our exports, but should also be able to participate in a large and rapidly expanding market.

However, the arguments against United Kingdom membership were also very strong. We should be surrendering independent control of our commercial policies to a European bloc, when our trading interests were world-wide. We should have to abandon our special economic relationship with the Commonwealth, including free entry for Commonwealth goods and the preferential system, and should instead be obliged to discriminate actively against the Commonwealth. We should have to devise for agriculture and horticulture new policies under which the burden of support for the farmers would be largely transferred from the Exchequer to the consumer, thus increasing the cost of living. Finally, we should sacrifice our loyalties and obligations to the members of the European Free Trade Association (E.F.T.A.), some of which would find it impossible to join the E.E.C. as full members.

CHAPTER 3

Years of consensus 1964–79

The period 1964–79 was notable for its consensus politics. Successive Labour and Conservative governments followed very similar policies. This was principally because they were beset by economic problems for which they could find few clear answers. Edward Heath's government tried briefly to diverge from the consensus, but circumstances soon ended the experiment. Overshadowing the period were the troubles in Northern Ireland, which successive governments struggled to resolve. Concurrent with political developments, significant social changes were occurring in British society. This chapter covers:

★ Wilson's government 1964–70
★ Heath's government 1970–4
★ Labour in office 1974–9
★ British relations with China and the USSR
★ British policies in Northern Ireland 1969–79
★ Social developments

Key dates

1964	Labour's election victory under Wilson	**1974**	Heath government defeated in election
1965	Race Relations Act		Wilson became prime minister
1966	Election gave Labour an increased majority	**1975**	Referendum on EEC membership
		1976	Callaghan succeeded Wilson as prime minister
1968	Immigration Act		
1970	Conservatives' election victory under Heath		IMF crisis
		1977	Lib–Lab pact
1971	Industrial Relations Act	**1978–9**	The 'winter of discontent'
1973	UK formally entered the EEC	**1979**	Labour's election defeat

Wilson's government 1964–70

▶ *What problems underlay Wilson's government?*

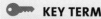
Sir Alec Douglas-Home's single year as prime minister from 1963 to 1964 was, as Conservative supporters admitted, an undistinguished time. The odd manner in which he had emerged as party leader and prime minister (see page 56) threw a shadow over his government and, although he was a man of considerable personal charm and courtesy, he did not compare well as a parliamentarian with Harold Wilson, Labour's leader. Douglas-Home invariably came off worse in the Commons' debates and **prime minister's questions**. It was no great surprise, therefore, that Wilson pulled away from Douglas-Home in the opinion polls, a development confirmed by Labour's victory in the 1964 general election.

Table 3.1 Results of the 1964 general election

Party	Votes	Seats	Percentage of vote
Labour	12,205,814	317	44.1
Conservative	12,001,396	304	43.6
Liberal	3,092,878	9	1.2
Others	348,914	0	1.3

Governments and prime ministers 1964–79

- 1964–70: Labour – Harold Wilson
- 1970–4: Conservative – Edward Heath
- 1974–6: Labour – Harold Wilson
- 1976–9: Labour – James Callaghan

The 1964 general election

The Labour Party's success, after thirteen years in opposition, suggested that the tide had turned in its favour. It presented a more youthful image, not simply because Wilson was a younger man than Home or Macmillan but because Labour seemed more in tune with young people and their idea of a progressive Britain. The notion of the 'swinging sixties' (see page 111) may have been largely a creation of the media but astute Labour politicians acknowledged its power as an image and were anxious not to appear unfashionable. Wilson also cleverly played on the contrast between himself as the plain, straight-speaking Yorkshireman and Home as the 'huntin', shootin', fishin' aristocrat' who was out of touch with ordinary people and their wants. Wilson tapped into the mood of the day by speaking of Britain's need to respond to the 'white heat of the technological revolution'. The situation was similar in many ways to 1945, when

Labour had successfully presented itself as the force of progress standing against the out-of-date political establishment.

Yet voters did not turn overwhelmingly to the Labour Party in 1964, any more than they had to the Conservatives in 1951. It was a close finish. There were even suggestions among some Conservatives that they might have won the 1964 election had Butler rather than Home been leader, an unprovable but arresting suggestion given how narrow the Labour victory turned out to be. The telling statistic was not the recovery of Labour but the falling away of support for the Conservatives. While Labour, compared with 1959, had slightly increased its share of the vote from 43.8 per cent to 44.1 per cent, the Conservative share had slipped six points from 49.4 per cent to 43.6 per cent. This was just enough to give Labour an overall majority of four seats. The Conservative decline indicated that, after thirteen years of the same party in power, a significant number of electors wanted a change. The Conservatives' decision to move closer to the principle of the planned economy had opened them to the charge that they were losing their traditional moorings and were ceasing to offer a distinct alternative to the Labour Party.

Reasons for Labour's victory in 1964

- Weariness and lack of spirit undermined the Conservative government after thirteen unbroken years in office.
- The scandals tainting the Conservative Party in 1963–4 (see page 53) weakened its claim to integrity and competence.
- The antiquated system which had produced Home as leader and prime minister damaged the Conservative attempt to project a modern image.
- Unemployment reached over 800,000 in 1963, denting Macmillan's earlier claim that Britain had 'never had it so good'.
- The government's humiliating failure in having its 1963 application to join the EEC rejected exposed how weak Britain had become internationally.
- The Labour Party presented a younger, 'with it', image that was in tune with the changing times.
- As a party leader, Harold Wilson presented a more dynamic image than Alec Douglas-Home.
- The Conservative government was the main target of satire that began to flourish in the early 1960s in the theatre and on radio and television.
- Wilson's skilful election campaign, in which he presented himself and his party as better fitted to lead the nation in the technological age that Britain had entered, edged him to victory.

Labour's difficulties in government

A factor that should be stressed at the outset is that Wilson's government was beset, as were all the administrations which followed, both Labour and Conservative, by constant economic difficulties. These arose from the fact that

Britain in the second half of the twentieth century was undergoing a major shift in its economic and social structure. It was changing from an industrial economy to a post-industrial one: manufacturing industries were shrinking while service and finance industries were expanding.

The transition was not smooth or consistent and so caused considerable social disruption. That, indeed, was the root cause of Britain's post-war difficulties. For all the talk of Keynesian planning (see page 6), the truth was that central and local government had only a marginal influence in shaping this transition. It was a case of responding to developments rather than directing them.

Such were Britain's difficulties in this period that some commentators used such terms as 'Britain in decline' or 'Britain, the sick man of Europe'. They meant that Britain had failed to match the growth rates achieved by the industrial economies of Western Europe, Japan and the USA. This was something that had become evident during the Macmillan years (see page 34) and was to continue to worry Wilson's and later governments. One explanation for Britain's relatively poor performance is that it spent too much on defence and too little on investment in industry. The figures in Table 3.2, which show the proportions spent on research and development (R&D), support this argument.

Table 3.2 Percentage of R&D budget spent on defence

State	1963–5	1966–70	1971–5	1976–9
Japan	0.9	0.9	0.7	0.6
Netherlands	1.9	2.3	2.0	1.6
Italy	2.6	2.4	2.1	1.9
West Germany	10.8	10.3	6.9	6.2
France	26.2	22.5	18.4	19.6
USA	40.6	31.9	27.7	25.4
Britain	34.5	25.6	28.9	29.3

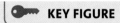 **KEY FIGURE**

George Brown (1914–85)

Minister of works 1951. Deputy leader of Labour Party 1960–70. Minister for economic affairs 1964–6. Foreign secretary 1966–70.

The National Plan 1964

Wilson's Labour government began confidently. A newly created department of economic affairs under **George Brown** drew up a National Plan, a programme for modernisation aimed at increasing industrial production and exports by encouraging co-operation between government, employers and trade unions. However, few of the expansive targets were met and by 1967 the National Plan had been quietly abandoned. But, in the interim, the electorate were sufficiently impressed by the government's modernising approach to give Labour a majority of 110 over the Conservatives in the 1966 election which had been called by Wilson after only eighteenth months in office. He had shrewdly judged that the growing popularity of the government would provide it with a comfortable working majority.

Table 3.3 Results of the 1966 general election

Party	Votes	Seats	Percentage of vote
Labour	13,064,951	363	47.9
Conservative	11,418,433	253	41.9
Liberal	2,327,533	12	8.5
Others	452,689	2	1.7

Tensions with the unions

Matters did not go well from the election onwards. Wilson was committed to the idea that inflation and Britain's balance of payments deficit were the major threats to Britain's economic progress, and that, consequently, wage and salary increases must be kept in check. As early as 1963, he had warned the Labour Party, trade unions and employers that they had to become more realistic in their approach to wage demands and settlements.

Convinced that his 1966 election success had given him a **mandate**, Wilson pressed forward with his ideas for cuts in government spending and a wage freeze. A Prices and Incomes Board was set up with the power to regulate pay settlements. Wilson's attitude disappointed the left of the party and angered the trade unions, which had hoped a Labour government would bring them benefits, not lectures on their need to be responsible and shore up the capitalist system. The leader of the Transport and General Workers' Union (TGWU, see page 104), Frank Cousins, whom Wilson had made his minister of technology in 1964, resigned over the creation of the Prices and Incomes Board.

The gap between government and unions became evident in a series of strikes over pay in 1966 and 1967, the most disruptive being lengthy stoppages by the seamen's and the dockers' unions. Wilson interpreted these as more than industrial disputes; he characterised them as a deliberate attack by a group of Marxist extremists on Britain's industrial well-being. In 1966, he spoke in the Commons of 'a tightly knit group of politically-motivated men who are now determined to exercise backstage pressures endangering the security of the industry and the economic welfare of the nation'.

Devaluation 1967

Wilson believed that the industrial troubles were a major factor in the increase in Britain's trade deficit, which had grown so large that in 1967 he felt he had to approach the **IMF** for another large loan, having already borrowed £1 billion from it three years earlier. Again, he blamed the trade union troublemakers, claiming that the government had begun to surmount the financial problems only to be 'blown off course by the seven weeks' seamen's strike'. The IMF loan was only a stop-gap, which, in Wilson's eyes, was a worrying sign that the government was losing control over its own finances.

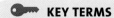 **KEY TERMS**

Mandate Popular backing for a particular policy.

IMF The International Monetary Fund. A scheme intended to prevent countries going bankrupt. It began in 1947 and by 1990 had been joined by over 150 countries. Each member state paid into a central fund from which it could then draw in time of need.

So concerned did Wilson become, that late in 1967 he took the step he had been determined to avoid since coming to power three years earlier – the devaluation of the pound. This involved reducing the exchange rate of sterling from $2.80 to $2.40. After the chancellor of the exchequer, James Callaghan, had announced the measure in the Commons, Wilson made a prime ministerial broadcast on television. In solemn tones, he informed the nation of what the government had been reluctantly forced to do. In an attempt to save face, Wilson assured viewers that devaluation did not mean the pound in their pockets was worth any less.

Perhaps, if devaluation had been introduced earlier and in a less theatrical way it could have been passed off as a mere financial adjustment. But Wilson, remembering that Attlee had had to devalue sterling in 1949, wanted to avoid the tag that Labour was the party of devaluation. However, by delaying the measure and then dramatising it, Wilson unwittingly made devaluation appear as a major political and economic failure by the government. That is how it was perceived by many inside as well as outside the Labour Party. A depressed Callaghan stood down as chancellor of the exchequer over it. The trade unions were angered by Wilson's attempt to lay most of the blame for the government's financial plight on the strikers. Interestingly, it is now recognised that Wilson had overestimated the seriousness of the balance of payments crisis. In fact, in the private sector of the economy there was no deficit but a substantial profit, as Table 3.4 shows.

Table 3.4 Britain's balance of payments 1963–9

Year	Balance in the private sector (in £ millions)	Balance in the public (government) sector (in £ millions)	Overall balance (in £ millions)
1963	+548	–619	+71
1964	–78	–666	–744
1965	+425	–677	–252
1966	+706	–754	–48
1967	+332	–793	–461
1968	+387	–785	–398
1969	+1,326	–924	+402

Commenting on the marked discrepancy between the private and public sectors, W.A.P. Manser, an influential economic historian, observed in 1971: 'For the cause of [Britain's] payments imbalance we need look no further than official activity. If there were no government spending, there would be no deficit and no balance of payments problem.' Nevertheless, whatever economic analysts might have concluded, Wilson was convinced at the time that Britain's sluggish industrial performance was largely caused by poor industrial relations. The strike figures appeared to support this belief. The Conservative governments (1951–64) had certainly been troubled by industrial action, but the number of stoppages grew in Wilson's time, undermining the idea that with Labour in power the unions would be easily appeased.

Table 3.5 Number of strikes and working days lost through industrial disputes

Year	Number of strikes	Days lost	Year	Number of strikes	Days lost
1951	1,719	1,694,000	1961	2,686	3,046,000
1952	1,714	1,792,000	1962	2,449	5,795,000
1953	1,746	2,184,000	1963	2,068	1,755,000
1954	1,989	2,457,000	1964	2,524	2,277,000
1955	2,419	3,781,000	1965	2,354	2,925,000
1956	2,648	2,083,000	1966	1,937	2,398,000
1957	2,859	8,412,000	1967	2,116	2,787,000
1958	2,629	3,462,000	1968	2,378	4,690,000
1959	2,093	5,270,000	1969	3,116	6,846,000
1960	2,832	3,024,000	1970	3,906	10,980,000

Labour and Europe 1967

It was economic fears at home that prompted Harold Wilson's government to make Britain's second attempt to join the EEC, four years after the French veto of the first application (see page 52). Wilson did this in the face of his party's continuing uncertainty on the issue. He feared that Britain would be left behind financially and economically by Europe unless it joined. Preliminary discussions with the EEC took place against the background of the sterling crisis which had led to devaluation. Backed fully by the Conservatives and the Liberals, but opposed by 36 Labour MPs, the government made its formal request. Again, on the same grounds as in 1963, the belief that Britain would be an obstructive member of the EEC, de Gaulle vetoed the UK's application. On this occasion, the annoyance of the other five members of the community with the French became quite open. However, this was of little consolation to Wilson; he had suffered the same humiliation that had befallen Harold Macmillan.

'In Place of Strife' 1969

The rebuff over Europe strengthened Wilson's determination to bring the unions into line. The climax of his campaign to make them accountable came in 1969 with the publication of a **White Paper**, 'In Place of Strife', a set of proposals aimed at preventing future strikes. The central proposal was for the introduction of a series of legal restrictions on the right to strike. Members of a union would have to be balloted and would have to agree by a clear majority on industrial action before a strike would be recognised as legal. Proposals were also included in the White Paper which obliged employers to keep to agreements and to consult the unions when major decisions were being contemplated. However, the unions were not impressed by this; they saw the supposed restrictions on employers as obvious attempts to make the strike controls more palatable to the employees.

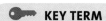 **KEY TERM**

White Paper A preliminary parliamentary statement of the government's plans in regard to a bill it intends to introduce.

**Barbara Castle
(1910–2002)**
Minister for overseas development 1964–5. Minister of transport 1965–8. Minister of labour 1968–70. Minister for social services 1974–6.

'In Place of Strife' never advanced beyond the White Paper stage. When it was put before the Cabinet by **Barbara Castle**, the minister of labour, it created immediate and deep divisions. The left asked bitterly why the government was contemplating a measure that undermined the principles for which the Labour Party was supposed to stand – protection of the unions. The party had come into being to resist restrictive laws on the workers and now it was being suggested that the laws should not be relaxed but tightened. There were allusions to the irony of Barbara Castle, a convinced left-wing Bevanite in her younger days, introducing the type of measure which one would expect from the Tories. It was the moderate James Callaghan, the Labour Party treasurer as well as the chancellor of the exchequer, who finally killed off any chance of 'In Place of Strife' proceeding by stressing the dangers to the party and government of alienating the trade unions, which still provided the bulk of Labour's funds.

The record of the Wilson government 1964–70

By 1970 there was a general feeling that Harold Wilson's first government had not lived up to expectations. The sharpest sense of disappointment was among traditional Labour supporters. They felt that the government had promised much but delivered little; it had entered office claiming to be a modernising, reforming government, but in practice had differed from its Conservative predecessors only in style, not in content. There had not been substantial change. Although certain sections of industry had been improved, it could not be said that the streamlining of British industry overall had been achieved. A leading social analyst, Peter Townshend, dismissed Labour's attempts at reform as 'hot compresses on an ailing body politic'.

Social reforms

While the government may have done nothing really new on the economic and industrial front, the same could not be said of its social reforms. In retrospect, these appeared groundbreaking (see pages 106–9):

- Race Relations Acts 1965 and 1968
- Abortion Act 1967
- Sexual Offences Act 1967
- Ombudsman 1967
- Commonwealth Immigration Act 1968
- Theatres Act 1968
- Abolition of the death penalty 1969
- Divorce Reform Act 1969
- The Open University 1969.

Roy Jenkins

1920 Born in Abersychan, son of a trade unionist

1948–87 Member of Parliament

1965–7 Home secretary

1967–70 Chancellor of the exchequer

1974–6 Home secretary

1977–81 President of European Commission

1982–3 Leader of the Social Democrat Party

2003 Died

Although Jenkins was home secretary for only two years initially, he had a profound effect on social attitudes. It is arguable that his liberal approach, which continued that of R.A. Butler, set the pattern for the rest of the century.

A man of refinement and high culture, a wine connoisseur and a distinguished historical biographer, Jenkins was less liberal and more orthodox in his economic policies as chancellor of the exchequer.

Never happy with the way the Labour left tried to impose what he regarded as their dated concepts on the Labour Party, he was one of the 'Gang of Four' who broke away in 1981 to form the Social Democratic Party (SDP, see page 152). It has been said that Roy Jenkins was New Labour (see page 178) before New Labour actually came into being, and that had he stayed in the Labour Party rather than breaking from it to form the SDP, he could have been a formative influence in the reshaping of New Labour.

Roy Jenkins as home secretary

The reforms listed above, particularly those relating to abortion, divorce, homosexuality, censorship and the death penalty, may be said to mark an important stage in the modernising of British social attitudes. They were largely the work of Roy Jenkins, home secretary between 1965 and 1967, who left such a mark on the home office that his successor, James Callaghan, simply continued with the programme that had been laid down. The measures were not always Jenkins' direct initiative: the abortion law, for example, was introduced by the Liberal MP David Steel. But it was Jenkins' support and encouragement of progressive social thinking that helped to create an atmosphere in which reform became acceptable.

Jenkins personified the tolerant, sophisticated attitudes that he wished to see become predominant in Britain. He was, of course, dealing with controversial issues. There were many in the population who were unhappy with these expressions of what became known as 'the permissive age'. They argued strongly that permissiveness could easily become an encouragement to socially irresponsible behaviour. Jenkins's response was to suggest that a more appropriate term for the times might be not the 'permissive' but the 'civilised age' (see page 107).

Criticisms of Wilson's first government

Even those who accepted the value of such social reforms tended to see them as isolated achievements. The people who had had the highest hopes of Harold Wilson – the left of the Labour Party and young people – were the most disillusioned by 1970. The left-wing critics complained that Wilson's government had either introduced or presided over the following:

- rising unemployment
- growing inflation
- wage controls
- attempted restriction of trade union freedoms
- immigration controls
- Britain's failed attempt to join Europe
- retention of Britain's nuclear weapons
- subservience to the USA in foreign policy.

The Vietnam War

A particular grievance of the left of the party was the government's support of the USA's involvement in the **Vietnam War**. In 1963 the USA, pursuing its 'containment' policy, based on the principle of not allowing Communism to spread, had become involved in what proved to be a long, drawn-out struggle in Indochina (south-east Asia). However, the ensuing war in Vietnam was never a simple conflict between good and evil. The various regimes that came to power in South Vietnam may have been anti-Communist but they were seldom genuinely democratic. The US governments met growing opposition at home to a war that became increasingly difficult to justify on strategic or moral grounds. Eventually, the USA withdrew all its forces from Vietnam in 1975, leaving the Communists victorious.

Although British forces took no part in the Vietnam War, Britain did give consistent diplomatic support to the USA. For many on the left, this was further evidence of Britain's subservience to the USA in foreign affairs. It was in protest against this that demonstrators in 1968 created the greatest civil disturbance in Britain since 1945 when they attempted to storm the US Embassy in London's Grosvenor Square. Wilson, unsurprisingly, condemned the violence as the work of people who simply did not understand international relations or Britain's financial position. Asked why he did not oppose the Americans over Vietnam, he replied angrily, 'We can't kick our creditors in the balls.' What he was saying in a crude way was that if Britain wanted to keep its hospitals, schools and welfare schemes, it could not afford to antagonise the country which, in effect, paid Britain's bills.

The end of Britain's 'east of Suez' role 1967–71

What found more favour with the left was the government's decision to end Britain's **east of Suez** stance. In 1967, Denis Healey, the defence minister, announced plans for the withdrawal of British troops from their bases in Borneo, Malaysia, Singapore and the Persian Gulf. This was planned to take effect by 1971. The withdrawal went ahead against the protest of the host governments, who lost both income and protection. The USA also strongly disapproved, arguing that Cold War tensions required a greater not a lesser commitment to the

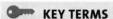

KEY TERMS

Vietnam War Fought from 1963 to 1975, it became the longest military struggle of the Cold War years. The USA sent forces to support the South Vietnamese governments in their resistance to invasion by Communist North Vietnam.

East of Suez A traditional shorthand way of referring to Britain's military commitments in the Middle East and Asia.

defence of the world's strategic areas. But a number of considerations combined to make Wilson's government determined to proceed with the withdrawal:

- The sheer cost of maintaining expensive bases was difficult to justify in a time of financial and economic difficulty at home.
- Exhausting military engagements in the 1950s and 1960s in Malaysia, Cyprus, Kenya and Aden, though largely successful, had stretched Britain's military resources to the limit.
- The Suez crisis had undermined Britain's confidence in playing the role of 'world police'.
- The process of giving up its former colonies and the abandonment of the vestiges of its empire (see page 46) made it wholly logical for Britain to withdraw from many of its military bases.
- Since Britain was still committed to the development of its nuclear weapons, it could still claim to be a world power notwithstanding its military cutbacks.

It was this last point in the list that continued to divide the Labour Party. Significantly, although the Conservatives had criticised the undermining of Britain's east of Suez role, Edward Heath's government after 1970 made no attempt to reverse the staged withdrawal that the Labour government had begun.

The 1970 general election

Despite internal party unrest and the loss of a number of by-elections, Wilson believed that Labour's basic support remained solid. That was why the result of the election he called in 1970 took him by surprise. He had not realised that his undistinguished economic policies, and his apparent failure to control the unions, had lost his government a significant degree of support among moderate voters. An extraordinary additional factor was Enoch Powell's contribution to Labour's defeat. Although Powell had been dismissed from the Conservative Party following his 'rivers of blood' speech (see page 110), his stand on immigration gained the Conservatives 2.5 million votes. The **psephologist** R.W. Johnson went so far as to claim that Powell won the 1970 election for the Conservatives: 'Of all those who had switched their vote from one party to another in the election, 50 per cent were working-class Powellites. Not only had 18 per cent of Labour Powellites switched to the Tories but so had 24 per cent of Liberal Powellites.' The result was a five per cent swing from Labour to Conservative, enough to put Edward Heath into office with a Commons' majority of 30.

 **KEY TERM**

Psephologist An expert on election trends and voting patterns.

Table 3.6 Results of the 1970 general election

Party	Votes	Seats	Percentage of vote
Conservative	13,145,123	330	46.4
Labour	12,179,341	287	43.0
Liberal	2,117,035	6	7.5
Others	903,299	7	3.1

Summary diagram: Wilson's government 1964–70

Wilson's narrow election victory 1964

- Conservative failings – tired and ageing image
- Wilson out-debated Douglas-Home
- Labour's young and enterprising image

Social unrest

- Government responded to racial violence with restrictive Commonwealth Immigration Act 1968

Labour's economic difficulties

Britain in transition:
- National Plan
- Manufacturing industries shrinking
- Service and finance industries expanding
- Rejection of UK's EEC application
- Union resistance to reform
- 'In Place of Strife' abandoned
- Inflation
- Unemployment
- Devaluation of the pound
- Rash of strikes

Overseas

- Costs and changing attitude to policeman role led to abandoning of Britain's east of Suez position
- UK gave diplomatic support to USA in Vietnam War

Shortcomings of the Wilson years

- Rising unemployment
- Growing inflation
- Conflict with trade unions
- Immigration controls
- Failure to join Europe

Election defeat 1970

- Undistinguished economic policies
- Failure to control the unions
- Devaluation
- Powell factor

Social reforms

- Role of Roy Jenkins ushered in the permissive age

② Heath's government 1970–4

▶ *What new style of government did Heath try to adopt?*

▶ *Who were the 'new right'?*

Heath's initial aim as prime minister

Edward Heath's position in 1970 was similar to Harold Wilson's six years earlier; he entered office with the aim of following progressive policies. He declared that he was adopting 'a new style of government' and that he intended 'to reduce the rise in prices, increase productivity and reduce unemployment'. Where Heath differed from Wilson was in his intention to break with the consensus that had broadly operated since 1945 in regard to state intervention in economic and social matters. This attitude was summed up in the term '**Selsdon Man**'; it referred to the new type of Conservatism, sometimes called the 'new right', that Heath had advocated in the run-up to the 1970 election. At a party strategy conference at Selsdon Park, Surrey, in January 1970, the Conservatives had

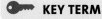

KEY TERM

Selsdon Man A symbolic anti-Keynesian, pro-market individual.

Edward Heath

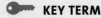

1916	Born in Broadstairs, the son of a builder
1950–2001	Member of Parliament
1965–75	Leader of the Conservative Party
1970–4	Prime minister
2005	Died

Grammar-school educated, Edward Heath was one of the talented young Conservatives who helped regenerate the party in the early 1950s. In 1960 Harold Macmillan gave him the task of negotiating the UK's entry into the EEC (see page 51). This work became the defining characteristic of his career.

In 1965, Heath became the first elected leader of the Conservative Party. However, this democratic distinction did not prevent his only period as prime minister, 1970–4, from being widely regarded as a failure. After two election defeats in 1974 (he lost three general elections out of four within a space of nine years), he was beaten in the party's 1975 leadership contest by Margaret Thatcher, with whom he had strained relations for the rest of his long career. He did not hold office again but remained in politics as a backbench MP.

In a tribute to Heath after his death, Thatcher commented that he had helped change the character of Conservative leadership 'by his humble background, by his grammar school education and by the fact of his democratic election'. To that could be added the enduring effect of his decision to lead Britain into the EEC in 1973.

agreed to promote a largely hands-off approach in matters of government direction and to encourage the people to use the new freedom to promote their own interests.

The change of approach was intended to be a liberating form of politics, but the Labour Party was quick to brand it as a return to right-wing reaction. Harold Wilson declared a month later that 'Selsdon Man is designing a system of society for the ruthless and the pushing, the uncaring. His message to the rest of us is: you're out on your own.' An important aspect of Heath's new approach was his decision to abandon an incomes policy; his government would not seek to impose a wage and salary freeze or interfere with pay settlements. Instead, **market forces** would be allowed to operate, allowing free bargaining between employers and workers. However, to make such bargaining genuine and fair it was important not to permit the trade unions to have unfair advantages. That was the reasoning behind the introduction of the 1971 Industrial Relations Act by Robert Carr, the minister of labour.

The Industrial Relations Act 1971

The Act was an extension of 'In Place of Strife', the measure which Wilson's government had considered in 1969 but had withdrawn in the face of party and trade union opposition (see page 71):

- It restricted the right of workers to strike by introducing a new concept of 'unfair industrial practice'.
- A National Industrial Relations Court (NIRC), with authority to judge the validity of strike action, was created.

KEY TERM

Market forces The natural laws of supply and demand operating without interference by government.

- Unions were required to put themselves on a government register if they wanted to retain their legal rights.

It was with the same object of giving freer rein to market forces that Heath appointed John Davies to head the new department of trade and industry (DTI). Davies was not a conventional politician; he came from outside Parliament having been director-general of the **CBI**. One of his first statements was that he intended to advise the government against helping 'lame ducks', referring to those companies and businesses which, despite performing badly, still expected public money to be spent on bailing them out.

🔑 **KEY TERM**

CBI Confederation of British Industry. Representing Britain's leading manufacturers and industrialists; although officially neutral in politics, it tended to side with the Conservatives.

A further example of the 'new right' approach was the policy followed by Anthony Barber as chancellor of the exchequer. Barber replaced Iain MacLeod, whose death in 1970 after being at the treasury for only a few weeks deprived the government of, arguably, its ablest minister. Barber's early measures included:

- income tax cuts
- reductions in government spending
- scrapping of the Prices and Incomes Board
- cuts in the subsidies paid to local authorities.

Whatever thanks Barber may have gained from the workers for lifting the restrictions on wage bargaining was more than lost by his tax concession to the wealthy and the cuts in government spending, the effects of which included a rise in council house rents. One particularly unpopular cut was the withdrawal of free milk for school children. This measure was piloted through by Margaret Thatcher, secretary for education, leading to opponents chanting, 'Margaret Thatcher, milk snatcher'. Whatever the economic argument might have been for the government's measures, they were a failure in public relations. The opposition seized the opportunity to condemn Heath's government for:

- abandoning the mixed economy
- weakening the welfare state
- undermining the principle of full employment
- putting economic calculation before social improvement.

These may have been exaggerated charges, but there was no denying that Heath's government had provided sufficient ammunition for Wilson to claim that he had been right in his interpretation of 'Selsdon Man' as an essentially reactionary force in politics.

Heath's U-turn

The Labour opposition had even more reason to mock when, within eighteen months of attempting his new style of government, Heath had to turn 180 degrees. Inflation, which had risen to fifteen per cent by the end of 1971, and declining industrial output destroyed the government's confidence that it could continue with its original policy. In 1972, the government announced that in an attempt to counter inflation it was returning to a policy of controlling prices and incomes. By then, it had also abandoned the notion of government non-interference in industrial matters. Contrary to John Davies' warning that the government would not help lame ducks, the DTI began to do precisely that. One of Britain's most famous companies, Rolls-Royce, had hit hard times. Its orders were falling and it was haemorrhaging money at an alarming rate. Rather than see the company, historically a beacon of British industrial success, go under, the government nationalised it in 1971. It was now to be sustained by government grants.

Subsidies were also granted to other private companies in difficulties, a major one being the Upper Clyde Shipbuilders. The threat that this Scottish company might be forced to close led to a determined resistance from the workers. Fearing that the industrial action, skilfully organised by Communist shop-stewards, might spill over into violence, the government backed down and authorised a subsidy of £34 million to be paid to keep the company going.

Problems with the unions

Having had to abandon his original hands-off policy, Heath now appealed to the unions to sit down with the government and the CBI and solve their common problems together. But it was too late for co-operation; too much had happened. The unions were suspicious and hostile. They asked the obvious question: why, if the government genuinely wanted partnership, had it introduced the 'union bashing' Industrial Relations Act in the first place?

As soon as the Act had been passed in 1971, the **TUC** had resisted by formally voting not to co-operate with the government's measures and calling on the individual unions to refuse to register. The unions responded with a collective rejection of registration. Such solidarity rendered it impossible to enforce or apply the Act. It made Heath and his Cabinet appear both incompetent and unrealistic and encouraged the more combative unions to increase their demands, something that was evident in the number of strikes that marred Heath's four years in government.

Table 3.7 Strike record during the Heath years 1971–4

Year	Number of strikes	Working days lost
1971	2,228	13,551,000
1972	2,497	23,909,000
1973	2,873	7,197,000
1974	2,922	14,750,000

It was the National Union of Mineworkers (NUM) that forced the issue. In 1972, in a joint bid to gain a wage increase and to highlight the increasing number of pit closures that threatened its members' livelihood, the NUM, led by **Arthur Scargill**, called a strike during which it effectively used **flying pickets** to prevent the movement of coal. This seriously disrupted fuel and electricity supplies and considerably reduced industrial production.

KEY TERMS

TUC Trades Union Congress: a federation of individual trade unions.

Flying pickets Teams of union members ready to rush to areas where strikes had been called to help dissuade or intimidate workers from going to work.

KEY FIGURE

Arthur Scargill (1938–)
Leader of the NUM from 1982 to 2002.

The three-day week 1973

Rather than give in to the miners, Heath hoped to defeat them by imposing severe limits on the use of fuel, thereby enabling the government to resist the NUM's attempted blackmail. Heath calculated that the government would be able to survive the strike longer than the miners. In December 1973 he announced that from the end of the year 'most industrial and commercial premises will be limited in the use of electricity to three specified days a week'. The situation could hardly have been more serious. The restrictive measures introduced by the government recalled the austerities of wartime and the late 1940s. Electricity blackouts interfered with industrial production and left ordinary people without light and heating for long periods. Sitting in candlelight and unable to cook, listen to radio or watch television, most people were well disposed neither to the miners nor to the government.

When the miners' dispute was eventually settled, the NUM gained a 21 per cent wage increase, nearly three times the amount that the employers had originally offered. The strike and its settlement marked a major defeat for Heath and his government. Emboldened by its success, the NUM again went on strike early in 1974 in pursuit of a further wage demand. This was too much for Heath. He called an immediate election on the issue of who ran the country: the miners or the government. The answer of the electorate was not what he had hoped for.

The 1974 (February) general election

While the election was not an overwhelming defeat for Heath, the results showed that a critical number of voters judged him to have been a failure; his government had achieved none of the economic goals it had set itself on taking office four years earlier:

- Rapid inflation had made the holding down of prices impossible.
- The wage demands of the unions, which in the majority of cases were accepted by the employers, and the large number of days lost through strikes, resulted in a decline rather than a growth in productivity.
- Unemployment had not been reduced. Indeed, 1972 marked the highest figure for joblessness since the depression in the 1930s.
- The resort to the three-day week in 1973 showed how far the government had fallen short of its aims.

The number of voters who felt disillusioned with the government was sufficient to give the Labour Party a narrow victory. The Conservatives gained a higher aggregate vote but the more telling figure was that their support had slipped by nearly seven points. Labour also lost ground electorally. Despite winning four more seats than the Conservatives, its popular vote dropped by six per cent. The impressive performance was by the Liberals, who increased their vote by over four million. Their fourteen seats were small reward for gaining well over half the vote achieved individually by the Conservative and Labour parties.

Table 3.8 Results of the February 1974 general election

Party	Votes	Seats	Percentage of vote
Conservative	11,868,906	297	37.9
Labour	11,639,243	301	37.1
Liberal	6,063,470	14	19.3
Northern Irish parties	717,986	12	2.3
Scottish Nationalists	632,032	7	2.0
Plaid Cymru	171,364	2	0.6
Others	260,665	2	0.8

The election gave Labour a majority of four over the Conservatives. With the support of the fourteen Liberal MPs, Harold Wilson was able to embark on his second period of government. But before turning to consider this, attention needs to be given to three other developments whose full effects were not felt until after Heath had lost office but which began during his period in government. These were:

- local government reform
- Britain's entry into the EEC
- the international oil crisis.

Reform of local government

Judged by its effects, one of the most significant of Heath's reforms was the Local Government Act (passed in two stages in 1972 and 1973), prepared and introduced by Peter Walker, the environment minister. This proved to be the most sweeping reform of its kind yet attempted; in reshaping the structure of local government the measures destroyed many historical administrative landmarks. Whole areas were subsumed into newly created regions and many familiar place names disappeared. There were protests, particularly from Conservatives on the right, that Walker's changes amounted in many cases to an attack on local identity.

Britain's entry into Europe 1973

Following de Gaulle's retirement as French president in 1969, the EEC had invited Britain to reapply. This gave Edward Heath the opportunity to fulfil his driving ambition of leading Britain into Europe. Ignoring the political implications of Britain's joining, he told his party that the economic situation made it essential that Britain became an EEC member. A typical expression of his ideas was contained in a speech in 1971 (see Source A, page 82).

According to Edward Heath in Source A, why did Europe overtake Britain in economic performance after the war?

SOURCE A

From Edward Heath's speech to the Conservative Party Conference in 1971, quoted in the Conservative Party Archive, www.bodleian.ox.ac.uk/cpa.

Twenty-five years ago much of Western Europe lay literally in ruins. Economic and industrial life had come to a standstill. For us here in Britain it was different. We were bruised, we were exhausted, but our economy and our industry remained intact. In Europe they were able again to start from scratch but we had to make do and mend. So it was not surprising when those countries, first matched and then overtook Britain in economic performance. A new world was already emerging; and it is to the credit of our Party that from an early stage we recognized that fact. Later we tried to join the united and prospering efforts of the major countries of Western Europe, but then Britain was foiled in the attempt by the veto of President De Gaulle. Our special strength is our stamina, in going on with what needs doing until it is done. We never know when we are beaten and that way we never are beaten. That is why Europe needs us.

Heath's government duly accepted the EEC's offer and signed the Treaty of Accession in 1972, which led to Britain's becoming a full member of the EEC on New Year's Day 1973. There is little doubt that Edward Heath regarded this as his greatest political achievement. Since the late 1950s, when Macmillan had asked him to be Britain's special negotiator with Europe, Heath had committed himself to obtaining Britain's entry. He had staked his reputation on it.

Advantages of Britain joining the EEC

- Gained access to European markets.
- Benefited from the final end of wartime antagonisms.
- As part of a European block, it stood a better chance of attracting global business.
- British regions were entitled to European development grants.
- British workers had the right to work in other EEC countries.
- Greater opportunity of movement for British people within Europe.

Disadvantages of Britain joing the EEC

- Britain was no longer able to buy cheap food from the Commonwealth.
- At the time of entry, Britain was classified as an advanced industrial economy. This meant that it had to make higher contributions to the EEC budget than it received in grants from Europe. By the early 1980s Britain was paying twenty per cent of the revenue raised by the EEC but was receiving only eight per cent of the expenditure.
- The European policy of supporting farmers meant that British consumers found themselves paying inflated prices.
- The Common Fisheries Policy severely restricted Britain's right to fish in its customary grounds and led to a significant reduction in its fishing industry.
- As a condition of entry, Britain had to impose a value-added tax (VAT) on most of the commodities which British consumers bought; VAT began in 1973 at eight per cent.
- In entering the EEC, Britain had joined a protectionist organisation that was already beginning to look dated now that the world was entering into the era of global markets.

That was why, having been invited to apply by the Six, Heath rushed to comply with their conditions of entry. Significantly, Britain's team of negotiators were instructed not to let their concerns about the political implications of entry deter them from continuing. One of the senior civil servants involved in the discussions later admitted that the possible loss of British sovereignty had been 'very much present in the mind of the negotiators', but they acted on the general understanding that 'the less they came out in the open the better': an example of the Establishment closing ranks.

The weakness of Britain's bargaining position

The Six knew that, notwithstanding Heath's personal ambitions, Britain had sought membership because it judged it could not survive economically on its own. This remains a highly controversial viewpoint. There are those who now argue that membership of the EEC, far from helping Britain, proved to be a brake on its progress. But, at the time, the majority view prevailing in government circles, though not in the Conservative or Labour parties, was that Britain could not afford to remain outside.

Britain could not negotiate from a position of strength in 1972. It had had no say in the setting up of EEC and, understandably, the existing members were not going to allow Britain as a late-comer to change the workings of the system they had created. One of the most significant EEC demands that Britain accepted was that Commonwealth food and goods would no longer enter Britain on preferential terms. Produce, for example, from Australia and New Zealand now had a European tariff placed on it that made it decreasingly profitable for those countries to sell to Britain or beneficial to Britain to buy from them.

> Study Source B. How has the cartoonist linked Britain's industrial troubles with its negotiations to join the EEC?

SOURCE B

A cartoon published in *The Observer* newspaper, 20 February 1972. Pompidou (right), the French president, says to Prime Minister Heath (with lamp, left): 'I was going to ask about all that technological know-how Britain will bring into Europe.'

It was true the EEC did permit a transition stage so that Britain and the Commonwealth countries could adjust to these changes, but the position was now clear. Britain had sacrificed its economic ties with the Commonwealth. There is a strong argument for regarding Britain's accession into Europe as an irreversible moment. Britain seemed resigned to the fact that it was a declining economic force whose only chance of survival was as a member of a protectionist European organisation.

The international oil price rise 1973

Heath had hoped that by joining Europe his government would be able to claw back some of the economic ground Britain had lost since 1970. But he was mistaken. Europe did not hold the key to British recovery. By a cruel twist the UK's entry into the EEC in 1973 coincided with the onset of an international crisis which showed that however Britain and, indeed, Europe might organise themselves, they were dangerously susceptible to events in the outside world over which they had no control.

Until the early 1970s, large multinational companies had controlled the production and distribution of oil and had provided the Western world with a steady supply of relatively cheap fuel. However, from the early 1960s, **OPEC** members began to establish greater control over their own oil industries. How strong OPEC had become was shown dramatically in 1973 when its Arab members chose to use oil as a weapon in their long-running conflict with Israel.

In retaliation for the West's support of Israel in the Arab–Israeli war, fought in October 1973, the Arab members of OPEC drastically reduced their oil supplies to those Western countries which they believed had sided with Israel. At the same time, OPEC sharply raised the price of its oil exports. Between 1973 and 1980 the cost of oil increased from $2 to $35 per barrel. The main target was the USA, but all the other Western states whose economies were heavily dependent on oil suffered. It was not simply fuel but all the many oil-based products, such as plastics, that became greatly more expensive. The result was rapid and severe inflation throughout the industrial world. In the decade after 1973, Britain suffered a severe recession.

The economic effects in Britain of the oil price rise

- The balance of payments deficit rose to £1 billion.
- The annual inflation rate rose to sixteen per cent.
- The value of sterling dropped to $1.57.
- The interest rate was raised to fifteen per cent.
- A record budget deficit occurred.
- Between 1974 and 1976 the unemployment figures more than doubled to 1.44 million and remained high for the rest of the decade.

OPEC Organisation of Petroleum Exporting Countries. Formed in 1961, it came to represent all the leading oil-producing nations, including the strategically vital Arab states of Bahrain, Iraq, Kuwait, Libya and Saudi Arabia.

Table 3.9 UK unemployment figures 1970–9

Year	Number
1970	628,000
1971	868,000
1972	929,000
1973	785,000
1974	628,000
1975	1,152,000
1976	1,440,000
1977	1,567,000
1978	1,608,000
1979	1,464,000

The unemployment statistics in Table 3.9 illustrate that although the oil crisis began during Heath's time in office, it was to be the Labour government of 1974–9 that would suffer the full force of these developments (see page 86).

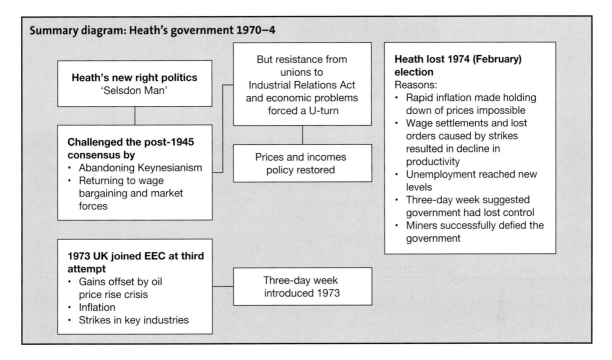

Summary diagram: Heath's government 1970–4

Heath's new right politics 'Seldson Man'

Challenged the post-1945 consensus by
• Abandoning Keynesianism
• Returning to wage bargaining and market forces

But resistance from unions to Industrial Relations Act and economic problems forced a U-turn

Prices and incomes policy restored

1973 UK joined EEC at third attempt
• Gains offset by oil price rise crisis
• Inflation
• Strikes in key industries

Three-day week introduced 1973

Heath lost 1974 (February) election
Reasons:
• Rapid inflation made holding down of prices impossible
• Wage settlements and lost orders caused by strikes resulted in decline in productivity
• Unemployment reached new levels
• Three-day week suggested government had lost control
• Miners successfully defied the government

3 Labour in office 1974–9

▶ *What problems confronted the Wilson and Callaghan governments between 1974 and 1979?*

From the beginning the Labour governments of 1974–9 suffered from three debilitating restrictions:

• the narrowness of Labour's overall majority in the Commons
• the grim effects of the rapid inflation that followed the oil price rise of 1973
• the struggle with the trade unions.

Labour's narrow Commons' majority

Although the second election in 1974 gave Labour a majority over the Conservatives of 42, its overall majority throughout its five years in office was never more than three seats. This tight margin made the government heavily dependent on the Liberal MPs and gave the Liberal Party an influence, eventually formalised in the **Lib–Lab pact**, that it had not enjoyed for half a century. There was some justice in this, since, in the two elections in 1974, the Liberals had won nearly twenty per cent of the popular vote.

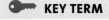

KEY TERM

Lib–Lab pact A 1977 agreement committing the Liberals to vote with the government in the Commons in return for the government's agreement to consult the Liberals on key issues. The pact lapsed in the autumn of 1978.

Table 3.10 Results of the October 1974 general election

Party	Votes	Seats	Percentage of vote
Labour	11,457,079	319	39.2
Conservative	10,464,817	277	35.8
Liberal	5,346,754	13	18.3
Northern Irish parties	702,094	12	2.4
Scottish Nationalists	893,617	11	2.9
Plaid Cymru	166,321	3	0.6

Inflation

The second problem was that the Labour governments of 1974–9 held office at a time when Britain began to suffer the worst effects of the rapid inflation that followed the oil price rise of 1973 (see page 84). The decline in the value of money and the growing debit in its trade balance threatened to make Britain bankrupt. In March 1976, for the first time in its history, the pound dropped below $2 in exchange value.

IMF crisis 1976

In September 1976, Dennis Healey, the chancellor of the exchequer, had to begin negotiating a loan of £3 billion from the IMF. The terms of the loan required Britain to make major cuts in its public expenditure. This outraged the left and the unions, who threatened to make trouble. In October, Healey had to delay a flight to Manila, where the IMF negotiations were being held, to rush to the Labour conference in an effort preserve party unity. He was only partially successful. A number of delegates jeered him when he appealed to them to show realism and accept that cuts in public expenditure were necessary in the country's interests.

Healey's rough reception showed that the long-running feud between the left and centre-right of the Labour Party was as fierce as ever. The left complained that the government was following policies which were indistinguishable from those of the Conservatives; it was trying to overcome Britain's financial and economic ills by policies shaped round the demands of international financiers. The centre-right counter-claimed that the government, by appearing so feeble in the face of threats from the trade union extremists, was in danger of losing its power to govern independently and was alienating itself from the ordinary voters of Britain.

Callaghan continued to try to face the left down. By 1979 the government, in line with the IMF demand, had reduced its spending programme by £3 billion. This helped to stabilise the financial situation but at the cost of increased unemployment, which reached 1.6 million in 1978. Commentators on both the left and right regarded these concessions to the IMF demands as marking a critical stage in the Labour Party's development. Labour's Tony Benn, for example, later claimed that the Cabinet's decision to give in to the demands of international bankers deprived a supposedly socialist government of the moral high ground and so opened the way for the Thatcher revolution of the 1980s (see page 120). Many others saw the IMF loan as further evidence of Britain's decline.

Labour and the unions

The government's failure to handle its economic problems without recourse to very large loans from the IMF related very closely to Labour's third abiding problem: its struggle to come to terms with the unions. The cuts in public expenditure and the resulting rise in unemployment that followed the IMF agreement embittered the trade unions and weakened their traditional loyalty to the Labour Party.

The credit the government had gained from repealing the Industrial Relations Act in 1974 was lost by its inability to persuade the workers to co-operate consistently with it. In many respects this was a repeat of the troubles that had stalked the Heath government (see page 76). The bitter aspect for Labour was that for a time after 1974 Wilson had seemed to be on co-operative terms with the unions. His good relations with Jack Jones, the moderate leader of the influential TGWU, promised much. There was frequent reference to a **social contract** between the government and the unions, but it produced little in the way of direct results. There were few examples of unions restricting their wage claims in accordance with it.

The referendum on Europe 1975

Harold Wilson was very conscious that the left wing of the Labour Party and the trade unions remained suspicious of the EEC. They regarded it as a capitalist club, necessarily hostile to socialism. It was to improve his relations with the unions that Wilson had pledged, while in opposition, that a future Labour government would renegotiate the terms of Britain's membership of the EEC. So it was that after being returned to office in 1974, his government began renegotiations in regard to agriculture, budget payments and Commonwealth imports. James Callaghan took the role of the government's chief representative. The exercise was largely a gesture since the talks produced no major changes. However, Wilson was able to claim that the renegotiations had opened the way for the British people to have a real choice on Europe. On the strength of this argument, he called a national referendum in 1975, the first consultation of its kind in British history. He had prepared the way for this in the Labour election manifesto (see Source C, page 38).

 **KEY TERM**

Social contract An informal 1972 agreement between Wilson and Vic Feather, the TUC general secretary, to the effect that when Labour was returned to power, the unions would follow a wage restraint policy in return for the adoption of pro-worker industrial policies by the government.

According to Source C, why is the Labour Party prepared to renegotiate the terms of the UK's relationship with Europe?

SOURCE C

From the Labour Party manifesto of February 1974, www.labour-party.org.uk/manifestos/1974/Feb/1974-feb-labour-manifesto.shtml.

Britain is a European nation, and a Labour Britain would always seek a wider co-operation between the European peoples. But a profound political mistake made by the Heath Government was to accept the terms of entry to the Common Market, and to take us in without the consent of the British people. This has involved the imposition of food taxes on top of rising world prices, crippling fresh burdens on our balance of payments, and a draconian curtailment of the power of the British parliament to settle questions affecting vital British interests. This is why a Labour Government will immediately seek a fundamental re-negotiation of the terms of entry. The Labour Party opposes British membership of the European Community on the terms negotiated by the Conservative Government. We have said that we are ready to re-negotiate. If re-negotiations are successful, it is the policy of the Labour Party that the people should have the right to decide the issue through a General Election or a Consultative Referendum. If these two tests are passed, a successful re-negotiation and the expressed approval of the majority of the British people, then we shall be ready to play our full part in developing a new and wider Europe.

In the campaign that preceded the referendum, the MPs were under no instruction from their parties as to which side to take. This produced an interesting cross-party divide. Although the government backed a yes vote, the bulk of Labour members were for coming out, and the majority of Conservatives and Liberals were for staying in. Prominent Labour pro-Europeans were Roy Jenkins and Shirley Williams, who shared a platform with Edward Heath and other leading Conservatives. The most conspicuous Labour opponents of Europe were Tony Benn, Michael Foot, Barbara Castle and Peter Shore.

In a remarkable move in the week before the referendum on 5 June 1975, the government sent a leaflet by post to all households. It was headed 'Britain's New Deal in Europe' and recommended that electors should vote to stay in the EEC.

According to Source D, why was the government urging the electorate to opt to stay in the EEC?

SOURCE D

From the government pamphlet of May/June 1975, 'Britain's New Deal in Europe', www.harvard-digital.co.uk/euro/pamphlet.htm#8.

'Her Majesty's Government have decided to recommend to the British people to vote for staying in the Community.'

Harold Wilson, Prime Minister

Dear Voter

This pamphlet is being sent by the Government to every household in Britain. We hope that it will help you to decide how to cast your vote in the coming Referendum on the European Community (Common Market).

Please read it. Please discuss it with your family and your friends.

We have tried here to answer some of the important questions you may be asking, with natural anxiety, about the historic choice that now faces all of us.

We explain why the Government, after long, hard negotiations, are recommending to the British people that we should remain a member of the European Community.

We do not pretend, and never have pretended, that we got everything we wanted in these negotiations. But we did get big and significant improvements on the previous terms.

We confidently believe that these better terms can give Britain a New Deal in Europe. A Deal that will help us, help the Commonwealth, and help our partners in Europe.

That is why we are asking you to vote in favour of remaining in the Community.

Historian Martin Pugh, writing in 1982, suggested that, when it came to polling day, the electorate, 'voted more out of fear of the consequences of leaving than out of enthusiasm for remaining in'. It was no great surprise that the results showed a large majority for Britain's staying in the EEC.

Table 3.11 Results of UK referendum on EEC membership, June 1975

Region	Total votes	'Yes' vote (%)	'No' vote (%)	Turnout (%)
England	21,772,222	68.7	31.3	64.6
Scotland	2,286,676	58.4	41.6	61.7
Wales	1,345,545	64.8	35.2	66.7
Northern Ireland	498,751	52.1	47.9	47.4
UK total	29,453,194	64.5	35.5	64.5

Opponents of the 'yes' vote argued that the referendum should have preceded Britain's entry, not followed it; Britain was voting on a *fait accompli*, not making a free choice. They also pointed out that, funded by the EEC, the 'yes' lobby had been able to spend twice as much on the campaign as the 'no' lobby, proportions which exactly matched the vote distribution.

The economic advantages that Britain expected to gain from entry proved illusory. The international oil price rise that began in 1973 had such a restrictive effect on the British economy (see page 84) that whatever gains might have accrued from being a member of the EEC were far outweighed by the inflation and economic downturn of the 1970s. It was also the case that in the period between 1958 and 1973, the year in which Britain formally joined the EEC, British exports to the EEC countries had more than doubled as a share of national income. Ironically, British exports to Europe declined after 1973. Thus,

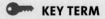 **KEY TERM**

Fait accompli An irreversible position already established.

having joined Europe in the hope of improving its economic status, Britain found that the net effect of its membership was greatly increased financial costs with no real trade benefits.

An issue which became contentious soon afterwards was that, at the time of the referendum, insufficient attention was given to the effect that membership of a federal union would have on British sovereignty. It should be emphasised that if the federal issue had been deliberately ignored or avoided this had not been Europe's fault. The members of the EEC made no attempt to hide the truth. They never denied that to join a federal union necessarily involved some loss of national sovereignty. **Jean Monnet** had spelt that out clearly as early as 1948: 'Only the establishment of a *federation* of the West, including Britain, will enable us to solve our problems quickly enough, and finally prevent war.' Robert Schuman (see page 13) had re-emphasised this point in 1950: 'Europe must be reorganised on a federal basis.'

Wilson's retirement in 1976

Despite his achievement in leading his party to victory in the two elections of 1974, Harold Wilson was in office for only two years. He resigned in March 1976 to be succeeded by James Callaghan as Labour prime minister. From time to time, there have been suggestions that Wilson's surprising decision to step down so early was because he wanted to leave office before the economic situation got worse, or because he was threatened with blackmail by the Soviet secret service over an affair he was supposedly having with his personal secretary. The less dramatic but more likely explanation is that the strains of office and leadership led him to keep to an earlier resolution that he had made to retire at 60.

Callaghan's problems

Wilson's declared intention had been to lead a Labour government that would break from the 'stop–go' economic policies associated with the Conservatives. But the effects of the 1973 oil price crisis destroyed any hopes he had of doing that. Callaghan fared no better after he took over. The industrial unrest that followed in the wake of the IMF crisis of that year set a pattern that was to continue throughout Callaghan's three years as premier. There was scarcely a month in which a strike did not occur; even the more moderate unions became involved. Angered by such moves as Callaghan's sudden announcement in December 1977 of a compulsory five per cent ceiling on wage rises, the unions became more sweeping in their demands and more aggressive in their methods.

It was around this time that foreign journalists coined the term 'the British disease' to describe the combination of poor employer–worker relations and constant industrial stoppages. The strike figures in Table 3.12 show how disturbed industrial relations became.

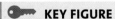 **KEY FIGURE**

**Jean Monnet
(1888–1979)**

A French foreign minister, regarded as the founding father of the EEC.

Table 3.12 Strike record during the Wilson and Callaghan years 1974–9

Year	Number of strikes	Working days lost
1974	2,922	14,750,000
1975	2,282	6,012,000
1976	2,016	3,284,000
1977	2,627	9,985,000
1978	2,349	9,306,000
1979	4,583	29,474,000

Among the most disruptive industrial actions were the following:

- A firefighters' strike in 1977 led the government to announce a state of emergency.
- A year-long strike beginning in 1977 at the Grunwick Film Processing Laboratories in north London involved mass picketing and violent clashes with the police.
- The workers at all 23 plants of Ford Motors went on strike in September 1979; the dispute was settled only by the Ford management giving in and granting a seventeen per cent pay rise.
- A lorry drivers' strike, called for January 1979, threatened the nation's food supplies; it was called off after the drivers gained a twenty per cent wage rise.

The 'winter of discontent' 1978–9

A particularly significant development was increased militancy among the public sector workers. Not wishing to miss out on the large pay settlements being achieved by many unions in the private sector, public service unions began to make demands. They felt they were the ones who suffered most from the government's cuts in public expenditure. It was their sense of grievance that intensified the industrial troubles and led to what became known as the 1978–9 '**winter of discontent**'. Taking their cue from the success of the haulage drivers, an alliance of public service unions, including the influential **NUPE** and **COHSE**, called for a day of action. On 22 January around 1.5 million workers responded by coming out on strike.

Following this impressive success, selective strikes were organised in areas calculated to attract the greatest media attention. The school meals service was disrupted, mounds of refuse were left to pile up uncollected and, perhaps most headline-catching of all, industrial action by grave diggers left dead bodies unburied. The media certainly sensationalised all this, but their depiction of a disrupted Britain was not all exaggeration. The Wilson and Callaghan governments had failed to meet their own expectations and the hopes of others. They had alienated large sections of their natural supporters and given encouragement to the opposition.

 **KEY TERMS**

Winter of discontent The term comes from the first line of Shakespeare's *Richard III*: 'Now is the winter of our discontent.'

NUPE National Union of Public Employees.

COHSE Confederation of Health Service Employees.

The economic problems the Labour administrations faced would have taxed any government. Yet it has to be said that Callaghan made matters worse during his period of government by appearing to allow things to drift. One example was his failure to call an election in the autumn of 1978, at a time when opinion polls showed that his government was picking up support. By waiting, he lost any room for manoeuvre, since there had to be an election no later than the autumn of 1979. His relaxed style of leadership had its attractions but it was not ideally suited to a time of crisis, where a more dynamic approach seemed necessary.

The 1979 general election

By the time Callaghan belatedly called the election in 1979, the Labour government had been gravely damaged by:

- economic and financial crises
- rising unemployment
- combative trade unionism
- political misjudgements.

The most serious of the government's political misjudgements was its treatment of the minority parties on whom its continuation in office had come to depend. In the autumn of 1978 it allowed the Lib–Lab pact to lapse (see page 85). With its tiny majority practically wiped out in by-election defeats, Callaghan's government was now reliant on the support of the Scottish Nationalist Party (SNP) in the Commons. However, when a referendum in Scotland in March 1979 failed to provide a clear mandate for **devolution**, the government dropped its proposal to introduce it. The SNP MPs immediately withdrew their support. The outcome was that on 28 March the government, with its majority gone, was defeated on a vote of no confidence. Obliged by this to call an election, Callaghan's government ended its six years in office in parliamentary failure. The Labour Party thus went into the election campaign in a low state of morale. The government's errors provided the opportunity for the Conservatives, under their new leader, Margaret Thatcher (who had ousted Edward Heath in 1975), to challenge Labour's hold on power.

KEY TERM

Devolution Granting to Wales and Scotland a significant measure of control over their own affairs by the creation of a separate parliament or national assembly.

Table 3.13 Results of the 1979 general election

Party	Votes	Seats	Percentage of vote
Conservative	13,697,690	339	43.9
Labour	11,532,148	269	36.9
Liberal	4,313,811	11	13.8
Plaid Cymru	132,544	2	0.4
SNP	504,259	2	1.6
Northern Irish parties	695,889	12	2.2

The 1979 result was not so much a matter of the Conservatives' winning the election as Labour's losing it. One of the most effective campaign posters in modern electioneering showed a long winding unemployment queue with

SOURCE E

How would you explain Source E's effectiveness as political propaganda?

The Conservatives' main election poster of 1979, voted 'the poster advertisement of the century' by the advertising trade magazine *Campaign*.

the caption, 'Labour isn't working'. For a significant portion of the electorate, this was a fair assessment of Labour's record. However, it would be inaccurate to describe Labour as having been swept from power by an angry electorate; indeed, it very nearly held its 1974 position in terms of votes and percentage support (see Table 3.13). But there was sufficient disillusion among the electors for them to give the Conservatives an eight-point increase in their 1974 showing and an additional 3 million votes. This provided the Conservatives with a comfortable majority of 70 over Labour and a majority overall of 43. It was enough to allow Margaret Thatcher to take office.

Summary diagram: Labour in office 1974–9

Underlying problems
- Small Labour majority in the Commons
- Grim effects of the oil price rise of 1973
- Struggle with combative trade unions

1975 EEC referendum confirmed UK's membership of EEC

Callaghan succeeded Wilson in 1976, but:
- 1976 IMF crisis deepened divisions in government and party
- Growing number of strikes 1977–9
- Industrial action by public sector unions led to 'winter of discontent'
- Labour government badly weakened by its failures to control the crisis
- End of Lib–Lab pact proved disastrous for Labour
- Door opened to Margaret Thatcher's Conservatives

British relations with China and the USSR

▶ *What factors affected Britain's relations with China and the USSR?*

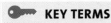

In the late 1960s, the People's Republic of China (PRC) was convulsed by the **Cultural Revolution**, a violent movement implemented by its leader Mao Zedong. The victims were not restricted to the Chinese people. In defiance of all the accepted rules of international diplomacy, a total of eleven foreign embassies were attacked and their employees assaulted. In 1967 the British embassy in Beijing was broken into and set on fire, and its staff physically assaulted. The attacks on foreigners were not confined within China. Amazing scenes occurred in London in 1967 when scores of staff members, all shouting Mao's name, came out of the Chinese embassy in Portland Place armed with sticks and machetes, which they waved threateningly at the police. Safe from arrest because of their diplomatic immunity, they demonstrated loudly and went back into their embassy building only after they had caused major disruption in the area.

Hong Kong

The London episode was part of the PRC's plan to use the Cultural Revolution to make trouble for Britain over its continuing possession of **Hong Kong**. In May 1967 Mao tried to turn a workers' strike in the colony into an anti-British demonstration. Chinese terrorists were sent into the colony to create havoc and so provoke British retaliation. In an eight-week period terrorist bomb attacks killed five policemen and injured scores of civilians. The Hong Kong authorities still did not resort to the extreme measures that Mao had expected, but he had largely succeeded in his aim of frightening the British into thinking that the PRC was preparing to take Hong Kong by force. He wanted to embarrass the British but not push things to the point where he would have to carry out his bluff.

Despite these episodes, Britain's relations with Communist China considerably improved in the 1970s. Two main factors help to explain this. One was the USA's abandonment of its support of Taiwan, dating back to the late 1940s, and its recognition of the PRC as the legitimate government of the whole of China. This had been followed by the official visit of President Nixon to Beijing in 1972. His historic meeting with Mao Zedong marked the moment when the previously hostile East–West relations began to improve. Britain, as the USA's ally, was wholly supportive of the US move. A second factor, strongly relating to the US initiative, was that soon after leaving office in 1974 Edward Heath had been the first major British politician to visit the PRC, where he was warmly welcomed as a Western statesman who was prepared to understand and co-operate with Communist China.

The Labour government of 1974–9 was able to build on Britain's improved relations with the PRC. The trade and diplomatic agreements Britain made with Communist China indicated that, while much still divided the countries, there were grounds for thinking that the old hostilities were easing.

The Soviet Union

It has to be stressed that China's willingness to improve its relations with the USA and Britain had a deeper purpose than merely a desire to be on better terms with the West. The softening of China's previously hard line was part of its strategy to undermine the USSR. The Chinese resented the Soviet policies of *détente* **and coexistence**, which they interpreted as a tactic to leave China internationally isolated. The PRC decided to outplay the USSR at its own game by achieving its own *détente* with the USA.

Britain's relations with the USSR in the 1970s span the period between the **Soviet invasion of Czechoslovakia** in 1968 and the **Soviet invasion of Afghanistan** in 1979. These two examples of the Soviet Union's determination to maintain its grip on its satellites and to use force to protect its borders led Britain to regard all Soviet moves as suspect. These suspicions were deepened by the activities of the **KGB**. The British authorities believed that there was strong evidence to show that East European dissidents were being hunted down in Britain. In 1978 Georgi Markov, an anti-Soviet Bulgarian, was killed in London in circumstances that strongly suggested he had been assassinated by agents of the Bulgarian secret service in collusion with the KGB. Markov died four days after being shot with a pellet laced with a lethal poison and fired from an umbrella tip. The Soviet and Bulgarian governments denied involvement and despite accusations made by other dissidents and witnesses, nobody was brought to account for the murder. The political impact of the episode was to harden British attitudes and increase its suspicions towards the USSR.

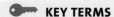 **KEY TERMS**

***Détente* and coexistence** An easing of antagonisms and a mutual recognition of each side's right to live in its own way.

Soviet invasion of Czechoslovakia In August 1968, the USSR, angered by the Prague Spring, the Czech government's attempt to liberalise its form of communism, sent forces into Czechoslovakia to suppress what it regarded as an anti-Soviet rebellion.

Soviet invasion of Afghanistan In 1980 Soviet forces began occupying parts of Afghanistan in an attempt to install a pro-Soviet regime there; a ten year war ensued before the Soviet withdraw having failed in its aim.

KGB The Soviet Union's espionage network.

Summary diagram: British relations with China and the USSR

PRC
- Cultural Revolution in PRC
- Attacks on British embassy in Beijing 1967
- Maoist demonstrations in London
- PRC challenges to British authority in Hong Kong

↓

USSR
- Hardening of Anglo-Soviet suspicion
- Result of Soviet invasion of Czechoslovakia 1968 and of Afghanistan 1979

Easing of tension in 1970s
- Nixon's visit to Beijing 1972
- Heath's personal visits welcomed in PRC

British policies in Northern Ireland 1969–79

▶ *How did British governments attempt to deal with the problem of Northern Ireland between 1969 and 1979?*

Britain's formal links with southern Ireland had ended in 1949 when, following partition (see the map on page 97), the Irish Free State became the sovereign Republic of Ireland. But one great problem remained: Northern Ireland. Constitutionally, it was part of the UK but its geography obviously made it part of the island of Ireland. This was an anomaly that Irish nationalists found objectionable. They claimed that the **1921 Treaty** had deliberately drawn the boundary between north and south so as to leave Northern Ireland with a predominantly Protestant population. In the six counties there were a million Protestants, identified politically as Unionists, to half a million Catholics, identified politically as nationalists or republicans. The Protestants had used their majority to dominate the separate parliament set up in 1921. They had then consolidated their political control by securing rights denied to the Catholic minority.

It was certainly the case that over the decades after partition Protestants came to monopolise the best housing, schools and jobs. The Catholic complaint was that this was a result of the political corruption in Ulster, which allowed Protestant councillors and officials to operate a system of favouritism and patronage. It was also said that constituency and ward boundaries were deliberately adjusted so as to maintain permanent Protestant majorities.

One area where local politicians could not control things was admission to higher education, since this was administered directly from London. By the end of the 1960s, nearly a third of the students at Queen's University, Belfast, came from the Catholic minority. It was from among such students that the Northern Ireland Civil Rights Association (NICRA) developed. Founded in 1967, NICRA condemned the **gerrymandering** of elections in Ulster and demanded the disbanding of the **B Specials** and a fair distribution of social and financial resources across the whole population. NICRA took as its model the black civil rights movement in the USA.

NICRA's first major public protest occurred in Dungannon in August 1968. In October of the same year a second demonstration, this time in **Londonderry**, Northern Ireland's most depressed economic area, ended in violence when the **RUC** baton-charged the marchers to break up what the authorities had declared to be an illegal march. This incident is often taken as marking the beginning of 'the troubles'.

KEY TERMS

1921 Treaty The Anglo-Irish agreement that had partitioned the island of Ireland between an independent south Ireland and Northern Ireland (loosely referred to as Ulster), which remained part of the UK.

Gerrymandering Manipulating constituency boundaries.

B Specials A wholly Protestant reserve police force on which the full-time police could call.

Londonderry A disputed place name; republicans call it Derry.

RUC Royal Ulster Constabulary; an almost exclusively Protestant armed police force.

Figure 3.1 Map of Ireland 1914–22. The 1921 Treaty settlement divided the island of Ireland into the Irish Free State and Northern Ireland (comprising the six counties). Northern Ireland is sometimes loosely referred to as Ulster, although historically Ulster had been made up of nine counties: the six shown plus Donegal, Cavan and Monaghan. The fact that Northern Ireland did not include these last three was highly important since it left the Protestants in a majority in the north.

'The troubles'

The term 'troubles' describes the cycle of violence dating from the 1960s to the 1990s whose main feature was terrorist conflict between the nationalists and the unionists, with British troops sent by London to attempt to preserve the peace. It should be stressed that mainstream nationalists and unionists always condemned the violence. It was the extremist groups within the two movements that resorted to terrorism.

Rival demonstrations showed the depth of Catholic–Protestant sectarian (religious) divide. In 1969, disorder grew as protest and counter-protest invariably resulted in violence. The Reverend Ian Paisley emerged as the leader of unyielding, anti-Catholic unionism that exploited Protestant bitterness. In the summer of 1969, the season of the traditional Protestant marches in Ulster, the first deaths occurred. Responsible politicians on both sides of the border and in London appealed for calm but both communities, Catholic and Protestant, were liable to be attacked by terrorists from the other side.

British troops sent to Northern Ireland 1969

In August 1969 James Callaghan, Labour's foreign secretary, took the momentous decision to send the British army to Northern Ireland to keep the peace. At first, the troops were welcomed by the Catholic community. Residents cheered and clapped as the soldiers encircled the Catholic Bogside area in Londonderry with protective barbed wire. This happy relationship was not to last. The **IRA**, which had been dormant, reorganised itself and took the lead in the struggle. However, not only did it resolve to attack unionism and head the Catholic nationalist protest movement, it also targeted the troops in Northern Ireland as representatives of the hated British imperialist government, seen as the root cause of Ireland's problems.

Internment, August 1971

The continuing violent disruptions convinced Edward Heath's government that the situation could be contained only by internment: arresting suspected troublemakers and holding them without trial. The aim was to remove the violent men from their communities and so reduce sectarian tensions. It had the opposite effect. Internment had the following results:

- increased tension in Northern Ireland
- a feeling among Catholics that they were being persecuted
- strained relations between the Irish government in Dublin and London
- the breaking of the cross-party understanding in the House of Commons over Northern Ireland, since many Labour MPs opposed internment and called for British troops to be withdrawn.

Bloody Sunday, January 1972

How little internment had improved matters became evident in 1972 when a prohibited civil rights march in Londonderry ended in carnage with fourteen demonstrators being shot and killed by British troops. The exact details of what happened and who was responsible remain disputed to this day. Over the years, there have been a number of official inquiries but none of their findings has been acceptable to republican sympathisers who want the British army to be condemned outright. The first inquiry, conducted by Lord Widgery, concluded that it was 'the shots that had been fired at the soldiers before they started the firing that led to the casualties'. This was seen by republicans as an attempt to whitewash the British army and condone its actions: 'Instead of justice we got Widgery.' The publication of the Widgery Report in May 1972 may be said to have made the situation worse:

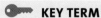

- It further convinced the Catholic population that the British government was hostile.
- It increased tensions between the London and Dublin governments.
- The gap between the IRA and the non-violent Social Democratic Labour Party (SDLP) widened.
- The gap between the moderate Official Unionist Party and the **DUP** led by Ian Paisley widened.

Before the Report appeared, Heath's government had taken the step of suspending the unionist-dominated **Stormont** Parliament and imposing direct rule of Northern Ireland from London. A year later, in an effort to produce a workable governing arrangement, Willie Whitelaw, Heath's Northern Ireland secretary, managed to persuade the rival parties to consider co-operating in a power-sharing experiment. In the Sunningdale Agreement of December 1973, backed by the London and Dublin governments, the SDLP, led by Gerry Fitt, and the Official Unionists, led by Brian Faulkner, agreed to form an executive which would govern Northern Ireland on behalf of both the Catholic and Protestant communities.

It was the first time since 1921 that Catholics had been offered a share in government, and for that very reason it frightened the majority of unionists. The general situation deteriorated; violence continued on the streets, usually involving the IRA and **loyalist** groups, with frequent IRA attacks on the police and army. The province became a highly dangerous place. Catholics continued to feel aggrieved over:

- unemployment, which always affected them the most
- the continued presence of the British army
- the slow progress in gaining their civil rights
- the way the law seemed tilted against them, as in the **Diplock Courts**.

The Protestant community felt no less aggrieved. They feared that such moves as the Sunningdale Agreement between London and Dublin were a cover for a sell-out of unionist Ireland. Such fears led to the creation of the Ulster Defence Force, drawn from loyalist extremists, the mirror image of the Provisional IRA.

Labour and Northern Ireland 1974–9

It was Harold Wilson's burden to be in power during one of the worst periods of the Ulster story. In May 1974, only three months after he had taken office, the province was paralysed by a massive fifteen-day strike organised by the pro-Paisley Ulster Workers' Council (UWC) in protest against the Sunningdale Agreement. Merlyn Rees, the Northern Ireland secretary, tried to take a tough line, refusing to negotiate with the UWC. Wilson backed him, referring in a television interview to the unionists as 'spongers'. It was no surprise when even the moderate unionist Brian Faulkner, who had signed the Sunningdale

KEY TERMS

DUP Democratic Unionist Party, which had broken away from the Official Unionist Party in 1971.

Stormont The building which housed the Northern Ireland Parliament.

Loyalist Anti-republican, pro-unionist.

Diplock Courts Set up in 1972 to hear cases without a jury, the aim being to avoid the problem of jury members' being intimidated.

Agreement for his party, declared that it was no longer workable and resigned from the executive. Power sharing seemed dead in the water.

Yet, despite the deep divisions in the province, Wilson did not despair of finding a solution. A Northern Ireland Act was introduced in 1974 which created a Constitutional Convention, a way of reintroducing the power-sharing principle. The first elections to the Convention in 1975 saw a 66 per cent turnout, a sign that the majority of the population were still willing to follow a peaceful, political path. However, when the 83 Convention members met they soon adopted their partisan positions. The Ulster Unionists presented a resolution prepared by Ian Paisley, declaring that they did not accept the right of republicans to take part 'in any future cabinet in Northern Ireland'.

In the face of such inflexibility there was little the SDLP could do. When the resolution was passed by a majority of three, the Convention lost any real meaning and the British government's formal dissolution of it in 1976, after barely a year in existence, was a recognition of what had already happened. In an attempt to maintain its hard-line policy towards terrorism, the government withdrew the 'special status category' for prisoners serving sentences in Northern Ireland for terrorist acts. In future they would be treated not as political prisoners but as common criminals.

Wilson and his successor, James Callaghan, continued to talk of finding a settlement but there were a number of factors that made this unrealistic:

- Since the IRA was the major culprit in the outrages and assassinations that occurred, including murders on mainland Britain, it was difficult to make political concessions to the legitimate nationalists without appearing to be giving in to terrorism. Indeed, in the face of a series of lethal IRA attacks in Britain in 1974, including the **Birmingham pub bombings**, the government introduced a **Prevention of Terrorism Act** in 1974.
- There were suggestions that, since the Labour majority was so small in the Commons throughout the 1974–9 period, the government could not afford to antagonise the Ulster Unionists, whose support might be needed in critical Westminster votes.
- The presence on the Labour backbenches of a number of MPs who openly supported the republican cause in Northern Ireland and the 'troops out' campaign compromised and inhibited the government.

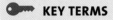 **KEY TERMS**

Birmingham pub bombings
On 21 November 1974, in separate explosions in two public houses in Birmingham's city centre, 21 people were killed and 180 seriously injured.

Prevention of Terrorism Act Gave the police and authorities considerably extended powers of search and arrest.

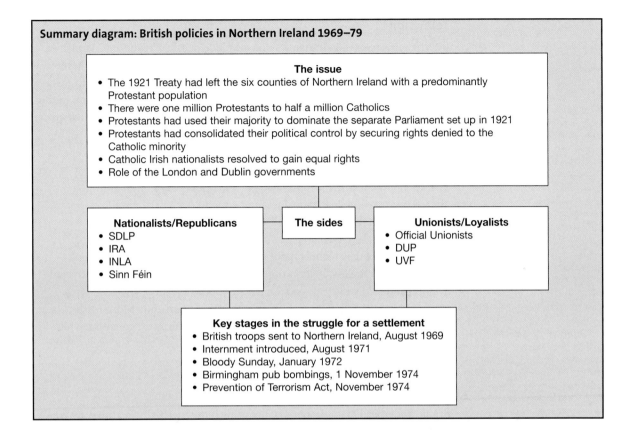

Summary diagram: British policies in Northern Ireland 1969–79

The issue
- The 1921 Treaty had left the six counties of Northern Ireland with a predominantly Protestant population
- There were one million Protestants to half a million Catholics
- Protestants had used their majority to dominate the separate Parliament set up in 1921
- Protestants had consolidated their political control by securing rights denied to the Catholic minority
- Catholic Irish nationalists resolved to gain equal rights
- Role of the London and Dublin governments

Nationalists/Republicans
- SDLP
- IRA
- INLA
- Sinn Féin

The sides

Unionists/Loyalists
- Official Unionists
- DUP
- UVF

Key stages in the struggle for a settlement
- British troops sent to Northern Ireland, August 1969
- Internment introduced, August 1971
- Bloody Sunday, January 1972
- Birmingham pub bombings, 1 November 1974
- Prevention of Terrorism Act, November 1974

 # Social developments

▶ *What were the main social developments in the period?*

The 1960s are regarded as a special period in British history. Often referred to popularly as the 'swinging sixties', they marked years of significant change in British social attitudes and behaviour. Some of these changes pre-dated the 1960s and many of the effects made their impact after the 1960s, but enough occurred in the decade to justify its being regarded as an especially formative and influential time. A point to emphasise is that the changes were intimately bound up with the scientific advances of the age.

Technology and science

The twenty years following the end of the Second World War saw remarkable advances in science and technology. These were not exclusive to Britain; indeed, many were initiated elsewhere, but they contributed notably to the development of British society, particularly in the areas of work and leisure. A selective list of the major technological advances indicates the scale.

Television

International television transmission was made possible by the 1962 launch of *Telstar*, a US satellite communications system. The British contribution to the success of the venture came in the shape of the Goonhilly Satellite Earth Station in Cornwall, developed by the early 1960s into the largest satellite station in the world; it provided over 60 communications dishes enabling worldwide television connections to be made.

Aerospace

The development of the jet engine to power commercial as well as military aircraft became an international phenomenon in the 1950s. A leading entrepreneur in this field was the De Havilland Company, based in Hertfordshire. The De Havilland *Comet* jetliner came into service in 1952. Although plagued by technical difficulties, which sometime proved tragic, the *Comet*, nonetheless, in its various modified forms proved a pioneer in civil aviation and sold widely abroad. One result of the advent of low-cost, long-range jet travel was that it revolutionised leisure opportunities for British people. Tony Fairbrother, a De Havilland spokesman, was hardly exaggerating when he remarked: 'the world changed from the moment the *Comet*'s wheels left the ground'.

Chemicals

Britain's chemical giant, Imperial Chemicals Industries (ICI), led the way in a wide range of scientific developments. Founded in 1926, ICI in the 1950s and 1960s, in addition to producing synthetic materials like Perspex, Crimplene and Lycra, began to develop a range of pharmaceuticals which included breakthrough drugs in the treatment of malaria, heart disease and certain forms of cancer. It also manufactured advanced forms of anaesthetics, disinfectants and pesticides. As well as improving living standards in Britain, such companies as ICI made a major contribution to the fight against disease and ill-health in some of the poorer countries of the world.

Britain's commitment to science is evident from the record of R&D expenditure in 1960 shown in Table 3.14.

Table 3.14 Relative spending on R&D as a percentage of GDP in 1960

USA 3%	USSR 3%	UK 2.3%	West Germany 1.5%	France 1.5%

Atomic energy

In 1947, the Labour government had made the momentous decision to make Britain a nuclear power (see the page 14), a commitment that was fully supported by the Conservatives when they came to power. This resulted in Britain's detonating its first atomic bomb in 1952 and its first hydrogen bomb in 1957. Having adopted nuclear power as a means of military defence, the decision was taken to develop it for civilian purposes. In 1954 the United Kingdom Atomic Energy Authority (UKAEA) was established; its role was to oversee policies for the civilian and defence use of atomic energy and for the development of research. By the late 1950s, an atomic research centre had been set up at Harwell and by 1962 a nuclear reactor at Dounreay was producing electricity for domestic use. However, in keeping with its defence remit, the UKAEA by 1958 had carried out over twenty nuclear weapons tests in selected areas of the Pacific. It was this aspect of the UKAEA's work that raised great moral issues and led to protest, in which the CND was the major voice (see page 113).

Motor cars

A particularly striking feature of technology was the extraordinary growth in the number of cars on British roads.

This growth intensified the need for more and better roads which in turn raised the issue of how Britain's transport structure was to be organised. The first stretch of the M1 motorway was opened in 1959. This was an impressive step in itself but it was clear that what was needed was an integrated transport plan. It was to achieve this that the British Transport Commission, which had been set up under the Attlee government in 1948, appointed Richard Beeching to draft a report on Britain's railways. His report, delivered in 1963, recommended sweeping cuts in the outdated system which, when acted on in the later 1960s, reduced the total length of railway lines from 13,000 to 9000 miles. The cuts followed the logic of closing lines that were underused or running at a loss. However, it was easier to close railway lines than it was to build roads. There was no equivalent master plan for the road system, which by its nature was much more difficult to design. The result was that no truly integrated plan emerged. Progress was piecemeal and halting.

Unsuccessful though the transport schemes may have proved, the attempts at road building in nearly every local authority invariably involved reconstruction and change. It was this that aroused the fears of those who came later to form an environmental movement. Environmentalism would not become a major cause until later decades (see page 222) but already, in its objections to ill-planned changes, it was part of that broad movement of protest that developed during the 1960s.

Responses to technology

Harold Wilson was very conscious of the great political importance of technology. In a keynote speech in the 1964 general election campaign he spoke of Britain's being forged in the 'white heat' of technological revolution. His words were an attempt to convince the electorate that the Labour Party he led was a progressive force in British politics, in sharp contrast to the old, Establishment-dominated Conservative Party that represented a Britain that was fast disappearing. Wilson made his point in practical terms by making a

Table 3.15 Number of privately owned cars 1950–65

Year	Number of cars
1950	2.3 million
1955	5.6 million
1960	9.2 million
1965	11.8 million

particular appointment to the government he formed after winning the 1964 election. He chose C.P. Snow as a parliamentary secretary in the newly formed ministry of technology, which was headed by Frank Cousins, the leader of the TGWU (see page 69). The significance of the appointment was that Snow over the previous eight years had become a leading critic of what he regarded as the anti-science Establishment that had such a preponderant place in British life.

In 1956 Snow, both a distinguished physicist and novelist, had written what proved to be a highly influential and divisive article. His argument was that post-war Britain was divided into 'two cultures'. One was a dated, self-regarding, coterie of intellectuals and writers, drawn from the humanities and arts in the universities, who made up the Establishment and who were wholly ignorant of science. The other was a progressive culture of scientists who understood the absolute necessity of Britain's adapting to the modern world of technology, but who were denied influence by the literary Establishment. Snow met many challenges from those who accused him of selectivity and exaggeration. However, Wilson chose to put his faith in Snow's analysis, and to pledge his party to be in the vanguard of technological progress. It was his political misfortune that Britain's economic circumstances did not permit him to pursue this.

Leisure

A key aspect of the march of technology was that it provided greater leisure opportunities for ordinary people. Much of this was based around the home, a consequence of the rapid spread of television. By the early 1960s four out of five homes had a television set. Nightly viewing joined the weekly cinema visit as defining characteristics of family leisure.

Equally influential in changing the nation's leisure habits was the huge increase in car ownership (see page 103). Having a car was one of the most liberating features for ordinary people in the twentieth century, giving individuals and families a sense of independence and opening access to a wide range of leisure pursuits.

Large crowds at sporting events, with football, rugby, speedway and cricket having the largest following, had been the norm until the late 1950s when people's possession of televisions and cars meant that traditional activities had to compete for participants and audiences. Most towns had an amateur dramatic society and choral societies and music continued to provide cultural outlets at a local level.

By 1955, 90 per cent of British workers took an annual two-week paid holiday. The seaside was the main venue for working-class families and holiday camps, such as Butlins, which had opened its first site in Skegness in the 1930s, grew in number and popularity. As earnings rose and disposable incomes grew, holidays abroad became possible. Travel companies offering package holidays brought travel within the range of ordinary families. Activities that before 1950 had been the preserve of the well-to-do were now available to most British people, another feature of the 'never had it so good' years.

Table 3.16 Percentage of homes with domestic appliances 1956–71

Year	Refrigerators	Televisions	Washing machines	Telephones
1956	8%	40%	20%	16%
1962	33%	80%	55%	40%
1971	69%	91%	64%	48%

The media

Although by the late 1950s radio and television broadcasts were fast becoming the chief means by which the public received information about national and international affairs, newspapers remained a powerful medium for influencing opinion and shaping attitudes. It was estimated that two-thirds of the adult population read a daily newspaper. The BBC and ITV were legally required to provide a politically neutral and balanced digest of the news but no such restrictions applied to the newspapers. It was for this reason that there were objections to the control of newspapers by those termed 'press barons'; wealthy men or families who individually controlled a range of newspapers. Examples of newspaper dynasties were:

- Harmsworth Press: owner of *The Times* and *Daily Mail*.
- Beaverbrook Press: owner of the *Daily Express*, the *Sunday Express* and London's *Evening Standard*.

Already, in the 1930s, there had been widely expressed concerns over the power that such ownership gave the papers' proprietors. This anxiety was restated in the post-war years. In response, a Press Council was set up in 1953. This was essentially a body of newspaper proprietors who came together as a voluntary organisation with the stated aim of encouraging the maintenance of the highest standards of journalism. However, the proprietors' essential purpose was to avoid being subjected to government control. One of their strong arguments against being regulated was that, however the papers were owned, taken together they fulfilled a very useful democratic function. The claim was that if the political leanings of the newspapers were taken into account, then on the centre-right were the *Telegraph*, the *Mail* and the *Express*; on the centre-left were the *Mirror* and the *Guardian*. In circulation numbers these two groups approximately matched each other, suggesting that the public were being well served in the balance of newspaper provision.

This neat argument became less convincing, however, with the buying in the late 1960s of *The Sun* by Australian newspaper magnate Rupert Murdoch. Within a few years he had turned an ailing paper into Britain's bestseller. What had begun life as a paper of the political left now began to veer to the right, thus distorting the previous national balance. Such developments raised an issue that was to continue to arouse controversy for the rest of the century and beyond: what was the proper role of the media in a modern democracy?

Table 3.17 Circulation of main national newspapers in millions 1947–76

Paper	1947	1956	1966	1976
The Sun	–	–	1.24	3.71
Daily Mirror	3.71	4.65	5.12	3.85
Daily Mail	2.08	2.07	2.32	1.76
Daily Express	3.85	4.04	3.98	2.55
Daily Telegraph	1.02	1.08	1.35	1.31
The Times	0.27	0.21	0.29	0.31
The Guardian	0.13	0.16	0.28	0.30
Financial Times	0.07	0.08	0.15	0.17

Equality

Table 3.18 Women as a percentage of those in higher education in the UK

1929	28%
1959	25%
1965	35%
1970	39%

Table 3.19 Women as a percentage of the UK's workforce

1951	31%
1970	35%
1990	43%

Significant progress for women was largely a response to the development of the feminist movement in the 1960s. It is hard to give a precise date to the start of this movement, but what was certainly important was the growth in the formal education of women at secondary and higher level. From this group came a literate, articulate demand for the recognition of the legal, social and economic equality of women. The outstanding voice was that of Germaine Greer, an Australia-born academic whose book *The Female Eunuch* (1970) provided the most powerful and convincing intellectual argument yet advanced for women's rights. At the forefront of the demand was an insistence that the law be changed in those areas where women suffered particular discrimination. It is in relation to such pressure that a number of critical legal changes were made. These did not appear until the 1970s (see box), but the groundwork had been laid in the preceding decade.

Laws passed during the 1970s to advance equality

- Equal Pay Act 1970: women were to receive the same rates of pay as men for doing work of equal value.
- Finance Act 1971: allowed the earnings of a married couple to be taxed separately if they so applied.
- Employment Protection Act 1975: denied employers the right to dismiss pregnant employees and required them to offer paid maternity leave.
- Sex Discrimination Act 1975: outlawed discrimination on grounds of sex in regard to employment, education and training, housing, provision of services, banking, insurance and credit. It also set up the Equal Opportunities Commission to monitor the working of the Act.
- Social Security Act 1975: provided a special maternity allowance fund.
- Social Security Pensions Act 1975: required pension schemes to be open equally to women engaged in the same work as men.

Although there is a natural emphasis on the success of feminism in bringing about legal change, equally important was the movement's insistence that there were many social injustices afflicting women which were beyond the scope of legislation since they belonged to the world of ingrained prejudice among women as well as men. What was needed, therefore, was a fundamental change of attitude in society at large. This is why feminism in turn has to be understood as part of a broad movement of thought that became particularly influential in the 1960s. This was made up of many strands but essentially what motivated it was the wish to remove traditional social and moral restraints. Where this tied in with feminism was in its approach to sexual questions. The 1960s saw changes that merited the term 'sexual revolution'. A development that advanced female emancipation far more rapidly than adjustments of the law or political arguments was the coming of 'the pill'. This female oral contraceptive, which was nearly 100 per cent reliable, became widely available in the 1960s. It was truly liberating. Possessed now of genuine control over their own fertility, women were in a position to shape their lives.

The Abortion Act 1967

The greater freedom gained from reliable contraception was complemented by the Abortion Act, which permitted the legal termination of pregnancy where two doctors certified that there was a serious risk to the physical or mental health of the mother, or a strong possibility that the child would be born with serious abnormalities. It was a highly controversial measure. Some moralists saw it as an assault on the sanctity of life, but most feminists hailed it as a major step in the liberation of women since it gave them 'the right to choose'. The dispute did not divide along gender lines; women were to be found on both sides of the debate.

By 2007 over 5 million abortions had taken place since the 1967 Act.

Table 3.20 Legal abortions in England and Wales 1968–90

Year	Abortions
1968	22,332
1975	106,648
1980	128,600
1985	141,000
1990	173,900

Permissiveness and censorship

The liberalising tendencies in society, as illustrated by the progress towards women's rights, were not universally applauded. Many people were disturbed by what they regarded not as an advance in freedom but as a move towards the abandonment of moral values. The term that became commonly used to describe this was 'permissiveness'. The battle over permissiveness can be examined in relation to three of the defining decisions and Acts of the 1960s: the *Lady Chatterley* case, the Abortion Act and the Sexual Offences Act. Not all these related specifically to women's rights but they helped to create an atmosphere in which the old taboos were broken down. Much of the 'swinging sixties' and the 'youth rebellion' was media hype, but there was enough reality behind the image-making to suggest that a significant change had occurred in British social attitudes. Women were often both the creators and the beneficiaries of this.

The *Lady Chatterley* case 1960

In 1959 the government had introduced the Obscene Publications Act. Not intended as a specifically liberalising measure, it nevertheless contained a clause that excluded from prosecution supposedly obscene works which were published 'in the interests of science, literature, art or learning'. In the following year, Penguin Books chose to test the new freedom by publishing D.H. Lawrence's *Lady Chatterley's Lover*, a 1928 novel which contained the frequent use of four-letter words and explicit descriptions of sexual activity. Penguin were promptly prosecuted for publishing an 'obscene' text. The trial became a test case and there are certainly grounds for regarding the not-guilty verdict as the beginning of the permissive age in literature. Those in the literary world largely rejoiced at the victory for free self-expression that the verdict represented and there was no doubt that publishers began to cover topics and writers began to use language they would not have risked before the trial.

Theatres Act 1968

This measure effectively ended theatre censorship by removing the outdated system by which plays had to be submitted to the Lord Chamberlain for approval before they could be performed. Given the greater literary freedoms, this seemed a logical step, although cinema censorship, in the form of age categorisation, remained in place.

Television

After the lifting of the restrictions on literature and theatre, it was noticeable that both television companies, BBC and ITV, were more relaxed in what they allowed to be broadcast. It was over the content of television programmes that the first organised resistance to permissiveness developed. Through an organisation she set up in 1963, the National Viewers' and Listeners' Association, Mary Whitehouse led a spirited attack on what she regarded as the debased standards and immorality of much of public broadcasting. She undoubtedly represented a strongly right-wing point of view. However, the proponents and opponents of greater freedom of expression did not divide along a simple left–right axis. Her efforts were matched by Lord Longford, a Labour peer, who campaigned in the 1960s and 1970s against the open sale and availability of pornography.

Sexual Offences Act 1967

For many libertarians, the crucial need if there was to be genuine sexual freedom in society was for homosexuality to be decriminalised. A major step towards this was the Sexual Offences Act. Introduced in 1967, the measure was based on the recommendations of the Wolfenden Committee report of 1958. It legalised male homosexual acts in private between 'consenting adults'. Female homosexuality was not mentioned in the Act, since this had never been illegal. The bill was not a government initiative, but was introduced by a private member, Leo Abse, who, convinced by the arguments of organised homosexual (**gay**) groups in publications such as *Gay News* (first published in 1962), presented a cogent and compelling case for implementing the liberalising measures recommended in the Wolfenden report.

Wider social tolerance and permissiveness

The greater tolerance that such measures as the Sexual Offences Act encouraged was also evident in other pieces of legislation which, while often controversial, did indicate that government and Parliament had recognised the need to extend rights and opportunities previously denied to the ordinary public.

Ombudsman 1967

A special Parliamentary officer, the Ombudsman (from the Swedish for 'a public advocate'), was appointed to whom ordinary citizens could appeal if they felt they had suffered from an abuse of authority by a government department.

Abolition of the death penalty 1969

The Act ending death sentences made permanent a measure passed in 1965 which had suspended the operation of the death penalty for an experimental four years. It removed the five remaining categories of offence for which the death sentence had been imposed. Given that opinion polls suggested that the majority of the population were for the retention of the death penalty, its abolition was an interesting example of Parliament's decision, in a free vote, to lead rather than follow public opinion on a moral issue.

Divorce Reform Act 1969

The Act allowed couples to divorce on the grounds of the 'irretrievable breakdown' of their relationship.

The Open University 1969

This new higher education institution was established to enable previously unqualified students to read for degrees by studying courses broadcast on radio and television. Harold Wilson later claimed this was his greatest achievement as prime minister.

Race

The riots and disturbances of the late 1950s (see page 42) had alerted government to the racial tensions in certain parts of Britain. It was in an attempt to deal with this, that Parliament had adopted three key measures; the Race Relations Acts of 1965 and 1968, and the Commonwealth Immigration Act of 1968.

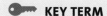

KEY TERM

Gay A term adopted by homosexuals themselves as a word that was free of connotations of stigma or disapproval.

Race Relations Acts of 1965 and 1968

Together, the Race Relations Acts were responsible for the following:

- prohibition of racial discrimination in public places and in areas such as employment and housing
- making incitement to racial hatred an offence
- setting up a Race Relations Board with the power to investigate complaints of racial discrimination
- setting up the Community Relations Commission to promote inter-racial understanding.

Commonwealth Immigration Act 1968

The Act prohibited new immigrants from settling in Britain unless they had family connections already established. Since the Act built on a previous measure introduced by the Conservatives in 1962, it was clear that both major parties had concluded that limitations on entry into Britain were necessary in the interests of peaceful community relations. It was to make that point that the Labour government had introduced Race Relations Acts in 1965 and 1968.

'Rivers of blood' speech 1968

In 1968 the race issue had been highlighted in a dramatic way, not by the government but by **Enoch Powell**, a prominent figure in the opposition. Powell was an intellectually gifted but maverick Conservative politician. An ardent nationalist, he came to regard unlimited immigration as a threat to the character of the UK. Ironically, it was while he was minister of health in Macmillan's government that he had presided over the recruitment of Commonwealth immigrants as nurses and hospital workers. However, in a notorious speech in 1968, he gave his vision of a future Britain shattered by racial conflict. Quoting *The Aeneid*, he prophesied: 'As I look ahead, I am filled with foreboding. Like the Roman, I seem to see "the River Tiber foaming with much blood".' The speech was condemned from all political sides and Edward Heath, the Conservative leader, felt obliged to dismiss him from the shadow cabinet. Although the speech made Powell popular with some working-class groups, such as the London dockers (see page 75), it effectively ended any possibility of his holding high office again.

Youth

One of the fruits of technology was that it provided young people with spending power and leisure time. This gave them a place in society that no young generation had ever before possessed. Teenagers and people in their twenties became a new type of social being. This meant they were wooed by advertisers eager in an age of intensifying consumerism to create a **niche market**. By the mid-1960s young people were spending over 60 per cent of their disposable income on clothes.

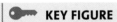

KEY FIGURE

Enoch Powell (1912–98)
MP 1950–87. Treasury secretary 1957–8. Minister of health 1960–3.

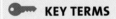

KEY TERMS

The Aeneid An epic poem by the Roman writer Virgil (70–19BC).

Niche market A particular section of society targeted by advertisers and manufacturers.

Drugs

In the early 1960s, some people began to experiment with **psychedelic** drugs. It was believed by their takers that they produced heightened physical and mental sensations which allowed them to enter new realms of reality. The drugs became particularly popular about the young middle class; they went with **cannabis** smoking and wearing of outlandish clothes as an expression of the **hippy** or **counter-culture** that young people embraced. There was no direct link between violence and drug taking. Nevertheless, those unhappy with the emergence of a counter-culture saw both developments as aspects of the social harm that came when the traditional taboos were disregarded.

Sex

In a society where the young were beginning to challenge the old ways, it was to be expected that sexual behaviour would quickly become an expression of protest and liberation. The availability of the contraceptive pill and of drugs provided an opportunity for experimentation that was eagerly seized by the young. The consequences can be measured in a number of ways:

- The rejection of monogamous marriage as outdated led to a great increase in premarital sex.
- The practice of couples opting to live together rather than marrying became more common.
- The right of women to choose to become single mothers became more accepted.
- Homosexual relations were regarded as being as normal and as legitimate as heterosexual relations.

These developments created distinctive social trends, as Tables 3.21 and 3.22 indicate.

The swinging sixties

In the 1960s there was an explosion of popular music, as the young, feeling free of the old restraints and with the time and money now available to them, bought cheap musical instruments and formed pop groups. Bands and bevvies of eager listeners proliferated. In what rapidly became a commercial boom time, recording companies rushed to sign up the more talented performers. The outstanding example of success was the Beatles, four young men from Liverpool whose catchy tunes and memorable lyrics came to symbolise the swinging sixties. Sharing their fame was George Best, a young Manchester United football player, whose skills and Carnaby Street lifestyle turned him into a superstar. In the 1960s Carnaby Street in London became the centre of fashion for the young. Its shops and boutiques sold the 'mod' and' 'hippy' clothing styles, created by such leading new designers as Mary Quant. The thousands who flocked daily to the area to buy clothes or simply to be seen there turned it into the 'coolest' location in London. As *Time* magazine put it, in an article published in 1966,

KEY TERMS

Psychedelic Hallucinatory drugs like LSD (lysergic acid diethylamide).

Cannabis A mildly addictive recreational drug; in a parliamentary debate in 1969 it was asserted that there were a million cannabis users and nearly 3000 users of the more damaging heroin.

Hippy Unconventional in appearance, language and behaviour.

Counter-culture A lifestyle based on the rejection of traditional social norms.

Table 3.21 Children born to unmarried mothers in the UK 1914–96

1914	3%
1970	10%
1988	25%
1996	34%

Table 3.22 Divorce rates in the UK 1939–70

Pre-1939	1 in 100 marriages
1960	1 in 10 marriages
1970	1 in 7 marriages

'Nothing illustrates the new swinging London better than narrow, three-block-long Carnaby Street, which is crammed with a cluster of the "gear" boutiques where the girls and boys buy each other clothing.'

There was a more troublesome side to the newfound youth freedoms. As was evident over the immigration issue, some young people readily turned to violence. The 1960s saw a continuation of the fight between rival mods and rockers. These for the most part were contrived affairs having no more point to them than an excuse for a punch-up, but they were worrying to government and local authorities and were much commented on in the foreign press as examples of an England ill at ease with itself. For much of the 1960s few of those in what the media tended to refer to in an imprecise way as the 'youth culture' had specific political aims, which was why the existing political parties were unappealing to them.

Young people did not have a single attitude of mind, of course, but their clothing and music could be interpreted as a broad protest against the system and the Establishment that operated in Britain. That sense of protest became focused in 1968 when the government of Harold Wilson, which at one time had prided itself on its youthful image, was confronted by a massive protest against its support for the USA in the Vietnam War (see page 74). Viewed in a wider context, the Grosvenor Square demonstration can be seen as part of a wave of protests that convulsed both the Western and Communist worlds in 1968. Historians note that although the protests had many strands, they can be interpreted collectively as marking a pivotal moment when people expressed their dissatisfaction with both oppressive communism and acquisitive capitalism.

Protest

The striking aspect of reforms and advances on the social front was they were the result of pressure from particular groups. For example, those advocating the introduction of women's rights or the decriminalisation of homosexuality believed that these aims could be achieved not by waiting for a major shift in public opinion but by pressing their particular demands in an organised way. The freedom campaigns of the 1960s pursued their objectives individually rather than as part of a broad reforming movement for social change. One implication of this was that people were losing faith in the traditional political parties as agents of social change. In the words of social historian Anthony Sutcliffe, writing in the late 1990s, 'A fragmentation occurred. The old structures of social class, convention and national character were in decline while associations linked to age, status and leisure interests were growing up.' To put it in simple terms: society does not change and grant rights to particular groups; particular groups gain rights by pressurising society into changing.

Organisations like those pressing for women's and gay rights were often presented by the press as part of the youth movement of the time. But, while the behaviour of many young people may have created the lively and challenging atmosphere, the leading figures in many of the movements were of mature years. The main spokesmen for CND, for example, were the future Labour Party leader Michael Foot and the distinguished philosopher Bertrand Russell (52 and 93, respectively, in 1965).

CND

In 1958 CND embarked on what became an annual Easter march which followed a 50-mile route from central London to the nuclear missile site at Aldermaston. The average number of marchers between 1958 and 1963 was over 100,000. The movement never formally attached itself to a political party although left-wingers in Labour and the trade unions were strongly represented in its ranks. Initially, its aim was radical but not revolutionary. Its strategy was to persuade the Labour Party to adopt unilateralism as an official policy which any future Labour government would be bound to implement. It was this that caused the Labour leaders such problems. Gaitskell, judging that CND, no matter how strong its moral convictions, was in a national terms only a small minority movement, calculated that for his party to embrace unilateralism would be a huge vote loser. Matters came to a head over this at the Labour Party conference in 1960 (see page 60). An interesting detail is that although CND was led by mature and middle-aged people, over half of those who went on the marches were aged under twenty.

University protests

The 1950s and 1960s saw a growth in the number of universities. Many of these became the scenes of protest. The concerns were usually localised in as much as they were about objections to university administration and course provision, but occasionally they took on a wider significance. One such took place at the London School of Economics in 1967 when some staff and students organised a ten-day occupation of the administration block in protest against the appointment of Walter Adams as director. Adams had previously been principal of University College Rhodesia, the colony that had declared UDI in 1965 (see page 47). This readiness to demonstrate on wider issues such as race was to become a feature of the protests of the 1970s.

Key charities

Several bodies, which were not in themselves primarily protest movements, played a role in awakening the public's social conscience by putting pressure on government for funding and support. Prominent among these were:

- Action on Child Poverty: a group concerned with helping destitute children whose families had fallen through the social services network.
- Shelter: committed to finding accommodation for homeless individuals.
- Release: a body that provided assistance for young people on drug charges.

Summary diagram: Social developments

Technology
- Advances in television
- Chemical industry
- Nuclear energy

Permissiveness and censorship
- *Lady Chatterley* case 1960
- Sexual Offences Act 1967
- Theatres Act 1968
- Abolition of death penalty 1969
- Divorce Reform Act 1969

Leisure
- Increased spending power
- Television
- Motor cars

Youth culture
- Swinging sixties
- Violent aspect

The media
- Social impact of television
- Struggle over control of the press

Race relations
Government policies aimed at balance between control and protection:
- Commonwealth Immigration Act 1968
- Race Relations Acts 1965 and 1968

Female advances
- The pill
- Divorce Reform Act
- Abortion Act
- Organised feminist movement

Protest
- Pervading but not centrally organised
- CND
- Grosvenor Square riot

Chapter summary

Wilson's government began by introducing a National Plan for recovery, but the need to borrow from the IMF led to the plan's abandonment. Returned to office in 1966, Labour introduced a prices and incomes freeze, but was met by union resistance in a series of strikes. A year later, financial problems obliged the government to devalue the pound. In an effort to improve industrial relations the government drafted a programme for limiting union powers, only for the Labour Party to reject the move. Greater success was achieved in social affairs, where Roy Jenkins presided over the move towards a permissive, more tolerant society.

Disappointed with Labour's overall record, the electorate returned the Conservatives under Heath in 1970. However, his attempts to follow 'new right' policies were overwhelmed by his conflict with the miners, which resulted in Conservative defeat in 1974, but not before he had taken the UK into Europe in 1973, a decision confirmed by a referendum introduced by Wilson in 1975. Callaghan's administration after 1976 saw industrial unrest culminate in the strike-ridden 'winter of discontent' of 1978–9, which proved a major factor in Labour's defeat in 1979.

During the period 1969–79, the successive Labour and Conservative governments wrestled with the seemingly intractable problem of an increasingly violent Northern Ireland.

The final section of this chapter surveys the remarkable social changes from the 1950s to the 1970s.

Refresher questions

Use these questions to remind yourself of the key material covered in this chapter.

1 What motivated the UK to make another application to join the EEC in 1967?

2 Why did Wilson's government of 1964–70 prove a disappointment to many of its supporters?

3 How progressive were the Labour government's social reforms in this period?

4 Why did Wilson's government not implement its 'In Place of Strife' proposals?

5 What factors explain the Conservative election victory in 1970?

6 What attitudes distinguished the 'new right'?

7 Why did Heath introduce an Industrial Relations Act in 1971?

8 Why was Britain able to enter the EEC at the third attempt in 1972?

9 What was the significance for Britain of the oil price rise of 1973?

10 Why was Labour able to win both general elections in 1974?

11 What was the outcome and significance of the 1975 referendum on Europe?

12 What developments led to the 'winter of discontent' of 1978–9?

13 How effective were the measures introduced in Northern Ireland by British governments between 1969 and 1979?

14 What major developments occurred in Britain in 1964–79 with regard to technology, leisure and the media?

15 What main forms did protest take in Britain in the 1950s and 1960s?

 Question practice

ESSAY QUESTIONS

1 'The social policies followed by the Labour government of 1964 to 1969 created the permissive society.' How far do you agree?

2 'By 1975 Britain's position in the world was in decline.' Explain why you agree or disagree with this view.

3 How seriously did the events of Bloody Sunday in January 1972 alter the situation in Northern Ireland?

4 'Callaghan's lack of action only prolonged the winter of discontent.' Assess the validity of this view.

SOURCE ANALYSIS QUESTIONS

1 With reference to Sources C (page 88) and D (page 88), and your understanding of the historical context, which of these two sources is more valuable in explaining why Harold Wilson's government recommended that Britain should continue its membership of the EEC?

2 With reference to Sources A (page 82), C (page 88) and D (page 88), and your understanding of the historical context, assess the value of these sources to a historian studying Britain's attitude towards the EEC between 1971 and 1975.

CHAPTER 4

The Thatcher revolution 1979–90

The final twenty years of the twentieth century were dominated by two main political developments: Thatcherism and New Labour. Thatcherism broke the consensus that had operated in Britain between 1945 and 1979 and profoundly altered many aspects of economic and political life. New Labour was a movement that began as an attempt by the Labour Party to accommodate itself to the changes that this revolution had brought. This chapter deals with the major elements in the story:

★ Thatcherism: the first stage

★ The Falklands War 1982

★ The miners' strike 1984–5

★ Thatcherism: the second stage

★ Foreign affairs and Ireland

★ The Labour Party during the Thatcher years

Key dates

1979	Margaret Thatcher came to power	1985	Kinnock's key speech at Labour Party conference
1980	Monetarism adopted		
1981	Riots in a number of cities	1986	Westland affair
	Serious slump		Supply-side economics adopted
1982	Falklands War		Single European Act
1983	Mrs Thatcher's second election victory	1987	Mrs Thatcher's third election victory
		1988	Mrs Thatcher's Bruges speech
	Neil Kinnock became leader of Labour Party	1989	Leadership challenge of Anthony Meyer defeated
1984–5	Miners' strike	1990	Poll tax crisis
1984	IRA bombing in Brighton		UK joined the ERM
1985	Riots in major cities		Lawson and Howe resignations

Thatcherism: the first stage

▶ *What were the main features of Thatcherism?*

Thatcherism

Margaret Thatcher gave her name to a new form of politics: Thatcherism. She was a striking example of a **conviction politician**. She had a strong aversion to the consensus politics that had developed in Britain since the Second World War. As early as 1968 she had attacked it as being devoid of principle and purpose since it tried to 'satisfy people holding no particular views about anything'. She regarded it as more important 'to have a philosophy and policy which, because they are good, appeal to a sufficient majority'.

Margaret Thatcher's Methodist upbringing and the influence of the ideas of Friedrich Hayek (1899–1992) and **Keith Joseph** gave her a set of beliefs that inspired her actions. Hayek was an Austrian economist and major critic of the Keynesian economic policies followed by most Western governments. He came to prominence with the publication of his book *The Road to Serfdom* (1944), in which he attacked the notion of state direction of the economy: 'The more the government plans', he wrote, 'the less can an individual plan, and when the government plans everything the individual can plan nothing'. He argued that the proper role of the state was not to involve itself in the welfare of its citizens but simply to provide the conditions of liberty in which individuals were free to make their own choices. He was a strong supporter of the **free market** (see page 77), which, he believed, was the best guarantee of economic and political liberty. He had a particular distrust of trade unions, whose power he regarded as a direct cause of unemployment and as a destroyer of democratic freedoms.

Mrs Thatcher's government may be regarded as part of the 'new right'. Her eleven years in office ended the consensus politics that had operated since 1945 and which she regarded as a form of creeping socialism. Her belief was not simply that the Labour governments had increased the power and control of the state but that the Conservatives had fallen into the same trap. Conservative governments had encroached on the free market, subsidised private and public companies, and permitted the growth of excessive trade union influence. Mrs Thatcher was angry with Heath for having abandoned his new right policies (see page 78) and reverting to the Keynesianism that she felt had damaged Britain after 1945.

As Margaret Thatcher saw it, the result of all this was inefficiency and low growth, made worse by a welfare system which undermined personal responsibility and created a dependency culture (see page 162). The nation was suffering from a malaise under which the hard-working members of society were subsidising the work-shy. Initiative was being stifled.

 **KEY TERMS**

Conviction politician Someone with strong opinions who acts out of principle rather than political expediency.

Free market An economic system in which the forces of supply and demand are allowed to operate naturally without regulation by the government.

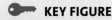 **KEY FIGURE**

Keith Joseph (1918–94)
A leading Conservative thinker who introduced Margaret Thatcher to the ideas of Hayek and encouraged her to adopt monetarist policies.

How effectively does Source A convey the idea of Margaret Thatcher competing in a male-dominated party?

SOURCE A

'One small step for Woman – a giant leap for womankind.' A cartoon from the *Daily Mail* celebrates Margaret Thatcher's success in defeating Edward Heath by 130 votes to 119 in the final vote in the Conservative leadership contest in February 1975. The other candidates depicted are (in descending order) Willie Whitelaw, James Prior, Hugh Fraser, Geoffrey Howe and Edward Heath. Heath took his defeat badly; he regarded her standing against him as an act of disloyalty. Ever after, in what a journalist called 'the longest sulk in history', he remained cool towards her, declining to serve in any of her Cabinets.

Ending the post-war consensus

The Conservatives' overall majority of 43 after the 1979 election was large enough to allow Margaret Thatcher to embark on a policy of radical change. Her intended solution to the problems she inherited was a return to the principle of individual accountability. The state, she believed, should no longer reward the incompetent and the half-hearted. It was false economics and bad social practice. In her memoirs, she defined the harm she believed had been done to Britain by a consensus politics that had allowed the state to play too large a part in people's lives. She was especially critical of Edward Heath, the man she had replaced as Conservative leader, who, she claimed, had pushed Britain further towards socialism than even the Labour governments had (see Source B).

Margaret Thatcher

1925 — Born the daughter of a grocer in Grantham

1943–7 — Read Chemistry and Law at Oxford

1970–4 — Minister for education and science under Heath

1975–90 — Leader of the Conservative Party

1979 — Became prime minister after election victory

1982 — Falklands victory

1983 — Second election victory

1987 — Third election victory

1990 — Resigned as prime minister and party leader

2013 — Died and received a ceremonial funeral

Margaret Thatcher was the first woman in British history to become a party leader and a prime minister. She held office continuously from 1979 to 1990. As a **populist**, she claimed to have a special understanding of ordinary people that bypassed party politics, a result of her youthful experience working in her father's grocery shop. Her politics are not easy to define in party terms. Her strong belief in the nation's paying its way and balancing the books made her much more a traditional Liberal than a Conservative. So, too, did her wish to reduce the power of the state and give greater opportunity for people to live their lives without government interference. Her economic policies were directed towards the same end. However, her policy of ending public subsidies led to a bitter struggle with the miners.

After Britain's recovery of the Falkland Islands under her leadership, she was likened by some to Winston Churchill in her ability to rouse the nation. Others who believed that she had deliberately provoked the war found her triumphalism after the British victory in 1982 repellent. However, her calm behaviour after the IRA tried to assassinate her in the Brighton bombing in 1984 enhanced her reputation. An ardent anti-Communist, she backed US President Reagan in his condemnation of the USSR as the 'evil empire'. Republicans in the USA suggested that her uncompromising attitude helped to bring about the end of the Cold War. Interestingly, for many in the Soviet bloc countries she became a symbol of freedom. In Poland, chapels and shrines were dedicated to her in gratitude for her support of Solidarity, the anti-Communist trade union movement. This was a bitter irony for those in Britain who believed she had trampled on the rights of trade unionists at home.

SOURCE B

From Margaret Thatcher, *The Downing Street Years*, HarperCollins, 1995, p. 6.

The Labour Party gloried in planning, regulation, controls and subsidies. It had a vision of the future: Britain as a democratic, socialist society, third way between east European collectivism and American capitalism.

The Tory Party was more ambivalent. At the level of principle, rhetorically and in Opposition, it opposed these doctrines and preached the gospel of free enterprise with very little qualification. But in the fine print of policy, and especially in government, the Tory Party merely pitched camp in the long march to the left. It never tried seriously to reverse it.

Ted Heath's Government proposed and almost implemented the most radical form of socialism ever contemplated by an elected British government. It offered state control of prices and dividends, and the joint oversight of economic policy by a tripartite body representing the TUC, the CBI and the Government, in return for trade union acquiescence in an incomes policy. We were saved from this abomination by the conservatism and suspicion of the TUC which perhaps could not believe that their 'class enemy' was prepared to surrender without a fight.

 KEY TERM

Populist A way of appealing directly to ordinary people that bypasses normal party politics.

According to Source B, what are Margaret Thatcher's objections to the policies of previous Labour and Conservative governments?

Mrs Thatcher's economic revolution

On taking up office in 1979, Margaret Thatcher's intention was nothing less than to change the economic basis on which Britain was run. This was part of her programme to end the consensus politics that had allowed Britain to slip into harmful social and economic habits. Among those she identified as the most serious were:

- high levels of government spending which led to borrowing, excessive taxation and inflation
- unnecessary government interference in the running of the economy
- the growth of bureaucracy which meant that civil servants and officials increasingly intruded into people's lives
- a combination of weak managements and powerful unions that had resulted in a continual increase in wages and salaries but a decline in productivity; this had led to inflation and lack of competitiveness.

Thatcher's economic policy is best understood as an attempt to reverse the harmful trends which, she believed, successive governments since 1945 had allowed to develop. Basic to all her efforts to achieve this was the restoration of the free market to replace the Keynesian system which British governments had followed since 1945. (Interestingly, her predecessor James Callaghan had previously hinted that he believed Keynesianism was dead.) She expressed this as 'taking government off the backs of the people'. Before any of this could be done, however, it was essential to tackle the major problem confronting Britain: inflation.

Monetarism

To bring inflation under control, the Thatcher government chose to adopt monetarism, a financial theory particularly associated with Milton Friedman, an influential US economist. Friedman taught that the root cause of inflation was government spending. It followed, therefore, that in order to control inflation, governments had to restrict the amount of money in circulation and reduce public expenditure. In keeping with Friedman's notions, the Thatcher government began to cut government spending, hoping that this would reverse the position in which Britain's **PSBR** was always in deficit. To control inflation further, interest rates were kept at a high level in order to deter irresponsible borrowing and keep the pound strong on the international financial market. The success of these measures was indicated by the fall in the rate of inflation from nineteen per cent in 1979 to five per cent in 1983.

While monetarism was successful in reducing inflation it did so at the price of job losses. As Table 4.1 shows, unemployment rose at a disturbing rate every year after 1980. This might have been acceptable had the drop in inflation been accompanied by economic growth. But the opposite was happening. In 1981, falling orders for manufactured goods had seen the start of an economic recession.

 **KEY TERM**

PSBR Public sector borrowing requirement. The public sector includes the whole of national and local government and the nationalised industries. The costs of running these is met from government revenue. If the revenue is insufficient, the difference is made up by borrowing. The gap between government revenue and government needs is known as the PSBR.

Table 4.1 Unemployment in Britain 1980–90

Year	Number
1980	2,244,000
1981	2,272,000
1982	3,097,000
1983	3,225,000
1984	3,284,000
1985	3,346,000
1986	3,408,000
1987	3,297,000
1988	2,722,000
1989	2,074,000
1990	1,850,000

Social unrest

In reaction to the recession, serious disturbances occurred in a number of English cities. In April 1981, in Brixton in south London, hundreds of black youths ran riot, burning shops and looting property. It was only with the greatest difficulty that the police eventually contained the trouble. In July similar violence occurred in the following cities:

- St Paul's region of Bristol
- Toxteth area in Liverpool
- Moss Side in Manchester.

Although local conditions helped to explain the disturbances, they were in a general sense a result of Mrs Thatcher's tough monetarist policies which had led to increased unemployment. The following common factors combined to ignite the troubles:

- Poor job prospects in the deprived inner-city areas.
- Alienation of young black people who felt they were discriminated against by the police, who, in a six-day period in April, in Brixton, had used the **'Sus' law** against more than 1000 people, the majority of whom were black.
- The high incidence of unemployment among school leavers. Overall, unemployment in Brixton was at thirteen per cent. It was estimated that unemployment for ethnic minorities in Brixton stood at 25 per cent and black youths in particular at 55 per cent.

The government did not always see the rioters as helpless victims of social and industrial change. There was a strong feeling on the right that the disturbances were deliberately started or exploited by political troublemakers. Comparing his father in the 1930s with the 'layabouts' of the 1980s, Norman Tebbit, the minister for employment, told applauding delegates at the 1981 Conservative Party conference: 'He didn't riot; he got on his bike and looked for work, and he went on looking until he found it.'

Tebbit was one of the tough guys in the Cabinet. Portrayed in the satirical television programme *Spitting Image* (see page 168) as a leather-clad, cosh-wielding enforcer, he was certainly one of Thatcher's staunchest supporters, who urged her not to allow the riots to deflect her from her policies. Such support certainly strengthened her resolve to keep to the promise made at the Conservative Party conference in 1980 when she had declared, to loud acclaim, 'the lady's not for turning'. This was a calculated act of defiance against the **'wets'**, ministers such as Francis Pym (defence), James Prior (employment) and Peter Walker (agriculture), who, worried by the effects of monetarism, had urged that the policy be abandoned or modified.

By 1982 the mounting social and economic problems had begun to threaten Mrs Thatcher's continuance in office. Opinion polls showed that the prime minister's personal popularity and that of her government had declined

KEY TERMS

'Sus' law A regulation that allowed police to 'stop and search' people suspected of criminal behaviour.

'Wets' Applied during the Thatcher years to those in the government and Conservative Party who opposed or were uncertain about the tough measures that Mrs Thatcher adopted.

significantly. Such developments led some Conservatives to doubt that they could win the next election. But in 1982 dramatic events took place that reversed all this: Britain went to war with Argentina over the Falkland Islands.

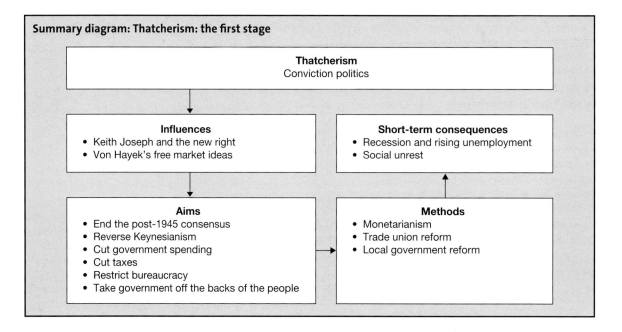

Summary diagram: Thatcherism: the first stage

Thatcherism
Conviction politics

Influences
- Keith Joseph and the new right
- Von Hayek's free market ideas

Short-term consequences
- Recession and rising unemployment
- Social unrest

Aims
- End the post-1945 consensus
- Reverse Keynesianism
- Cut government spending
- Cut taxes
- Restrict bureaucracy
- Take government off the backs of the people

Methods
- Monetarianism
- Trade union reform
- Local government reform

② The Falklands War 1982

▶ *Why did Britain go to war over the Falklands in 1982?*

The crisis over the Falklands Islands provided Margaret Thatcher with an opportunity to reveal a facet of her character that otherwise would have remained hidden. She became an outstanding war leader. Her commanding conduct and demeanour during the Falklands conflict so added to her reputation that she regained a popularity (sometimes referred to as 'the Falklands factor') that enabled her to stay in office until 1990, winning the elections of 1983 and 1987 along the way.

The Anglo-Argentinian dispute

The legal ownership of the islands had long been disputed between Argentina and Britain. The historical arguments over who had sovereignty were complicated. Britain's position was that the Falklands had legally been a British dependency since 1833. What was not in dispute in 1982 was that 98 per cent of the population of some 2000 islanders wished to remain under the British flag. This was the point constantly emphasised by Margaret Thatcher. It gave her the justification for insisting that 'sovereignty is not negotiable'. Yet, it should

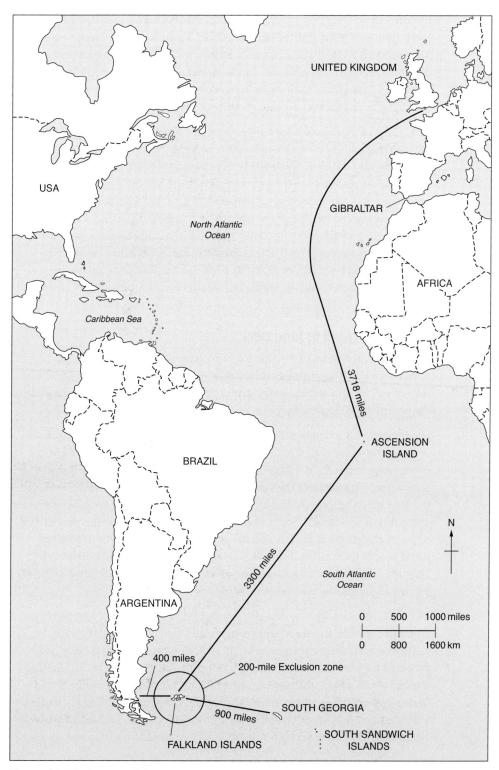

Figure 4.1 The location of the Falkland Islands and the route of the military task force from Britain.

be noted that Thatcher's government had at first been willing to discuss a compromise with Argentina. Nicholas Ridley, a minister at the foreign office, had proposed 'a leaseback' agreement by which Britain, while maintaining ultimate sovereignty over the Falklands, would allow Argentina to administer the region as its own. However, any chance of a settlement on these terms was destroyed by Argentina's decision to attempt to take the islands by force.

In a precipitate move on 2 April 1982, General Galtieri, the Argentine dictator, eager to make his four-month-old regime acceptable to the people, ordered the seizure of the Falklands. Some 4000 troops invaded the islands and quickly overcame the resistance of the garrison of 80 Royal Marines. This act of aggression was condemned by all parties in Britain, but whereas the Labour opposition wanted the British response to be channelled through the United Nations (UN), which formally condemned the Argentine invasion, Margaret Thatcher was adamant that it was entirely a matter for Britain to resolve. Its sovereignty had been affronted and its people in the Falklands put under occupation. It was, therefore, entitled to take action. She immediately ordered the retaking of the Falklands.

The conflict, April to June 1982

On 8 April a British task force, having been assembled in only four days, sailed from Portsmouth and Southampton. On 25 April South Georgia, which Argentina had also seized, was recaptured. Air strikes began on 1 May against the occupying Argentine forces on the Falklands.

Having placed a 200-mile (320-km) exclusion zone around the islands, Britain began its naval campaign on 2 May. In an action that caused considerable controversy in Britain, the Argentine cruiser *Belgrano* was sunk by a British submarine. Opponents of the war asserted that the prime minister had ordered the *Belgrano* to be torpedoed even though it was sailing out of the exclusion zone at the time it was struck. The accusation was that she had done this deliberately to wreck the efforts of the UN secretary general to bring about a negotiated settlement of the conflict. Thatcher's defence was that, in a war situation, the *Belgrano*, regardless of its position and heading, remained a real threat to British personnel. Ships, she pointed out, can always turn round.

Two days after the *Belgrano* had been sunk, HMS *Sheffield* was destroyed by an Argentine missile. In subsequent engagements, two British frigates were also destroyed and others damaged in air attacks. However, the Royal Navy had prepared the way effectively for British troop landings to begin on 21 May. By the end of the month, the two key areas of San Carlos and Goose Green had been recaptured. The climax came with the liberation of the Falklands' capital, Port Stanley, on 14 June. Argentina then surrendered. The conflict had claimed the lives of 255 British and 665 Argentine servicemen. Although some people found it tastelessly jingoistic, Mrs Thatcher's cry of 'rejoice, rejoice' at the news of the task force's victory found an echo with the population at large. She was likened to Churchill in her ability to inspire the nation in wartime.

Having regained the Falklands through force of arms, Britain established a permanent garrison on the islands to guarantee their security. Margaret Thatcher let it be known she had no intention now of negotiating them away: 'Our men risked their lives for the British way of life, to defend British sovereignty. I do not intend to negotiate on the sovereignty of the islands in any way except for the people who live here.'

Political benefits for Mrs Thatcher

Margaret Thatcher's reward for her leadership during the Falklands crisis came in the 1983 election. She won an overwhelming victory carried by the surge of popularity that the war had brought her. In contrast, the opposition who had opposed military action found itself in the unenviable position of trying to attack the government while at the same time supporting the servicemen and women who were actually fighting the war. It proved an impossible act to bring off and leaders Michael Foot and Neil Kinnock suffered a dip in their personal standing.

Table 4.2 Results of the 1983 general election

Party	Votes	Seats	Percentage of vote
Conservative	13,012,315	397	42.4
Labour	8,456,934	209	27.6
Liberal	4,210,115	17	13.7
Social Democrat	3,570,834	6	11.6
Scottish Nationalists	331,975	2	1.1
Plaid Cymru	125,309	2	0.4

Impressive though her electoral success was, Mrs Thatcher's achievement has to be put in context. What she had done was to recover the support that the opinion polls suggested she had lost in the early 1980s and restore herself and her party to the position they had held in 1979. The real explanation for the Conservative victory in 1983 was the remarkably poor performance of the Labour opposition, which saw its total vote drop by 3 million and its share of the vote fall by nearly nine per cent. To understand why this happened we need to examine the fortunes of the Labour Party during the Thatcher years (see pages 151–4).

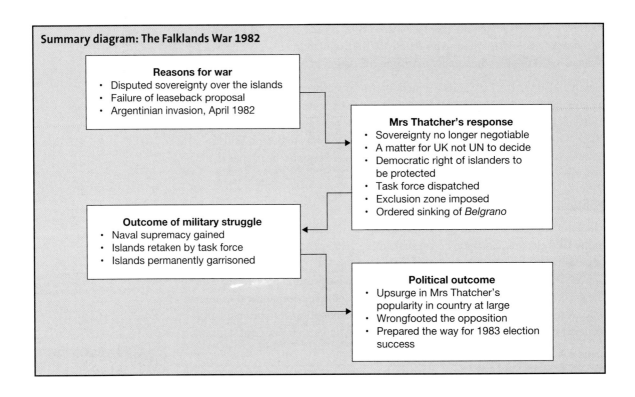

Summary diagram: The Falklands War 1982

Reasons for war
- Disputed sovereignty over the islands
- Failure of leaseback proposal
- Argentinian invasion, April 1982

Mrs Thatcher's response
- Sovereignty no longer negotiable
- A matter for UK not UN to decide
- Democratic right of islanders to be protected
- Task force dispatched
- Exclusion zone imposed
- Ordered sinking of *Belgrano*

Outcome of military struggle
- Naval supremacy gained
- Islands retaken by task force
- Islands permanently garrisoned

Political outcome
- Upsurge in Mrs Thatcher's popularity in country at large
- Wrongfooted the opposition
- Prepared the way for 1983 election success

③ The miners' strike 1984–5

▶ *What circumstances brought about the confrontation between Thatcher's government and the coal miners?*

Margaret Thatcher's insistence on the nation's paying its way meant that subsidies would not normally be used to shore up ailing industries, a practice for which she had sharply criticised Edward Heath. Her argument was that, while sympathy might lead one to help enterprises that were in difficulties, it had always to be remembered that public subsidies, by definition, came from the public purse. This meant that other areas would be deprived of resources to pay for the failing ones. 'Robbing Peter to pay Paul' made no sense economically if Peter was productive and Paul unproductive. This merely rewarded the inefficient at the expense of the efficient. It was such arguments that lay at the heart of the government's dispute with the miners, which came to a head in 1984.

Crisis in the coal industry

Throughout the twentieth century the British coal industry had been in recurrent crisis. The basic fact was that coal was increasingly becoming costly and difficult to mine. Nationalisation in 1948 had not altered this (see page 7).

Indeed, there was a case for saying that a lack of government investment since then had added to the problem. For some time, Britain had been importing coal from abroad. With the exception of a few pits producing particular types of coal, British mines by the 1970s were running at a loss.

The government's case for pit closures

The government under Margaret Thatcher declared its unwillingness to put further public money into an industry which had little real chance of being able to recover its place in a competitive market. Her argument was that not to take hard measures when necessary simply delayed the inevitable; it was better to face the situation now and lessen the consequences of closure by large redundancy settlements than pretend things could get better.

The miners' case against closures

The miners' unions and other analysts advanced a strong counter-argument. They asserted that, with a proper investment programme backed by a genuine government commitment to coal as a long-term power source, large parts of the British coal industry still had a profitable future. Moreover, they pointed out, it was not simply a matter of economics. The social consequences of widespread pit closures would be catastrophic. In areas such as south Wales, Yorkshire and Durham, coal was not simply an industry; it was a way of life. Whole communities were dependent on it. If the local mine closed, the local community would cease to exist.

Development of the dispute

These opposing points of view became personalised in the leading protagonists in the coal strike of 1984–5. The **NCB** had recently appointed as its chairman Ian McGregor, an unsentimental Canadian manager, whose remit was to cut out the non-profitable parts of the coal industry. He was faced by the equally uncompromising NUM leader, Arthur Scargill, the man who had brought down Edward Heath in 1974 (see page 79), who was determined to resist pit closures.

Although the government claimed to be neutral in the dispute and concerned solely with upholding law and order, it fully backed McGregor and the NCB. Indeed, there were grounds for suggesting that the government deliberately encouraged a showdown with the miners as part of its campaign to bring the trade unions to heel. Anticipating a prolonged strike, the government had made careful plans. Norman Tebbit, the employment minister, had already steered through two Employment Acts in 1980 and 1982, intended as the first steps towards weakening union power. The measures:

- forbade mass picketing
- outlawed the 'closed shop', the requirement that all workers in a particular plant or factory had to be union members
- declared industrial action illegal unless the workers had voted for a strike in a formal ballot.

 **KEY TERM**

NCB The National Coal Board, the body with overall responsibility for running the industry.

In addition to undermining the miners' legal defences, the government had taken the practical step of stockpiling coal and coke at the fuel stations and drafting emergency plans for importing further stocks should the need arise. The strike, which began in 1984, lasted a year and saw violent clashes between striking miners and the police, the worst occurring in June at 'the Battle of Orgreave' in South Yorkshire. Strikers tried to prevent coke-filled lorries leaving the Orgreave coking works. An estimated 6000 pickets struggled for hours against some 7000 policemen before finally being overcome. There were 93 arrests, and 51 strikers and 72 policemen were injured. Scargill struggled to keep the strike going by his rousing speeches.

SOURCE C

From Arthur Scargill's presidential address to the NUM conference, July 1984, reported in *The Times* newspaper, 12 July 1984.

Through the police, the judiciary the social security system – whichever way seems possible – the full weight of the state is being brought to bear upon us in an attempt to try and break this strike. … On the picket lines, riot police in full battle gear, on horseback and on foot, accompanied by police dogs, have been unleashed in violent attacks upon our members … Throughout this dispute … it has been clear that the Board's negotiators are manipulated in every move by the Prime Minister, who seems obsessed with trying to defeat the National Union of Mineworkers … .

Ours is a supremely noble aim: to defend pits, jobs, communities and the right to work. We are now entering a crucial phase in our battle for the survival of this industry. For the first time since the strike began, even the pundits and the experts have started to admit that the pendulum is swinging in favour of the NUM. The sacrifices and the hardships have forged a unique commitment among our members. They will ensure that the NUM wins this most crucial battle in the history of our industry.

According to Source C, how did the Thatcher government try to break the miners' strike?

Despite the miners' resistance at Orgreave and Scargill's attempts to rally his forces, the strike had petered out by early 1985, leaving a legacy of bitterness and recrimination.

Reasons for the strike's failure

- Arthur Scargill's abrasive manner alienated other unions within the mining industry. The notable example was the Nottinghamshire miners who defied his appeals and continued working throughout the strike, preventing it from becoming solid.
- Scargill's persistent refusal to hold a ballot of the NUM members made it appear that he was undemocratically forcing his union into a strike.
- Few other trade unions were willing to support the strike.
- The government, which backed the NCB throughout, had made careful preparations to maintain essential fuel stocks and supplies.

- The Labour opposition did not perform well. Although some on the left wholly supported the striking miners, party leader Neil Kinnock tried to take a middle path, condemning violence but being sympathetic towards the strikers' cause. It was unimpressive and did not convince voters that Labour had a consistent attitude to the strike.
- Tebbit's Employment Acts gave the NCB and the government powerful restraints on the strikers.
- The police were largely successful in enabling strike-breakers to get into work and delivery lorries to get through picket lines.
- Coal was no longer the vital fuel source for ordinary people the way it had been in previous generations, as more people turned to using oil and gas. The strike, therefore, never made the impact the strikers had hoped.
- Since coal was of declining industrial importance there was a sense in which the strike was a parting gesture. It seemed to belong to an age that had passed.

The miners' defeat marked a major success for the government's anti-union campaign and encouraged other employers to begin resisting union demands. Worker power was on the decline. This was clearly evident in 1986 in the failure of the **print workers**, despite prolonged and desperate efforts, to prevent Rupert Murdoch, a press baron and the proprietor of the Times Newspaper Group, from obliging them to accept new technology and modified working practices. Murdoch followed the tactics of Eddie Shah, a newspaper owner in Manchester, who in 1982 had used the legal powers granted to employers under the new Employment Acts to break the power of the print unions. Since the miners and the printers were arguably the strongest unions in Britain, their defeat marked a major success for Margaret Thatcher's industrial policies. It also strengthened her resolve to overcome the other forces in Britain, such as those local governments which she regarded as undemocratic and economically wasteful.

Impact of the miners' strike

The effects of the strike went beyond the mining industry and its regions:

- The disturbing scenes of violence between strikers and police regularly seen on television divided public opinion. Polls suggested that 65 per cent of people supported the government and the police, 35 per cent the miners. Commentators suggested that these figures reflected the divide in the nation at large between the minority of people who lived and worked in the areas of declining industry and the majority whose livelihoods no longer depended on the old staple industries. In simplified terms, the divide was between the two nations, the north and the south.
- Social commentators suggested that the violent clashes that frequently accompanied the strike stimulated a general lawlessness in Britain, as evidenced by further riots in some of Britain's cities in 1985.

 **KEY TERM**

Print workers Among the highest paid workers in British industry, they were reluctant to accept work practices based on new technology that threatened their job security.

- The failure of the strike allowed the planned closures to go ahead at greater speed. The result was job losses, redundancy, social disruption and the decline of traditional mining communities.
- The violent nature and the ultimate failure of the strike convinced the majority of people that action of this kind was no longer an appropriate way of settling industrial issues in modern Britain.
- The failure of the miners gave heart to employers who wanted to convert their workers into accepting modern ways and new techniques.
- Since the NCB's victory was really the government's victory; Mrs Thatcher was encouraged to think that, if the government kept its sense of purpose and determination, other opponents could be defeated.

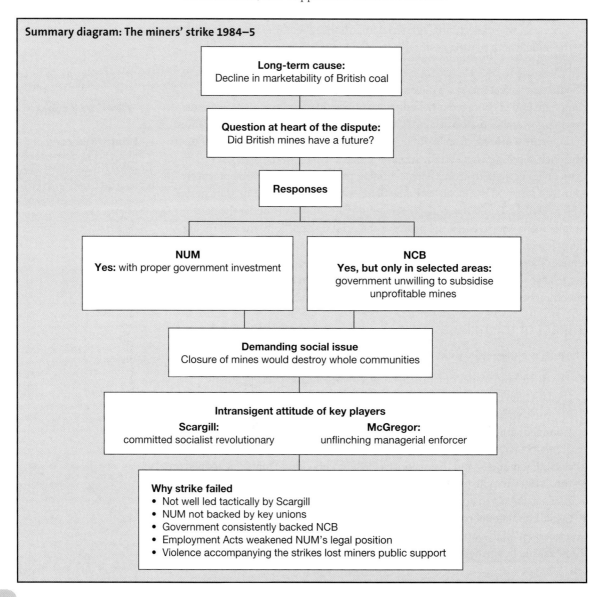

Summary diagram: The miners' strike 1984–5

Long-term cause:
Decline in marketability of British coal

Question at heart of the dispute:
Did British mines have a future?

Responses

NUM
Yes: with proper government investment

NCB
Yes, but only in selected areas:
government unwilling to subsidise unprofitable mines

Demanding social issue
Closure of mines would destroy whole communities

Intransigent attitude of key players
Scargill:
committed socialist revolutionary

McGregor:
unflinching managerial enforcer

Why strike failed
- Not well led tactically by Scargill
- NUM not backed by key unions
- Government consistently backed NCB
- Employment Acts weakened NUM's legal position
- Violence accompanying the strikes lost miners public support

Thatcherism: the second stage

▶ *What were the essential features of supply-side economics?*

Despite Margaret Thatcher's impressive victory in the 1983 election and her earlier declaration that she was 'not for turning', the severity of the recession obliged the government to modify its financial policies.

Supply-side economics

Although monetarism was never formally dropped as a policy, from the mid-1980s it was in practice largely abandoned. In its place, the government began pursuing supply-side economics. This approach rested on the belief that Keynesian policies had distorted the operation of the economy by attempting to create demand artificially. Supply-side economists argued for a return to incentives; people would work harder and more productively if they were allowed to keep more of their earnings. This would stimulate the economy. Chief among the policies the supply-siders advocated were:

- reducing taxation so as to provide employees with a greater incentive to work
- encouraging competition in order to lower prices
- limiting the powers of the trade unions so that they could not block productivity or prevent the modernisation of industry
- cutting wasteful welfare payments as a way of saving public money and reducing dependency.

The adoption of supply-side economics marked a shift of emphasis rather than a basic change in Margaret Thatcher's original policies. It was still part of her broad programme for establishing the free enterprise economy.

Deregulation

A critical move towards free enterprise was made with the introduction of a policy of deregulation. This was a concerted effort to remove the financial and legal restrictions that Margaret Thatcher believed had prevented efficiency and profitability in many areas of social and economic activity. Among the chief areas included in the deregulation programme were the following:

- Finance: credit and exchange controls were abolished.
- Transport: bus companies were deregulated to encourage competition.
- Education: schools were entitled to opt out of the state sector and become responsible for their own financing.
- Health: hospitals were required to operate an 'internal market' by taking control of their own finance and matching needs to resources.

Housing: the 'right to buy'

One of the most notable aspects of deregulation and one on which both opponents and supporters of Thatcherism focused was the right, granted by the Housing Act of 1980, to council house tenants to buy the homes that they were renting. Critics argued that it undermined the principle of social housing and reduced the stock of available properties. Defenders argued that it provided incentive and rewards for those poorer members of society who previously would have had no possibility of becoming property owners. Mrs Thatcher viewed the right to purchase council houses as a flagship of her economic policies; it was a further move towards the ideal of Britain as a property-owning democracy (see page 36). Along with the growing numbers of ordinary people who were taking out building society accounts and thus becoming small-scale shareholders, it represented her belief in enlightened capitalism as the great bond that could unite all classes of society. It certainly proved a popular move among its target audience; by 1985, over 800,000 tenants had begun to purchase the properties they had previously rented. In overall terms, the figure for home ownership was 68 per cent of the population by 1990, an increase of 15 per cent since 1981.

KEY TERMS

Privatisation The selling of nationalised (government-owned) concerns fully or in part to private buyers and investors.

Shareholders Investors in companies or public utilities, such as electricity and gas.

North Sea oil This resource had begun to be tapped in the late 1970s and turned Britain from a net importer to a net exporter of oil.

Table 4.3 Government revenue derived from privatisation 1979–89

1979–80	£377 million
1985–6	£2.6 billion
1988–9	£7.0 billion

Privatisation

Deregulation was complemented by a policy of **privatisation**. As well as providing the state with large additional funds, the policy aimed at increasing 'popular capitalism' by giving a much greater number of ordinary people the chance to become **shareholders**. Between 1979 and 1990 the number of shareholders in Britain rose from 3 million to 9 million.

Of the 50 enterprises sold off during the Thatcher years, the largest were:

- British Airways
- British Steel
- British Coal
- Cable & Wireless
- British Telecom
- Regional electricity and water boards.

Table 4.3 shows how much revenue was raised by this policy.

Financial deregulation encouraged banks and building societies to advance larger loans to their customers. A significant part of the money borrowed was then spent on consumer goods from abroad. The result was that between 1980 and 1989 Britain's balance of payments deficit rose from £16 billion to £47 billion.

North Sea oil

One of the most contentious privatisation measures was the selling off of **North Sea oil**. In 1976, the Labour government had established the British National Oil Corporation as a means of keeping North Sea oil under public control. However, beginning in 1982, Margaret Thatcher's government sold off its majority shareholdings to the private sector. The argument advanced in justification was that despite the considerable revenue gains for Britain since 1976, world oil prices in the 1980s had entered a period of long-term decline. Critics, however, complained that the government had squandered a national asset for short-term gain. They saw deregulation as part of a broader irresponsibility on the government's part that threatened to destroy large parts of Britain's industrial economy, as was evident in the increase in unemployment in British manufacturing industries.

The debate over deregulation and privatisation

The government's defenders argued that greater unemployment did not necessarily prove national decline. They claimed that redundancy, although obviously painful for those experiencing it, was part of a necessary modernising process. The firm measures adopted by the Thatcher governments obliged British industry to shed the wasteful practices that had formerly hindered it. Streamlining and cost-effective techniques resulted in higher productivity since fewer workers were involved.

Such arguments were of little comfort to those people who had lost their jobs. They were unimpressed by the figures which revealed that between 1979 and 1989 manufacturing productivity grew at an annual rate of 4.2 per cent – the highest growth rate in British industrial history and also some way ahead of Britain's European partners. Some writers, such as historian Alan Sked, have gone so far as to suggest that Britain in the 1980s, like Germany in the 1960s, had achieved an economic 'miracle'. This claim should be examined in the light of the following tables indicating some of the key aspects of economic performance in the period 1979–90.

The growth of small businesses in Britain is part of the explanation why, by 1990, it had a higher growth rate than the other countries of the EEC (see Table 4.5). This was in spite of the serious industrial recessions Britain experienced in 1981 and 1987 that produced a serious balance of payments deficit by the late 1980s.

Table 4.4 Number of industrial workers in Britain 1970–90

Year	Number
1970	9 million
1980	7 million
1990	4 million

Table 4.5 Comparison of GDP growth rates 1950–89

Time period	Britain	European average
1950–79	1.8%	3.9%
1979–89	2.1%	1.9%

Table 4.6 Rise or fall in real wages of workers 1979–94

Britain	France	West Germany	USA
26%	2%	3%	–7%

Table 4.7 Job creation in the UK 1979 and 1989

Businesses	1979	1989
Number of self-employed	1,906,000	3,497,000

Table 4.8 The UK's balance of payments (in £ millions) 1978–90

Year	Amount	Year	Amount
1978	1,162	1985	2,888
1979	−525	1986	−871
1980	3,629	1987	−4,983
1981	7,221	1988	−16,617
1982	4,034	1989	−22,512
1983	3,336	1990	−18,268
1984	1,473		

A factor to stress is that throughout the period of the Thatcher government, North Sea oil brought billions of pounds into the Treasury. Arguably, it was this, rather than genuine economic growth, that funded the unemployment and benefit payments that the recession of the 1980s necessitated. Critics of Thatcherism claimed that it was this revenue that made possible the income tax cuts in which the government took great pride. A combination of North Sea oil and privatisation saved Thatcher's government from bankruptcy, enabling it to overcome the recessions that its monetarist policies had created.

Figure 4.2 shows that the highest point of oil revenue came in 1985, but governments continued to draw considerable income from North Sea oil until 2007, when revenue began to fall following the realisation that the natural oil and gas supplies were beginning to decline.

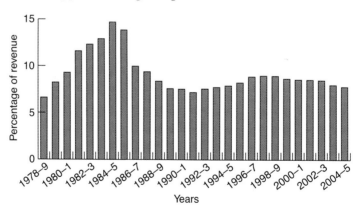

Figure 4.2 Proportion of UK revenues from oil and gas.

Taxation under Thatcher

One of the government's proudest boasts was that the Thatcher years were a period of low taxation. However, it is clear from Table 4.9 that, although there certainly was a significant reduction in income tax rates during Mrs Thatcher's years in office, the overall tax bill for ordinary people had not greatly altered. This was because of increases in indirect taxes, such as National Insurance contributions, VAT and local rates.

Table 4.9 Percentage of gross income taxed for people on average earnings in 1979 and 1990

	Single person		Married person with two children	
	1979	1990	1979	1990
Income tax	25.0	20.3	18.8	12.9
National Insurance	6.5	8.0	6.2	8.0
VAT	2.7	5.1	2.5	5.0
Indirect taxes	8.1	7.1	8.1	7.1
Rates/poll tax	3.1	2.4	2.8	4.9
Totals	45.4	42.9	38.4	37.9

In 1987 a feature film was released in the USA, entitled *Wall Street*, which, while not being explicitly about Thatcherism, was widely interpreted as a critique of the prevailing mood of the times in President Reagan's USA, where he was pursuing economic policies very similar to Margaret Thatcher's. The film's main character was an unscrupulous financier, who, in his pursuit of personal wealth, rode roughshod over anyone who got in his way, destroying their income and livelihood. He justified his behaviour in these terms: 'Greed, is good. Greed is right; greed works. Greed, in all its forms has marked the upward surge of mankind.'

Opponents of Thatcherism seized on this statement as being a precise description of the amorality of a system that allowed the powerless in society to be abused and exploited by the powerful. Defenders responded by pointing out that the film was fiction made by people of the political left, intent on putting the worst interpretation on **Reaganism**. Their reply was that, far from being exploitative, Thatcherism had given the powerless the opportunity to regain control over their lives by loosening the grip of the state over them.

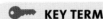 **KEY TERM**

Reaganism
The conservative social and economic policies followed by the Reagan administration in the USA 1981–9.

The Westland affair 1986

In 1986, the Westland affair revealed a division within the government. Westland was an ailing British helicopter company which Michael Heseltine, the defence secretary, proposed to save by making it part of a European consortium which would include British Aerospace, the recently privatised company. However, Leon Brittan, the industry secretary, put forward an alternative package which involved the takeover of Westland by a US company, Sikorsky. When Mrs Thatcher chose to back the Sikorsky option, Heseltine stormed out of the Cabinet. His resignation on 9 January was followed two weeks later by Brittan's when it was revealed that his department of industry had put pressure on British Aerospace to withdraw from the European consortium. Nobody came out of the affair with credit. The Labour opposition were quick to suggest that the affair showed up two unattractive aspects of Margaret Thatcher's style of government: her bullying of the Cabinet and her readiness to give in to US pressure.

The 1987 election

The internal squabble over Westland did not greatly harm the government's standing with the voters. In 1987 Thatcher achieved her third consecutive electoral victory. Although the results showed some recovery by the Labour Party from its disastrous performance in the 1983 election (see page 125), the government maintained its share of the popular vote and despite losing 22 seats still had an overall majority of 100 in the Commons.

Table 4.10 Results of the 1987 general election

Party	Votes	Seats	Percentage of vote
Conservative	13,763,747	375	42.2
Labour	10,029,270	229	30.8
Liberal/SDP	7,341,275	22	22.6
Plaid Cymru	123,589	3	0.3
Scottish Nationalists	416,873	3	1.4
Northern Irish parties	730,152	17	2.3
Others	151,517	1	0.4

Local government reforms

Margaret Thatcher interpreted the election success as a mandate for pressing on with her reforming policies, particularly in regard to local government. In 1988 a series of changes in local authority finances were introduced:

- A system of standard spending assessments (SSAs) enabled central government to control local government expenditure levels.
- Councils were also required to adopt 'compulsory competitive tendering', that is, to contract out their services to the companies that could provide the best service at the lowest price.

The government hoped that these changes would be welcomed by the general public, who would see that the financial changes would create 'more gainers than losers'. For Mrs Thatcher, the financial adjustments were a further step in her plan to bring local government into line with her ideas of public accountability. She believed that public institutions, whose primary purpose, after all, was to serve the public, had to be made more responsive to the needs of the people. This was especially true of local government. She knew that many local authorities were unpopular. Only a minority of people (sometimes under 25 per cent) voted in local elections. This had allowed socialist groups to dominate areas such as the London boroughs and the city councils in Liverpool and Manchester. These were among the high-spending Labour authorities that she had successfully attacked by breaking up the metropolitan councils and abolishing the Greater London Council in 1983.

Education

Margaret Thatcher also regarded her 1987 election victory as a mandate for the most significant educational reform since the 1944 Butler Act (see page 4). The Education Reform Act of 1988 had essentially the same purpose as her local government reforms; namely, to make the service provider, in this case the schools, more responsive to the needs of the consumer, in this case the children and their parents. Introduced by Kenneth Baker, the education minister, the principal provisions of the 1988 Act were:

- The principle of local management of schools was introduced, under which schools were entitled to free themselves from direct financial control by the local education authority (LEA). School budgeting could now be taken over by the head teacher and the school governors.
- Primary and secondary schools could also opt to become grant maintained schools, which allowed them to become independent of their LEAs and be financed directly by central government.
- A National Curriculum was introduced, containing 'core' subjects, such as English and Maths, and 'foundation' subjects, such as Geography, History and Art.
- In their teaching, schools were to cover a set 'key stages', aimed at achieving a number of prescribed learning aims.
- Where local conditions allowed, parents could specify which school they wanted their children to attend.
- League tables, showing the examination results achieved by schools, were to be published.

The poll tax 1989–90: the beginning of the end

Margaret Thatcher's extraordinary period as prime minister came to an end in 1990. Two particular issues largely explain this. One was the misjudgement she made over the **poll tax**; the other was the opposition she met from within her own Cabinet over her policy towards Europe (see page 140). Her difficulties can be read as a sign that after a decade in office she was losing her political touch. Furthermore, she was not helped by being deprived of the moderating influence of Willie Whitelaw, the deputy prime minister who had retired from politics in 1987 after suffering a stroke. It is arguable that some of the errors she made might have been avoided had Whitelaw still been there to offer his common-sense advice.

Mrs Thatcher judged that the general public would continue to support her as she continued with her drive for accountability in local government (see page 136). It was such thinking that led to the community charge, which was introduced into Scotland in 1989 and a year later into England and Wales. The poll tax, as it was better known, has been described as 'a reform too far'. Few issues in British domestic politics have excited such public anger. Yet it was

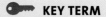

KEY TERM

Poll tax A flat-rate levy to fund local services, to be paid by all adults resident in the local area, not just owners of property; introduced into Scotland in 1989 and into England and Wales in 1990.

never intended to arouse controversy; it was meant to be a rationalising of the existing system of raising money through rates, which nearly everybody agreed was unfair. For, example a single pensioner living alone might well be charged the same rates as a household of four wage-earners living in a property of equal value. The plan was now to tax people, not property.

KEY TERM

Think-tank A body of specialists working together in a research organisation.

The idea of a community charge or poll tax in place of the rates came originally from the Adam Smith Institute (ASI). The ASI was a Conservative **think-tank**, which challenged the idea that the state should redistribute resources in society by taxing the rich and providing for the poor; it argued that the free play of market forces was the best way of fulfilling people's needs. It was this viewpoint which led to the ASI's suggestion that, since there would be 38 million poll-tax payers, compared with only 14 million ratepayers, payment for local services would be much more evenly and justly spread. Moreover, if everybody had to pay for local services then everybody would become much more conscious of the quality of the services provided.

Impressed by this reasoning, Mrs Thatcher reckoned that the community charge would help make local authorities answerable to their 'customers', who would be the people now paying for the services. Her hope was that local electors would embrace the poll tax and then go on to vote out high-spending Labour councils and vote in 'responsible' Conservative ones. This was a serious miscalculation. The opposite happened. The poll tax created fury in the country at large, providing a cause around which her opponents rallied, and alienating some of the Conservative Party's staunchest supporters.

'One-nation Conservatives'

There were a number of Conservative MPs, Edward Heath and Michael Heseltine being the most prominent, who had become unhappy with Margaret Thatcher's approach. They argued that the government should use redistributive taxation to help the disadvantaged members of society. For these 'one-nation Conservatives', as they were called, the poll tax's main disadvantage was that it was a regressive tax, that is, as a flat-rate levy it bore hardest on the poorest. They believed that the riots that had occurred in various English cities in the 1980s held a message (see page 121). Although the disturbances had complex causes they could be interpreted at least in part as an expression of the disaffection of many people, particularly the young unemployed, from Thatcherite Britain.

Unfolding events showed that the government had misjudged the situation. The public saw it as a new tax imposed by a grasping government intent on trapping everybody in the same net. The government did, in fact, list a large number of exemptions from payment for those on low incomes, but these concessions were lost sight of in the furore that the poll tax aroused. Opposition to the charge when it was introduced was immediate and organised. Millions of people refused or avoided payment.

Opposition spreads

The significant feature of all this was that opposition came from across the political spectrum. The far-left group Militant tendency, which had caused such trouble for the Labour Party in the early 1980s (see page 152), revived itself to form the All-Britain Anti-Poll Tax Federation. The Scottish National Party ran a successful 'can't pay, won't pay' campaign. Although the Labour Party and the Liberals did not openly encourage non-payment, they savaged the government over the issue.

More disturbing for Mrs Thatcher was the reaction of many in her own party. She had had a forewarning of this in 1988 when several Conservative backbench rebellions against the poll tax had occurred, the most worrying arising from a Conservative backbench proposal that the tax be modified 'in the interests of fairness'. When the charge came into force in England in March 1990, it was on average double the original estimate. At this, even the respectable middle classes, previously Margaret Thatcher's staunchest allies, began to protest. The most serious disturbance came in March 1990 with a violent anti-poll tax demonstration in London's Trafalgar Square.

A further irony was that, in the event, the poll tax cost two and a half times more to collect than the rates had. In an effort to keep down poll tax levels, the government 'charge-capped' a number of authorities (mostly Labour, but also some Conservative). This involved compelling them to reduce their budgets even if it meant cutting services, a result that stood on its head the original notion of improving local government services in the interest of the 'customer'. Critics had strong grounds for asserting that the whole exercise had been aimed not at encouraging greater local democracy but at imposing the will of the central government on the local authorities. The poll tax was abolished in 1991 by John Major, Mrs Thatcher's successor (see page 167), and replaced with a new council tax, based on the value of a home within eight assessment bands.

Summary diagram: Thatcherism: the second stage

Methods
- Deregulation
- Decentralisation
- Privatisation

Aim
To create economic growth by:
- Reducing taxation
- Providing incentives
- Encouraging competition
- Limiting trade union powers
- Cutting wasteful welfare payments
- Creating accountability

Key areas affected
- Local government
- Social services
- Education

Consequences
- Unemployment in some areas
- Job creation in others
- No real reduction in taxation
- Growth in GDP
- Increase in real wages
- Large increase in inflation

The poll tax 1989–90
- Proposed to tax people not property
- Policy misjudged the public reaction
- Met fierce resistance from all classes in Britain
- One Nation Conservatives rebelled
- Violent anti-poll tax demonstration in London in March 1990
- Marked beginning of the end of Thatcher government

The debate over Thatcherism

For
- Made UK face economic reality
- Encouraged initiative and entrepreneurship
- Created the conditions of growth
- Created new jobs
- Advanced popular capitalism
- Developed the notion of accountability

Against
- Encouraged individualism and greed
- Ignored the needs of the more vulnerable in society
- Caused unemployment
- Led to a recession

 Foreign affairs and Ireland

▶ *What impact did Margaret Thatcher have on international affairs?*

▶ *What approach did Margaret Thatcher adopt towards Northern Ireland?*

Mrs Thatcher and Europe

When Margaret Thatcher came into office in 1979 she was confronted by the record of Britain's poor economic performance in the 1970s, caused at least in part by the difficult adjustments that had had to be made on entering the EEC. She later claimed that she had not been initially anti-EEC but when she realised how much waste and inefficiency there was in the Brussels bureaucracy and how much Britain was disadvantaged she felt compelled to speak out. The centralising bureaucratic character of Europe ran counter to the revolution she was trying to bring about in Britain. Her main concerns were as follows:

- Protectionism, the principle on which Europe operated, was outmoded in an age of economic globalism.
- Europe was obsessed with a dated concept of centralisation when that polity was clearly collapsing in the wider world (for example, in the USSR, which disintegrated between 1989 and 1991).
- The disparity between the budget payments made by the separate member states rewarded the inefficient nations and penalised the efficient and productive ones.

The issue of federalism

Mrs Thatcher's response was to emphasise the virtues of national sovereignty and free enterprise. She was also disturbed at a deeper level by the threat that European federalism held for Britain:

- She stressed how young the European institutions were; none of them pre-dated 1945, whereas Britain's governmental system had evolved over centuries.
- She felt that Europe could easily become the prey of creeping socialism and bureaucracy because in the final analysis the EEC was not subject to genuine democratic control.

These fears were not new. They had shaped the attitude of both Labour and Conservative parties as early as the 1950s when the first moves were taken towards forming a European Union (see page 49). What made Margaret Thatcher appear particularly hostile was her manner. She carried over into her discussion with European ministers the adversarial style of debate which she had learned in British politics. But this was out of place in a European context. Direct confrontation was rare between European ministers and officials. They tended to get things done by compromise, concession and private agreements. Such techniques irritated Thatcher and she was not reluctant to show it.

Britain and the EEC budget

The ground on which she chose to defend the British position most strongly was that of Britain's disproportionately high payments to the EEC budget. She defined her position in her memoirs (see Source D, page 142).

Her battling had some success; the EEC reluctantly authorised a reduction in Britain's budget payments. But her dislike of the centralising process within Europe remained. She was at her most forthright in attacking the notions of **Jacques Delors**, whom she regarded as typical of the unelected and unaccountable bureaucrats who were making the rules for Europe. In a landmark speech at Bruges in 1988, she condemned 'the erosion of democracy by centralisation and bureaucracy' (see Source E, page 142).

 KEY FIGURE

Jacques Delors (1925–)
European Union president from 1985 to 1995 and a strong federalist.

According to Source D, what are Margaret Thatcher's concerns about Britain's contributions to the EEC budget?

SOURCE D

From Margaret Thatcher, *The Downing Street Years*, HarperCollins, 1993, p. 62.

Britain's unique trading pattern made her a very large net contributor to the EC [European Community] budget – so large that the situation was indeed unacceptable. We traditionally imported far more from non-EC countries than did other Community members, particularly of foodstuffs. This meant that we paid more into the Community budget in the form of tariffs than they did. By contrast, the Community budget itself is heavily biased towards supporting farmers through the Common Agricultural Policy: indeed when we came into office more than 70 per cent of the budget was spent in this way. The CAP was – and is – operated in a wasteful manner. The dumping of these surpluses outside the EC distorts the world market in foodstuffs and threatens the survival of free trade between the major economies. The British economy is less dependent on agriculture than that of most other Community countries; consequently we receive less in subsidy than they do.

SOURCE E

According to Source E, what does Thatcher understand by 'a European super-state'?

From Margaret Thatcher's speech to the College of Europe in Bruges, 20 September 1988, www.margaretThatcher.org/document/107332.

[I]t is ironic that just when those countries such as the Soviet Union, which have tried to run everything from the centre, are learning that success depends on dispersing power and decisions away from the centre, there are some in the Community who seem to want to move in the opposite direction. We have not successfully rolled back the frontiers of the state in Britain, only to see them re-imposed at a European level with a European super-state exercising a new dominance from Brussels.

Certainly we want to see Europe more united and with a greater sense of common purpose. But it must be in a way which preserves the different traditions, parliamentary powers and sense of national pride in one's own country; for these have been the source of Europe's vitality through the centuries.

Her Bruges speech was widely regarded as a rallying cry to all those who wished to prevent the absorption of national identities into a centralising Europe. It was a piece of populism; she was trying to appeal over the heads of Europe's bureaucrats to the ordinary people in France and Germany as well as to the British.

The Single European Act 1986

Despite her fighting words, the great paradox was that it was Margaret Thatcher who presided over the process by which Britain was drawn ever closer into Europe. It was she who in 1986 accepted the Single European Act, which marked the biggest step towards a centralised Europe that had yet been taken. The main terms of the Act were as follows:

- The signatory countries committed themselves to closer monetary and political union.
- The principle of supranationality (the subordination of individual member states to the EEC) was established.
- The right of individual member states to veto majority decisions was abolished.

The Exchange Rate Mechanism

Margaret Thatcher was also in office when Britain agreed to enter the **ERM** in October 1990. She had been told by her financial experts that it would provide a means of fighting inflation. In the event it did the opposite and in 1992 a monetary crisis obliged Britain to withdraw from the ERM.

Thatcher claimed later that she had been misled into entering the ERM in 1990 by her former chancellor of the exchequer, Nigel Lawson, and her foreign secretary, Geoffrey Howe. Both ministers were to play an important role in the weakening of her position as prime minister and party leader. In 1989 Lawson had resigned when he found that Mrs Thatcher was taking more notice of Alan Walters, whom she had appointed her special economic adviser, than she was of him as chancellor. Howe, a pro-European, made a similar charge, claiming that the prime minister's aggressive anti-Europeanism was distorting his attempts as foreign secretary to smooth Britain's entry into the ERM.

On 31 October 1990, on Margaret Thatcher's return from a top-level European meeting in Rome where she had openly declared that Britain would never join the single currency, she stated emphatically to the Commons: 'The President of the Commission, Monsieur Delors, said at this conference that he wanted the European Parliament to be the democratic body of the Community, he wanted the Commission to be the Executive, and he wanted the Council of Ministers to be the Senate. No, No, No!'

Howe's resignation speech, November 1990

It was in the wake of this that Howe, feeling his position had been made untenable, resigned. In his resignation speech in the Commons on 13 November 1990, he revealed the serious divisions within the Conservative Party over Europe. Those who witnessed it said the speech took its power from its understatement. Read in Howe's characteristically flat unemotional tones, which expressed sorrow rather than anger, it amounted to a devastating criticism of the prime minister for her obstructive attitude towards European development, and her undermining of his position. He likened himself to a batsman arriving at the wicket only to find that his bat had been broken by the team captain. Howe's measured criticism of Margaret Thatcher proved devastating. It was the prelude to the leadership struggle that led to her resignation in November 1990 (see page 158).

KEY TERM

ERM The Exchange Rate Mechanism introduced by the EEC in 1979, as a system for bringing European currencies much closer together in value as preparation for the eventual adoption of a single European currency.

Mrs Thatcher and Hong Kong

In 1842, China had granted Britain the island of Hong Kong on a permanent basis. In 1860, Britain formally added Kowloon, the harbour directly facing Hong Kong island, to its permanent possessions. The third piece of territory, Kowloon peninsula, on which the harbour stood, was gained by Britain in 1898. This last piece, known as the New Territories, was not granted to Britain in perpetuity but only on a 99-year lease.

The British colony of Hong Kong as formed in 1898 was to develop during the following century into one of the most prosperous cities in the commercial world. After 1949, when the Communists, led by Mao Zedong, had taken over mainland China, Hong Kong became a haven for those fleeing from Communist rule. Thousands of businessmen and bankers, who brought their wealth with them, settled in Hong Kong and quickly turned it into a world centre of manufacturing, commerce and finance.

Yet, the People's Republic of China (PRC) could take deep satisfaction from the thought that under the terms of the 1898 agreement, Hong Kong would return to China in 1997. **Deng Xiaoping** anticipated that it would add a huge asset to his modernisation plans for China.

There was a problem, however. Opinion polls showed that 95 per cent of the Hong Kong people wanted to stay British. Would Britain use this as a

KEY FIGURE

Deng Xiaoping (1904–97)

Leader of the PRC from 1978 to 1997, his policies prepared the way for China to become one of the world's major economic powers.

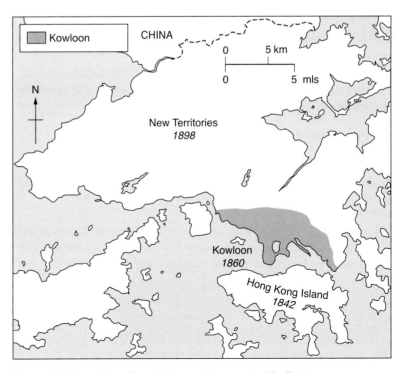

Figure 4.3 Hong Kong. Dates indicate when acquired by Britain.

justification for resisting China's claim? In strictly legal terms, Britain had a case for doing so. According to the earlier treaties, Kowloon and the island of Hong Kong were permanent British possessions. It was only the New Territories that were leased. The PRC expected to meet difficulties and prepared for a long diplomatic battle. PRC–UK talks began in 1979. Margaret Thatcher was personally involved in the negotiations from 1982 onwards. Deng Xiaoping took a hard line. He told her: 'I would rather see Hong Kong torched than leave Britain to rule it after 1997.'

Britain was not in a strong bargaining position. The idea of giving up the New Territories but keeping Hong Kong and Kowloon was not really an option. It was the New Territories that supplied Hong Kong with its essential water and power supplies. The logistical problems of supplying the island by any other means were insurmountable. Deng was not exaggerating when, in one sharp exchange, he threatened that Chinese forces 'could walk in and take Hong Kong later today if they wanted to'.

Deng knew that he also held the moral high ground. The British had originally acquired the colony through superior military strength, forcing China to sign away Hong Kong against its will. It was, said Deng, an example of colonialism at its most exploitative. The *People's Daily* commented bitterly: '150 years ago, to maintain its drug trafficking in China, Britain launched the aggressive **Opium War** against China, during which it carried out burning, killing, rape, and plunder on Chinese soil.'

The Joint Declaration 1984

Aware of its military and moral weakness, all Britain could work for was a compromise that would give Hong Kong some form of legally binding protection after it returned to China. This came in the form of the Sino-British Joint Declaration, signed in December 1984:

- Britain agreed that on the expiry of the lease on the New Territories in 1997 all the areas that made up Hong Kong would return to the PRC.
- In return, the Chinese Communists declared that Hong Kong after 1997 would be treated as a 'Special Administrative Region' (SAR) until 2047. This would leave its capitalist economic structure unaltered.

Hong Kong's democrats

Difficulties arose during the period leading up to the 1997 handover. A particularly demanding problem was the opposition of Hong Kong's democrats, who felt that the Declaration would not give them sufficient protection post-1997. However, Britain seemed intent on causing as little fuss as possible by not pressing Beijing on the democracy question. Since the Hong Kong handover was now inevitable, there were more important things Britain should be looking towards. Among these was the maintenance of good relations with China, whose billion-plus population offered huge commercial prospects for Britain.

 **KEY TERM**

Opium War In a series of wars in the middle years of the nineteenth century, Britain had forced China to buy large quantities of opium, a humiliation which remained a basic historical reference point for many Chinese in explaining their suspicion towards the West.

Mrs Thatcher: the iron lady

It is a remarkable fact that at the end of her period in government Mrs Thatcher was far more popular abroad than she was at home. This was because as a staunch anti-Communist, she had played no small role in bringing about the collapse of the Soviet Union and the end of the Cold War. Her populist instincts served her well in this regard. She sensed that Communism no longer represented the will of the people in those countries where Communist regimes were still in power. Although she was prepared 'to do business' with the Soviet Union in commercial matters and got on well personally with its leader, Mikhail Gorbachev, whom she met on a number of occasions, she never budged from her conviction that Communism as an ideology was the enemy of freedom.

As early as 1976, her attitude had earned her the nickname 'the iron lady' in the Soviet press. The title was intended as a disparaging allusion to her opposition to Communism, but Margaret Thatcher delighted in it, viewing it as a recognition of her firmness of purpose. As prime minister, Margaret Thatcher made a number of visits to the Eastern bloc, including Poland, Hungary and the USSR itself. For many people in those countries she became a symbol of freedom. In Poland, for example, chapels and shrines were dedicated to her. This was principally because of her open support throughout the 1980s for Solidarity, the Polish trade union movement. Led by its chairman, Lech Wałęsa, Solidarity fought a running battle with Poland's Communist government, demanding recognition as an independent movement free from control by the authorities. Its successful resistance to attempts to suppress it was a major factor in encouraging anti-Communist, anti-Soviet movements throughout the Eastern bloc, which culminated in the '**velvet revolution**' of the late 1980s.

There was some shaking of heads in Britain. Critics asked how the prime minister could reconcile being pro-trade union abroad and anti-trade union at home (see page 127). Defenders suggested that it was all a matter of freedom; she was against trade unions when she regarded their actions as a threat to liberty, but supported them when they promoted liberty.

Mrs Thatcher and Ronald Reagan

Margaret Thatcher's powerfully expressed anti-Communism chimed well with the prevailing view in the USA. It so happened that her leadership of Britain in the 1980s coincided with the presidency of Ronald Reagan. The two leaders had a special affinity. Reagan had been greatly impressed by Thatcher's resolute handling of the Falklands crisis in 1982. Their liking for each other and their shared attitudes personalised the special relationship between Britain and the USA. The modern British historian Peter Clarke neatly conveyed the personal, ideological and economic bonds between them in this extract from *Hope and Glory Britain 1900–1990* (Allen Lane, 1996):

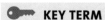 **KEY TERM**

Velvet revolution In the face of popular nationalist opposition, the USSR abandoned its authority over the countries of Eastern Europe without a fight; this resulted in the collapse of the USSR itself in 1991.

Nowhere was Thatcher more warmly received than in the USA. … An idealized USA was held up by Thatcherites as a model of society based on the free market, minimal government, anti-Communism, the mighty dollar and Almighty God. After Ronald Reagan was elected President in 1980, Thatcher found a real ally, with her trenchant expositions of their common outlook complemented by his benignly bemused concurrence. This was indeed a special relationship, which helped to inflate Thatcher's international standing.

While they might have disagreed over aspects of foreign policy, they were of one mind over the Cold War's big questions. They agreed that the West had to remain fully armed with nuclear weapons. One result of this was Britain's buying from the USA, at an initial cost of £10 billion, Trident missiles to replace the obsolete Polaris variety (see page 51). In addition, Britain agreed in 1981 to allow the USA to install its Cruise missiles at the US air force base at **Greenham Common**, a decision that led to a major resurgence in the CND movement (see page 113).

While the left in both countries accused Reagan and Thatcher of crudely oversimplifying the issues, the effect of the UK–USA's unyielding front towards international Communism in the 1980s was to put great pressure on the Soviet Union, whose attempt to keep up in the arms race with the West exhausted it militarily and financially. In 1983 Reagan announced the development of a Strategic Defence Initiative (popularly known as 'Star Wars') which when fully operational would give the USA complete protection against missile attack. This may have been exaggeration, but it convinced the USSR that it could no longer keep pace with the West. This proved a major factor in the USSR's eventual disintegration in 1991. Thatcher had played a part in winning the Cold War for the West.

The special relationship that Margaret Thatcher had helped to renew was to prove a significant factor in the subsequent administrations of John Major and Tony Blair when Britain and the USA acted together in a number of critical international issues.

Mrs Thatcher and Ireland

In 1979, the year she took office, Margaret Thatcher was made all too aware of the task facing her in Northern Ireland. In March, two months before she became prime minister, Airey Neave, the man whom she intended to make her Northern Ireland secretary, was killed when a bomb planted under the bonnet of his car exploded as he drove out of the Commons' car park. The killers were the **INLA**, an extreme breakaway group from the IRA, which claimed responsibility in a released statement: 'Airey Neave, got a taste of his own medicine when an INLA unit pulled off the operation of the decade and blew him to bits … The nauseous Margaret Thatcher snivelled on television that he was an "incalculable loss" – and so he was – to the British ruling class.'

KEY TERMS

Greenham Common Became the site of a women's peace camp which picketed the base from 1981 to 2000, a graphic example of the extra-parliamentary protests against government policy that were a feature of late twentieth-century politics.

INLA Irish National Liberation Army, whose republicanism was part of its programme for Marxist world revolution.

Five months later it was a member of the royal family who fell victim. At the end of August, Earl Mountbatten, uncle of the Prince of Wales, was blown up by a bomb smuggled aboard his holiday yacht in County Sligo. The explosion also killed Earl Mountbatten's daughter and grandson, and two others in the holiday party. The murders were synchronised with the detonation of two remote-control bombs at Warrenpoint in Northern Ireland which killed eighteen British soldiers of the parachute regiment. The troops were deliberately targeted because the IRA considered that particular regiment to have been responsible for 'Bloody Sunday' in 1972 (see page 98).

The INLA was right in thinking that Thatcher would take a tough stance over Northern Ireland. But her approach did not exclude negotiation and co-operation where these were thought possible. In 1980 she had a number of meetings with Charles Haughey, the Irish *taoiseach*, with a view to establishing 'closer political co-operation' between Dublin and Westminster.

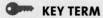

KEY TERM

Taoiseach Gaelic for prime minister.

Death of Bobby Sands 1981

Such gains as were made on the diplomatic front were overshadowed by developments in Northern Ireland itself. In March 1981, in protest against the refusal of the authorities in the Maze prison to treat him as a political prisoner, Bobby Sands, a convicted bomber, went on hunger strike. Mrs Thatcher told the authorities to stand firm in the face of such coercive martyrdom. The result of the intransigence on both sides was that Sands died after refusing food for 66 days. Sands became an iconic figure to the nationalists of Northern Ireland. Yet, despite the intense anger towards the British government that his death aroused among them, there was a more positive consequence; Sinn Féin, the legitimate republican party, began to pick up votes in elections. Although Sinn Féin was the political wing of the IRA, the growing willingness of nationalists and republicans to use the ballot box was at least a sign that violence was not looked on as the only recourse.

The Brighton bombing 1984

A political solution was still a long way off, however. This was dramatically illustrated on 12 October 1984, when Mrs Thatcher narrowly escaped being assassinated in the IRA bombing of the Grand Hotel in Brighton. The bomb had been concealed in a bathroom wall three weeks earlier and was timed to go off in the early hours of the morning when most of the Cabinet, who were using the hotel as a base during the Conservative Party conference, were expected to be there. In the event, five people were killed, none of them ministers, and 30 others injured. Later that day Thatcher gave an impressive performance, insisting that the conference must go on and declaring that democracy would never bow to terrorism.

Anglo-Irish Agreement, August 1985

A major step towards democracy was taken a year later with the signing of the Anglo-Irish Agreement by Margaret Thatcher and the Irish premier, Garrett Fitzgerald. It contained three main provisions:

- The Republic recognised Northern Ireland as being constitutionally a part of the UK.
- The British government gave an assurance that it supported full civil rights for all in Northern Ireland and acknowledged the strength of nationalist desires for a united Ireland.
- The two governments committed themselves to close co-operation over cross-border security matters.

With hindsight, the Agreement can be seen as an important stage in the advance towards a peaceful settlement. However, at the time, it was bitterly condemned by many of those it most closely concerned. Mrs Thatcher, who had genuinely intended it to be a basis for reconciliation in Ulster, was shocked at the vehemence of the response; she recorded that it was 'worse than anyone had predicted.' The reasons for opposition to the Agreement were as follows:

- The unionists objected to the involvement of the Irish government in Northern affairs, fearing that it gave encouragement to the notion of a united Ireland under the rule of Dublin. At a massive unionist rally in Belfast a few days after the signing of the Agreement, Ian Paisley cried out emotionally, 'Thatcher tells us that the Republic must have some say in our Province. We say never, never, never, never.' The unionist MPs showed their bitterness by resolving not to attend Westminster, copying a tactic that Sinn Féin had continually used.
- The republicans rejected the Agreement for a similar but opposite reason; its terms confirmed the very thing they were fighting against: Northern Ireland's continuation as a part of the UK. They pledged themselves to continue 'the armed struggle'.
- Some members of Thatcher's government were unhappy with the Agreement on the grounds that it might be wrongly interpreted as a concession by the government towards the men of violence in Northern Ireland. Ian Gow, the housing minister, resigned, although he continued to be on good terms with the prime minister. In 1990, he paid the ultimate price for his tough line on Ulster when he was blown up outside his home in Sussex by an IRA car bomb.

Massacre at Enniskillen 1987

The IRA's commitment to 'armed struggle' was murderously expressed in November 1987 when it exploded a bomb at a Remembrance Day service in Enniskillen in Northern Ireland. Eleven people were killed and 60 others, including women and children, maimed. So poignantly tragic was the fate of these innocent victims that there were many in both the Catholic and Protestant communities who openly doubted that any cause could ever justify such suffering. The IRA, however, stated that the carnage would not deter it from its mission. Its official terse comment was 'The British Army did not leave Ireland after Bloody Sunday.'

'Death on the Rock' 1988

The undeclared war continued. In March 1988, in the British colony of Gibraltar, the **SAS** shot and killed three IRA members before they had time to detonate a car bomb intended to decimate British troops at a changing of the guard ceremony. There was official disquiet, although little public sympathy for the victims, when eyewitness accounts suggested that they had been shot without warning. At the funeral of the three a week later in Belfast, a crowd of some 5000 attenders were fired on by Michael Stone, a loyalist gunman; three died and another 50 were injured. Three days later two off-duty British soldiers drove, presumably by mistake, into an area where an IRA parade was being held. They were dragged from their car by the crowd and killed.

In October 1988, in an effort to deny the terrorists 'the oxygen of publicity', Margaret Thatcher's government imposed a broadcasting ban on the IRA. This involved blanking out the voices of terrorists and their supporters, and substituting actors' voices. As even the government later reluctantly admitted, it was all rather pointless since the IRA personnel could still be seen and their message heard.

Measures to bring stability

Bitter reading though the catalogue of death made, behind the violence that obviously caught the headlines efforts continued to be made to bring stability to Ulster. In the final years of Thatcher's government, the following measures were introduced:

- 1987: the Central Community Relations Unit was established to foster greater contact and understanding between Catholics and Protestants.
- 1989: the Fair Employment Act required employers who had more than 25 workers on their books not to discriminate when allocating jobs and promotions.
- 1990: the Northern Ireland Community Relations Council extended the support and resources granted to the Community Relations Unit three years earlier.

These minor advances kept alive the idea that the government was not totally consumed with the fight against terrorism in the province; it had time for the smaller things. But as the number of outrages and the death toll mounted, it was evident to all that only a political solution could end Northern Ireland's agonies.

Summary diagram: Foreign affairs and Ireland

Europe
- Opposition to protectionism, centralisation and federalism
- Won rebate for Britain over EEC budget
- Accepted Single European Act 1986
- Accepted ERM
- Thatcher's Bruges speech 1988 rejected European superstate
- Thatcher's anti-Europeanism led to Howe's resignation 1990

The iron lady
- Strongly anti-Communism but prepared 'to do business' with Gorbachev
- Admired by East Europeans for her encouragement of velvet revolutions
- Special relationship with Reagan
- Britain bought US Trident missiles
- Reagan–Thatcher pressure on Soviets a factor in collapse of the USSR

Hong Kong
- Joint Declaration 1984
- Conceded China's main demands
- Hong Kong to be returned to China in 1997
- Hong Kong democrats ignored

Ireland
- 1979: Murder of Airey Neave deepened resolve to resist terrorism
- 1981: Death of Bobby Sands followed refusal to make concessions
- 1984: Thatcher survived Brighton bombing
- 1985: Anglo-Irish Agreement
- 1987: Enniskillen massacre; continued IRA commitment to 'armed struggle'
- 1987: Central Community Relations Unit established
- 1988: 'Death on the Rock': SAS action illustrated Thatcher's uncompromising approach
- 1989: Denied terrorists 'oxygen of publicity': censorship imposed on IRA representatives

---

6 The Labour Party during the Thatcher years

▶ *Why was the Labour Party unable to mount an effective challenge to Thatcherism?*

If Margaret Thatcher had a profound effect on her own party, her impact on the Labour Party was hardly less significant. The 1980s were a disastrous decade for the Labour Party.

Labour's problems

- Between 1979 and 1992 Labour lost four elections in a row.
- The last year of James Callaghan's administration in 1978–9 witnessed the 'winter of discontent', a series of damaging strikes by public service workers (see page 92).
- The Labour Party's strong links with the unions were seen by the voters as a contributory factor to the industrial strife, and to Labour's inability to govern. This view held for the next thirteen years. The electorate no longer seemed to regard Labour as a party of government.

- In many respects Labour was its own worst enemy in this period. It presented an image of a divided party more concerned with its own internal wrangles than with preparing itself for government.
- A major problem was the split between the left and right of the party. Callaghan had been a moderate but he was followed as leader in 1980 by **Michael Foot**, whose election marked a success for the left-wing backbench MPs.

The Labour left

Apart from Foot himself, the outstanding spokesman of the left was Tony Benn. He had been born Anthony Wedgwood Benn, the heir to Lord Stansgate. However, true to his democratic principles, he renounced his peerage and remained a member of the House of Commons (see page 56). He was a minister under both Wilson and Callaghan but despite gaining a loyal following on the left of the party was never able to convert his popularity into a successful bid for the leadership. Moderates regarded him with suspicion and the right-wing tabloid newspapers portrayed him as a dangerous representative of the 'loony left'. From the 1960s, he was a consistent opponent of Britain's membership of EEC and later the European Union (see page 170), regarding these bodies as undemocratic and unrepresentative.

Benn had interpreted Labour's defeat in 1979 as a sign not that the party was too left wing but that it was not left wing enough. He urged the party to embrace genuinely socialist policies instead of tinkering with capitalist ideas. As a step towards achieving this, he led a campaign to change the party's constitution. At Labour's 1980 and 1981 conferences, the left forced through resolutions that required all Labour MPs to seek reselection by their constituencies. The aim was to give greater power to left-wing activists who, although being a minority in the party overall, were disproportionately stronger in the constituencies.

The Social Democratic Party

Benn hailed the changes as a victory for party democracy, but for Labour moderates it signalled the takeover of the party by extremist groups, such as the **Militant tendency**. Believing that the party was allowing itself to be divorced from people's real needs by pursuing an unrealistic political agenda, a number of Labour MPs broke away in 1981 to form a new Social Democratic Party (SDP). The most prominent among these were Shirley Williams, David Owen, William Rodgers and Roy Jenkins, known as the 'Gang of Four'. Although they had all held posts in the Labour governments of the 1970s, none of them had been happy with what they perceived to be the Labour Party's domination by the trade unions and its anti-Europeanism. They had stifled their feelings and gone along with the main policies of Wilson and Callaghan. But three connected factors convinced them that the time had come for them to make a complete break:

- Labour's election defeat in 1979
- the election of Michael Foot as leader in 1980
- the Labour Party's constitutional changes that had pushed it still further to the left.

The defectors claimed that the SDP would be a radical but not a socialist force in British politics. Their hope was that it would attract disaffected members from both the Labour and Conservative parties. In alliance with the Liberals, the SDP gained a quarter of the popular vote in the 1983 election. But, despite such early success, it was never able to establish itself as a credible alternative to the major parties. By the early 1990s the SDP had formally merged with the Liberal Party to form the Liberal Democrats.

The 1983 general election

Led by Michael Foot, the Labour Party suffered a heavy defeat in the 1983 election. The reasons are clear:

- Foot led the party and the campaign in an uninspiring way.
- The party was weakened by its serious and public internal disputes.
- The party's ill-thought-out manifesto was largely a concession to its left wing and in particular to the CND. Among its pledges was the promise to abandon Britain's independent nuclear deterrent and reintroduce nationalisation. The Labour MP Gerald Kaufman wittily, if despairingly, described the manifesto as 'the longest suicide note in history'.
- Margaret Thatcher was riding high on the Falklands factor (see page 125).
- The apparent pacifism of Foot and Kinnock during the Falklands War made the Labour Party look unpatriotic at a time of national crisis (see page 125).

Kinnock's reforms

Neil Kinnock replaced Michael Foot as party leader in 1983. This was to prove a turning point in Labour's fortunes. Although Kinnock had earlier been on the left of the party, he was realistic enough to appreciate that the hard left path was unlikely to lead Labour back to power. He began a wide-ranging policy review which rejected many of the programmes, such as unilateralism, which the party had saddled itself with under Foot. A key moment came in 1985 at the annual party conference when Kinnock denounced the Militant tendency councillors, such as those in Liverpool and Manchester, whose extreme activities had earned the contempt of the electorate. He told the party that it had to adapt to the real world or it would be condemned to permanent powerlessness (see Source F, page 154).

There is a strong argument for regarding Kinnock's conference speech in 1985 as having destroyed the SDP. By advancing the notion of a party wedded to reform but determined to avoid extremes, he had stolen the SDP's clothes. A reformed but still radical Labour Party meant there was no need for an SDP. It has also been suggested that had the Gang of Four shown patience and waited they would have found that Kinnock's Labour Party perfectly fitted their ideas.

SOURCE F

From Neil Kinnock's speech at the 1985 Labour Party conference, http://ukpolitics.org.uk/node/376.

Implausible promises don't win victories. I'll tell you what happens with impossible promises. You start with far-fetched resolutions. They are then pickled into a rigid dogma, a code, and you go through the years sticking to that, out-dated, misplaced, irrelevant to the real needs. I'm telling you, you can't play politics with people's jobs and people's services or with their homes. [outbreak of booing in the hall] Comrades, the voice of the people – not the people here; the voice of the real people with real needs – is louder than all the boos that can be assembled. Understand that, please, comrades. In your socialism, in your commitment to those people, understand it. The people will not, cannot, abide posturing. They cannot respect the gesture-generals or the tendency-tacticians.

They know life is real, life is earnest – too real, too earnest to mistake a Conference Resolution for an accomplished fact; too real, too earnest to mistake a slogan for a strategy; too real, too earnest to allow them to mistake their own individual enthusiasm for mass movement; too real, too earnest to mistake barking for biting. I hope that becomes universal too.

Yet in battling with the left and laying the base for the modernisation of the Labour Party, Kinnock had sacrificed his own party-political future. He had, in effect, to execute a series of U-turns, on nationalisation, on the nuclear issue and on Europe. These were courageous moves on his part and unavoidable if his party was to progress, but the consequence for Kinnock personally was that he was never again fully trusted either by his party or by the electorate. He stood down after his second election defeat in 1992. His successor, John Smith, was very popular in the party but had little time to build on this before his premature death in 1994. Smith was succeeded as leader by Tony Blair (see page 178).

> ? According to Neil Kinnock in Source F, what political mistakes have been made by Labour Party extremists?

Summary diagram: The Labour Party during the Thatcher years

Difficulties of its position

- Took time to live down the memory of the 'winter of discontent'
- Internal divisions between left and right a continual source of weakness
- Michael Foot a disappointment as a leader – unable to inspire the party or engage with the electorate
- Angered by the prevailing influence of CND, Militant tendency and the unions, a section of the party split away to form the SDP in 1981
- The party came badly out of the Falklands War in 1982 – its objection to military intervention was read by the electorate as lack of support for those fighting the war
- The party's disastrous performance in the 1983 election showed how out of touch the party had become

Kinnock's reforms

- Began the painful process of trying to reshape the party to win the centre ground
- His 1985 speech a landmark in the evolution of what was to become New Labour
- Helped to nullify the SDP
- But in making the necessary policy adjustments was seen as abandoning his previous principles
- The distrust this excited was evident in the election defeats of 1987 and 1992

Chapter summary

A conviction politician, Margaret Thatcher took office determined to end the post-war consensus. Her monetarist policies challenged the prevailing Keynesian orthodoxies. However, the restrictions on government expenditure led to recession which caused unemployment, social unrest and a sharp fall in her popularity. But rapid recovery in her ratings came in 1982 with her leadership of Britain's successful war with Argentina over the Falklands. Her opposition to subsidising ailing industries led to the miners' strike of 1984–5.

Accepting that monetarism had not produced the desired results, the government adopted supply-side policies aimed at encouraging individualism and growth in the private sector and greater accountability in the public sector. Mrs Thatcher's determination to defend what she regarded as the country's interests was evident in her resistance to federalism in Europe and to terrorism in Northern Ireland. Acknowledged as an international stateswoman, Margaret Thatcher's close ties with President Reagan helped to bring the end of the Cold War following the collapse of Soviet control in Eastern Europe. The opportunity for political exploitation that government failings presented was largely spurned by a Labour Party whose internal dissensions compromised its ability to act as an effective opposition. It was Thatcher's own mistakes over the poll tax and Europe that fatally weakened her position.

Refresher questions

Use these questions to remind yourself of the key material covered in this chapter.

1 What did Thatcher understand by the post-war consensus?

2 In what sense was Mrs Thatcher an economic revolutionary?

3 In what ways was Thatcherism a reversal of Keynesianism?

4 What impact did monetarism have?

5 What political benefits did Mrs Thatcher derive from the British victory in the Falklands War?

6 What issues were at stake in the miners' strike of 1984–5?

7 What was meant by 'supply-side economics'?

8 What was the policy of deregulation and privatisation intended to achieve?

9 How was the principle of 'accountability' applied in the government's reforms of local government and education?

10 Why did the poll tax arouse such widespread opposition?

11 What attitude did Thatcher's government adopt towards Northern Ireland?

12 What part did Mrs Thatcher play in the ending of the Cold War?

13 What developments led to the formation of the SDP in 1981?

14 Why did Labour perform so poorly in the 1983 election?

15 How did Neil Kinnock attempt to reform the Labour Party?

 Question practice

ESSAY QUESTIONS

1 To what extent was the practice of consensus politics undermined during the period of the Thatcher governments 1979–90?

2 How successful were the monetarist policies introduced by the Thatcher government?

3 'The Falklands War proved to be Margaret Thatcher's greatest asset as prime minister.' Assess the validity of this view.

4 How far do you agree that the Labour Party was its own worst enemy in the period of the Thatcher governments?

SOURCE ANALYSIS QUESTIONS

1 With reference to Sources B (page 119), D (page 142) and E (page 142), and your understanding of the historical context, assess the value of these sources to a historian studying Mrs Thatcher's political convictions.

2 With reference to Sources D (page 142) and E (page 142), and your understanding of the historical context, assess the value of these sources to a historian studying Margaret Thatcher's beliefs in relation to her policies.

CHAPTER 5

From Thatcherism to New Labour 1990–2001

It has been said that all political careers end in failure. Certainly Margaret Thatcher's fall in 1990 brought her down from the heights of power and popularity she had enjoyed earlier. So remarkable had her eleven years in office been that they left a legacy that could not be ignored; she had made a revolution. The question then arose: how would those who came after her handle the legacy she had bequeathed? After an interlude in which John Major extended the period of Conservative government to eighteen years, New Labour came to power under its young leader Tony Blair, who was to take Britain into the new millennium. These developments are treated as the following themes:

★ The fall of Margaret Thatcher 1990

★ Margaret Thatcher's legacy

★ John Major's government 1990–7

★ New Labour 1994–7

★ Tony Blair's first administration 1997–2001

The key debate on *page 165* of this chapter asks the question: What was Thatcherism?

Key dates

1990	Poll tax crisis	1992	UK withdrawal from ERM
	UK joined ERM	1993	Euro-rebellion and ratification of Maastricht Treaty
	Howe's resignation		
	Mrs Thatcher resigned after failing to win the leadership contest	1994	Blair became Labour Party leader
	Major became prime minister	1995	Major won party leadership election
1991	Citizen's Charter		NATO intervention in Bosnia
	Coalition forces liberated Kuwait	1997	Labour election victory
1992	Maastricht Treaty	1999	NATO intervention in Kosovo

The fall of Margaret Thatcher 1990

▶ *What issues brought down Margaret Thatcher in 1990?*

Given the anger aroused by the government's inept handling of the poll tax (see pages 137–9), it was no surprise that the Conservatives lost all four by-elections held in 1989 and 1990. In April 1990, opinion polls showed that Labour had gained a twenty-point lead over the Conservatives. The polls also revealed that Margaret Thatcher's personal popularity rating was lower than at any other time in her eleven years as prime minister. Such developments led a growing number of people in her party to question whether they could win the next general election if she were still their leader. This feeling was intensified by the disagreements within the Cabinet over the economy and Europe, as evidenced by the Lawson and Howe resignations (see page 143).

Leadership contest, November 1990

It was in this atmosphere that Michael Heseltine, who had been resentful towards the prime minister ever since the 1986 Westland affair (see page 135), decided in November to mount an open challenge for the leadership. Mrs Thatcher had easily survived a challenge in 1989 when a pro-European backbencher, Anthony Meyer, had formally stood against her. Yet the fact that 33 MPs voted against her and 25 others abstained suggested to some, including Heseltine, that her popularity was waning and that a heavyweight in the party such as he might be able to unseat her should the opportunity arise.

The poll tax and the Lawson and Howe resignations appeared to have provided that opportunity. Heseltine announced his candidacy for the leadership of the party. Although in the ensuing contest Margaret Thatcher won the first ballot by 52 votes she regarded the narrowness of the margin as evidence that she had lost the confidence of two out of five of the Conservative MPs. She took an individual sounding of her Cabinet colleagues. With a few exceptions, they all told her, some openly weeping, that her time was up. So, she withdrew from the second ballot and announced that she would resign as soon as her successor was chosen. By the time the second ballot was held John Major and Douglas Hurd had entered the race. This scuppered Heseltine's chances. He had gone a long way to removing Thatcher only to find that the majority of the parliamentary party did not really want him. They preferred the stolid John Major to the more flamboyant Michael Heseltine.

The Conservative Party had decided that after eleven years of Margaret Thatcher, they wanted a safer, even if duller, leader. She felt betrayed. She had not, she said, been dismissed by a vote of Parliament, still less by the people at an election, but by a cabal of the leading Conservative MPs. 'It was treachery, treachery. It is something I will never forget and never forgive.'

Table 5.1 Conservative Party leadership election results 1990

Ballot	Date	Candidates and votes		
First ballot	20 November	Heseltine 152	Thatcher 204	
	22 November	Mrs Thatcher announced she would resign		
Second ballot	27 November	Heseltine 131	Major 185	Hurd 56

Summary diagram: The fall of Margaret Thatcher 1990

Reasons for weakening of Margaret Thatcher's position
- Opinion polls showed growing unpopularity following the poll tax
- Disputes over the economy – Lawson's resignation
- Disputes over Europe – Howe's resignation

↓

Leadership election forced by Heseltine
- Thatcher won first ballot by too narrow a margin
- After consulting colleagues Thatcher withdrew from second ballot
- Resigned as leader once Major had won second ballot

---

2 Margaret Thatcher's legacy

▶ *What were the main features of the Thatcher revolution?*

The bitterness and recrimination that accompanied Margaret Thatcher's resignation in November 1990 did not alter the fact that her period in office had been of huge significance. She had changed the political, economic and social agenda of British politics. Deeply controversial though her policies were, the governments that came after her, those of John Major (1990–7) and Tony Blair (1997–2007), were profoundly affected by what she had done.

Thatcherism

It is worth listing the chief features of Thatcherism since all subsequent governments followed policies that were either a continuation of, or a reaction against them:

- abandoning consensus politics
- replacing Keynesianism with the free market
- reducing the power of the state and giving greater opportunity for people to live their lives without government interference
- limiting the power of the trade unions
- making local government answer more directly to people's needs
- restoring the notion of social accountability, the idea that effort should be rewarded and lack of effort penalised.

Margaret Thatcher did not, of course, achieve all her aims. Her mistakes over the poll tax, when she misjudged the attitude of ordinary people, showed that her populist instinct could seriously let her down. There are also many fascinating paradoxes about her; what she wanted was sometimes contradicted by what she did. There are four particular examples:

- She intended to reduce taxes but in fact Britain's tax bill went up under her leadership (see page 135).
- Despite her determination to cut government spending, when she went out of office public expenditure was at record high levels, and in 1992 the government was having to borrow heavily to finance a public sector borrowing requirement of nearly £30 billion. This was largely because her policies had led to unemployment, thereby increasing the government's need to borrow to pay for social security and other welfare benefits.
- She promised to reduce the power of central government but, in practice, broadened and increased it, there being more government departments and more civil servants in 1990 than there had been in 1979.
- She appeared to be anti-European but she took Britain deeper into Europe (see page 142).

'A woman but not a sister'

Feminists have also pointed to another paradox. Some of her strongest critics were women, who complained that she was 'a woman but not a sister', a reference to her unwillingness to support the women's movement for equality. She certainly did little to promote women in politics, appointing only one woman to her Cabinet, Linda Chalker, as minister for overseas development in 1986. It has been suggested that this was because as the lone woman she wanted to exploit her femininity among her male colleagues, free of competition from other women. A weightier charge is that in eleven years of government she made no effort to introduce structural changes to advance the role of women in politics and society.

Against that, it might be said that in the end what really mattered historically about Margaret Thatcher was not what she did but what she was. In 1966, only nine years before she became party leader, she had been one of only seven female Conservative MPs out of a total of 266. For a woman to lead a political party for fifteen years, to remain prime minister for eleven, and to be acknowledged internationally during that time as an outstanding stateswoman were extraordinary achievements. She had successfully stormed the fortress of male dominance. After her, things would never be the same again.

Thatcherism and social attitudes

Margaret Thatcher's disinclination to support broad movements like feminism was consistent with her idea that social responsibility was an individual matter, not a group affair. The rights of the individual and the family should take precedence over abstract notions of social good. In her social attitudes she was much more of a Victorian Liberal then a modern Conservative. She often expressed admiration for what she called 'Victorian virtues'. The wish to restrict the power of the state and to prevent the irresponsible spending of public money were key aspects of her approach. It was, she believed, false sentiment to spend public money to maintain systems or institutions once they had become wasteful and expensive.

SOURCE A

'If you want to stay living round here you're going to need loadsamoney!' A mocking comment from 1988, published in the *Daily Mirror*, on the **yuppy** world created by Thatcherite economic policies. The scene is set in London's docklands, which in the 1980s was redeveloped as an expensive residential area. In the cartoon Thatcher is behaving in the manner of the character 'Loadsamoney', an aggressive yuppy, created by the television comedian Harry Enfield.

Study Source A. How accurate is this depiction of the prime minister's financial and social aims?

KEY TERM

Yuppy An acronym for 'young upwardly mobile professional person'.

'No such thing as society'

Margaret Thatcher aroused a storm when, in an interview printed in a women's magazine in October 1987, she remarked, 'there's no such thing as society'. Her critics seized on this as evidence of her lack of compassion and her wish to encourage unbridled individualism. The left-leaning newspaper *The Guardian* reprinted the interview on its front page. Opponents said that her statement illustrated why she was willing to cut government spending on social welfare. She defended herself by quoting how her statement had continued in the original interview (see Source B, page 162).

According to Source B, what is Margaret Thatcher's understanding of social responsibility?

SOURCE B

From an interview with Margaret Thatcher in *Woman's Own*, 23 September 1987, www.margaretthatcher.org/document/106689.

I think we've been through a period where too many people have been given to understand that if they have a problem, it's the government's job to cope with it. 'I have a problem, I'll get a grant.' 'I'm homeless, the government must house me.' They're casting their problem on society. And, you know, there is no such thing as society. There are individual men and women, and there are families. And no government can do anything except through people, and people must look to themselves first. It's our duty to look after ourselves and then, also to look after our neighbour. People have got the entitlements too much in mind, without the obligations. There's no such thing as entitlement, unless someone has first met an obligation.

Mrs Thatcher claimed that her purpose had in fact been to emphasise self-reliance and the individual's responsibility towards society. She was defending the family as the basic social unit. In her memoirs published in the early 1990s she described the social ills she had had in mind: 'Welfare benefits, distributed with little or no consideration of their effects on behaviour, encouraged illegitimacy, facilitated the breakdown of families, and replaced incentives favouring work and self-reliance with perverse encouragement for idleness and cheating.'

It might be thought that such convictions would have made her government eager to reform the welfare state. It is true that certain steps were taken. To tackle what Mrs Thatcher called the 'why work?' problem, her reference to the **poverty trap**, the government introduced a measure taxing short-term income relief. It also imposed a five per cent cut in unemployment, sickness, injury, maternity and invalidity benefits. However, the government's public spending cuts were largely restricted to her first administration in the early 1980s. This was because unemployment remained so high during her eleven years in office that it necessitated not a decrease but a major increase in unemployment payments.

KEY TERM

Poverty trap The dilemma facing the low paid; if they continued working they were penalised by being taxed, which reduced their net income to a level little higher than if they simply drew unemployment benefit.

Principal non-contributory benefits paid by the state

- *Income support*: for those of working age who are unable to work, or to those who have inadequate pensions. It has been called 'the safety net of the welfare state'. In the late 1990s income support was costing over £13 billion annually.

- *Invalidity benefit*: for those medically certified as being physically or mentally unable to work. Between 1982 and 1998 the number of recipients trebled from 600,000 to 1.8 million, at a cost of £5.2 billion per year.

- *Housing benefit*: rent and rate rebates for those on inadequate incomes.

- *Child benefit (previously called family allowance)*: a weekly amount paid to parents (usually the mother) for each child. This was a universal payment, that is, there was no means testing. By 1998 this was costing £6 billion per year.

- *Family income supplement*: provided a cash benefit for poorer families with children.

The remarkable fact is that Margaret Thatcher's governments spent more on welfare than any previous administration. As Figure 5.1 shows, between 1977 and 1994, government expenditure on social security and welfare rose by 60 per cent in real terms.

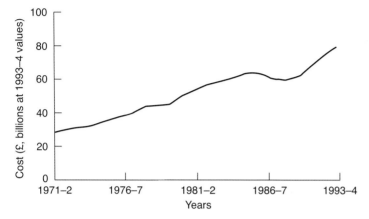

Figure 5.1 A graph showing the real growth in social security benefit expenditure 1971–94.

How greatly the Conservatives under Margaret Thatcher and her successor John Major were committed to financial provision for welfare services can be gauged from Table 5.2, which illustrates the order of priorities in benefit provision and government spending.

Table 5.2 Government expenditure 1993–4

Area	Amount (in £ billions)	Percentage of total expenditure
Social security	£65.0	26.6%
Environment	£38.9	15.9%
NHS	£29.9	12.2%
Local government	£24.2	9.9%
Defence	£23.5	9.6%
Scotland	£13.9	5.6%
Education	£9.5	3.9%
Northern Ireland	£8.4	3.5%
Wales	£7.2	3.0%
Foreign and overseas	£6.5	2.7%
Transport	£6.4	2.6%
Home Office	£6.1	2.5%
Employment	£3.7	1.5%
Trade and industry	£2.6	1.1%
Agriculture	£2.6	1.1%

Mrs Thatcher's unpopularity

Despite her government's large-scale welfare spending, Margaret Thatcher's 'no such thing as society' statement and her belief in public accountability largely explain her unpopularity in intellectual circles. Institutions, including higher education, were subjected to the same demands of accountability as other areas of public life which were receiving government funds. On the grounds that her policies were undermining education, Oxford University, in a controversial gesture in 1983, voted to deny her the honorary degree that had traditionally been conferred on prime ministers.

There was a further aspect to this. Margaret Thatcher's distrust of those intellectuals who, she felt, said much but did little made her the target of attacks from the 'chattering classes', a term denoting those broadsheet and television journalists who were strongly influenced by the welfarist notions that had become the received thinking among social scientists. Such thinking had become an important part of the consensus which had dominated politics after 1945. In challenging that Establishment orthodoxy, Mrs Thatcher aroused resentment among those academics and politicians who believed that the Beveridge Report and Keynesianism had become indispensable to Britain's social and economic well-being. Her questioning of these notions gave her an uncaring, hard-hearted image that damaged her reputation and lessened her popularity.

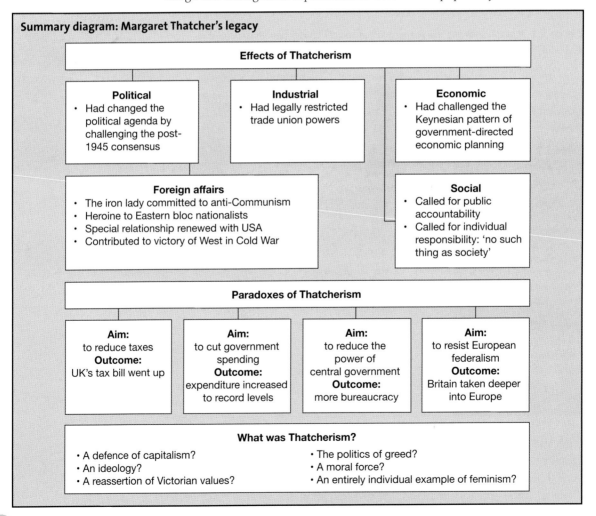

Summary diagram: Margaret Thatcher's legacy

Effects of Thatcherism

Political
- Had changed the political agenda by challenging the post-1945 consensus

Industrial
- Had legally restricted trade union powers

Economic
- Had challenged the Keynesian pattern of government-directed economic planning

Foreign affairs
- The iron lady committed to anti-Communism
- Heroine to Eastern bloc nationalists
- Special relationship renewed with USA
- Contributed to victory of West in Cold War

Social
- Called for public accountability
- Called for individual responsibility: 'no such thing as society'

Paradoxes of Thatcherism

Aim: to reduce taxes
Outcome: UK's tax bill went up

Aim: to cut government spending
Outcome: expenditure increased to record levels

Aim: to reduce the power of central government
Outcome: more bureaucracy

Aim: to resist European federalism
Outcome: Britain taken deeper into Europe

What was Thatcherism?
- A defence of capitalism?
- An ideology?
- A reassertion of Victorian values?
- The politics of greed?
- A moral force?
- An entirely individual example of feminism?

Key debate

▶ *What was Thatcherism?*

In 1989 a Leicester University student was asked to define Thatcherism. At the end of his long essay, he wrote 'I don't really know what Thatcherism is. I just wish it would go away.' His frustration at not being able to give a precise answer is understandable. Historians and political analysts offer a range of definitions. This is because Thatcherism could be legitimately studied in a number of ways:

- as a set of policies that Thatcher followed while in government, such as monetarism and privatisation
- as a set of personal characteristics peculiar to Margaret Thatcher, such as determination, forcefulness and self-belief
- as a set of political attitudes, such as a dislike of socialism and consensus politics
- as a set of moral convictions, such as a belief in individualism and public accountability
- as a style of leadership as party chief, prime minister and international figure
- as a set of achievements, such as victory over Argentina and the miners.

It should be stressed that each approach is equally valid. Indeed, most of the categories overlap. Writing in 1989, Hugo Young, a voice of the liberal left, observed that Mrs Thatcher 'gave her name to the age in which we live. Thatcherism is unique: not perhaps as a set of ideas, but as the only "ism" attached to the name of a British prime minister.'

Henk Overbeck, a Dutch Communist, gave a clear Marxist definition of Thatcherism as a front for the forces of capitalism.

EXTRACT 1

From Henk Overbeck, *Global Capitalism and National Decline*, Routledge, 1989.

Thatcherism is a reasonably coherent and comprehensive concept of control for the restoration of bourgeois rule and bourgeois hegemony in the new circumstances of the 1980s. The central elements in the Thatcherite concept are the reorientation of Britain's foreign policy and its redefinition of its place in the world; its attack on the position of the trade unions and the Labour Party (Thatcher aims to eliminate 'socialism' as a serious political force); the restructuring of the role of the state in the economy; and finally a reordering of the balance of power between different factions of capital in Britain.

In 1991, Martin Loney, a representative left-wing writer, took a less determinist but equally committed view of Thatcherism as avarice: 'The Thatcher government proclaimed the new national philosophy should be based on the unfettered pursuit of self-interest: the politics of greed.' Approaching things from a centre-right position, S.R. Letwin in 1992 took a different view. He saw

Mrs Thatcher's policies as a direct response to the wishes of the people: he asserted that her government answered to 'a deeply felt public demand to be liberated from a tyranny had made it impossible for Britain to know from one day to the next what stoppage would produce chaos in their daily life.'

In 1989 a respected centre-left political analyst, Dennis Kavanagh, judged Thatcherism to have been essentially a destructive force that ended consensus: 'I see postwar British politics between the late 1940s and the 1980s being, as it were, made and unmade by the Attlee and the Thatcher governments.' Peter Riddell, an analyst from the political centre ground, suggested in 1983 that the essential dynamic of Thatcherism was not political but moral: 'Thatcherism is an instinct, a set of moral values rather than an ideology.'

The legacy of Thatcherism was thoughtfully described in the 1990s by two voices, one from the left and one from the right. Tony Benn observed that 'the Prime Ministers who are remembered are those who think and teach, and not many do. Thatcher influenced the thinking of a generation.' Patrick Minford, an economist and admirer of Thatcher, suggested that her years in office had seen 'a peaceful revolution' in the British economy: 'Virtually no area of activity has remained untouched by the drive to reinstate market forces and reduce government intervention.'

Charles Moore, in his biography of Margaret Thatcher, suggested that Thatcherism was best understood not as an ideology or a set of policies but as an aspect of Thatcher herself. For him, the defining element was the Falklands crisis, to which she responded not simply as a politician but as a woman.

EXTRACT 2

From Charles Moore, *Margaret Thatcher*, Penguin, 2014, volume 1, pp. 752–3.

The Falklands War brought out Mrs Thatcher's best qualities – not only the well known ones of courage, conviction and resolution, but also her less advertised ones of caution and careful study ... Because she knew nothing about war before the crisis broke, she approached the subject modestly. Those who worked closely with Mrs Thatcher at that time noted that she was remarkably free of the long winded digressions and tendency to lecture which were common at other times ... She cared passionately for the cause and the people involved. In this, her sex was important. She was the first female war leader with executive power in the British Isles since Elizabeth I, and the first ever in a democratic age. She felt a maternal identification with the men whom she was sending into battle, and they responded with a chivalrous devotion, a desire to protect her as a woman and an embodiment of the national spirit.

A much less admiring view was advanced by the distinguished historian Kenneth Morgan, who argued that Thatcherism was best defined as the policies Margaret Thatcher actually followed, particularly during her second term.

EXTRACT 3

From Kenneth O. Morgan, *The People's Peace*, Oxford University Press, 1999, pp. 468–9.

Governments often lose momentum in their second term … Mrs Thatcher was determined that this would not happen to her. On the contrary, from the Queen's Speech of November 1983 onwards, she turned her second term into a crusade of increasing radicalism, the doubts and hesitancies of the first administration mostly shed. It was in those years that the main contours of 'Thatcherism' as a phenomenon were firmly established. It is on these years that the government's historical reputation will surely be based … To an increasing degree, the government and its outlying establishments bore the Prime Minister's stamp.

In many key directions the new radicalism now showed itself in full. Much the most notable of these novelties was the policy of the privatization of industries and utilities. After 1983, the 'frontiers of the state' were, in this respect at least, rolled back as they had not been since 1945.

> In the light of the different interpretations in Extracts 1–3, how convincing do you find the view of Thatcherism as a revolution?

There is clearly no final resolution on how Thatcherism as a multifaceted movement is to be defined and how its historical reputation is to be judged. In studying Thatcherism as a historical movement we are necessarily studying Margaret Thatcher as a historical figure, about whom there is never likely to be agreement.

4 John Major's government 1990–7

▶ *What issues confronted John Major's government?*

Margaret Thatcher had been the dominant political figure of her time, capable of arousing both intense admiration and deep dislike. John Major was not in the same mould. For some, this was his attraction. He did not have the abrasive, combative character of his predecessor. Yet personally likeable though he was, he was not an inspiring figure. Despite having held key ministries in the Thatcher government, he had not held them long enough to create a lasting impression. The historian John Keegan, in 2004, described Major's government as 'one of the dreariest administrations of the century'.

Political satire

Since the theatrical revue 'Beyond the Fringe' in Harold Macmillan's day (see page 32), satire had become one of the most public forms of political criticism.

A fortnightly magazine, *Private Eye*, which first appeared in 1961, soon established a reputation, through its cartoons, comments and selected news items, for mocking the pomposity of public figures or exposing the absurdities of their behaviour. Any celebrity was fair game but politicians, given the nature of their work, were most likely to feel the satirists' lash.

Such shows and journals helped to create a critical atmosphere, but it was when television became involved that satire entered a boom period. Television was especially powerful since it came into everybody's home. Two programmes, ITV's *Spitting Image* and the BBC's *Yes Minister*, were aired in the 1980s. *Spitting Image* was a puppet show which presented leading political figures in distorted but very recognisable caricatures in a set of short sketches. For example, John Major was portrayed as a literally grey figure, boringly consumed with the unimportant details of life. The tone of the script can be gauged from one of the programme's most memorable lines. In a sketch set in a restaurant where the Cabinet were dining, Mrs Thatcher was doing the ordering. Having named her dishes, she was asked by the waiter, 'And for your vegetables?' Looking at her colleagues, she replied, 'Oh, they'll have the same as me.'

Yes Minister, which ran for 21 episodes between 1980 and 1984, was gentler in its comedy, which perhaps made all the more credible its description of the civil service Establishment running rings round government ministers. However, it is an open question as to whether satire always hit its targets. Many of those satirised welcomed it as a form of publicity. Norman Tebbit was known to enjoy *Spitting Image*'s portrayal of him as the leather-clad thug in Thatcher's Cabinet (see page 121), while Margaret Thatcher eagerly accepted the chance to play herself in an episode of *Yes Minister*, even rewriting some of the script.

Spitting Image ran from 1984 until 1996, but finished when its producers felt that the scripts no longer matched the quality of the puppetry. That was not, however, the end of televised political satire. In 2005 Blair's government was subjected to a realistic – some critics said brutal – depiction in the BBC's *The Thick of It*, which was full of swearing and crude behaviour and portrayed a world of amoral spin doctors and self-seeking ministers. Whether the parody went too far in its cynicism was a matter of judgement, but there was little doubt that it contributed to the public perception of politics as an increasingly dishonest business.

Major's domestic record

Knowing that an election had to be called within eighteen months, Major made little attempt to modify the policies he had inherited. With only the slightest hint of criticism of his predecessor, he declared on taking office that he wanted to build 'a country that is at ease with itself'. To this end he took two main steps:

- The unpopular poll tax, which was already doomed before Margaret Thatcher had left office, was quietly withdrawn in 1991.

- In the same year Major announced that his government would base its approach on a new 'Citizen's Charter', which read as a watered down version of Thatcherism: 'The Citizen's Charter is about giving more power to the citizen. It is a testament to our belief in people's right to be informed and choose for themselves.'

The 1992 election

Until the week before polling day on 8 April 1992, it was generally assumed, even by some Conservatives, that after thirteen years in power the government would lose. However, the Labour Party led by Neil Kinnock conducted a poorly judged campaign. Having in the early part of the campaign successfully promoted itself as the caring party, it assumed from the opinion polls that it was going to win. This was evident in an ill-conceived rally in Sheffield in the week before the election. Aping the razzmatazz style of US politics, the Labour campaigners put on an extravaganza with blaring music and announcements and spotlights picking out shadow cabinet members who walked to the platform through ranks of cheering admirers. The climax came with Neil Kinnock bounding up to the rostrum and exchanging repetitive shouts with audience as if he were at an American convention. Kinnock later admitted that the triumphalism had been both premature and rather tasteless, although he disputed that it had cost Labour the election.

More seriously, Labour damaged itself by presenting a shadow budget that seemed to threaten large increases in taxation. John Major exploited this by literally standing on a soap-box and suggesting in a homely way that only the Conservatives could be trusted to run the economy. *The Sun* newspaper was sufficiently convinced to switch its support from Labour to Conservative. This defection to the Conservatives of one of the main voices of popular opinion was a blow to Labour and helped explain the late and decisive swing to John Major.

Table 5.3 Results of the 1992 general election

Party	Votes	Seats	Percentage of vote
Conservative	14,092,891	336	42.0
Labour	11,559,735	271	34.2
Liberal Democrats	5,999,384	20	17.9
Plaid Cymru	154,439	4	0.5
Scottish Nationalists	629,552	3	1.9
Northern Irish parties	740,485	17	2.2
Others	436,207	0	1.3

The result was much closer than in 1987. Labour increased its vote by 3.5 per cent and its seats from 229 to 271. But this was not enough to defeat the Conservatives, who, despite losing 40 seats, still had an overall majority of 21.

The Maastricht Treaty 1992

One issue over which Major did adopt a different approach from his predecessor was Europe. He wished to show that he was a good European. He took a momentous step by signing up Britain to the Maastricht Treaty in February 1992, the declared aim of which was 'to create an ever-closer union among the peoples of Europe'. Its main terms were as follows:

- full European integration
- common European foreign policy
- common European defence policy
- European Central Bank
- single European currency , 'the euro', to be adopted by 1999 (Britain obtained an opt-out clause on this, which it exercised in 1999)
- the treaty to come into effect in November 1993, with the EEC being renamed first the European Community (EC) and then the European Union (EU).

The Exchange Rate Mechanism

In late summer 1992, a crisis developed over the Exchange Rate Mechanism (ERM). The ERM had been devised as a system for reducing inflation. This was to be done by creating parity between the various European currencies by pegging them to the value of the Deutschmark (DM), Europe's strongest currency at the time, rather than let them find their market value. When Britain joined the ERM in 1990 (see page 143) the exchange value of the pound sterling had been DM2.95. This was unrealistically high and caused British exports to become overpriced.

Worse was to follow. In September 1992, international bankers, sensing that the pound sterling was overvalued, began to speculate against it on the money markets. The pound began to fall sharply. In a desperate effort to maintain the pound at the level required by the ERM, Norman Lamont, the chancellor of the exchequer, raised interest levels from ten per cent to fifteen per cent and sold off £30 billion of the UK's foreign reserves. It was all to no avail. The pressure on the pound was too great. Major's government did the only thing it could; on 16 September 1992, known afterwards as 'Black Wednesday', it withdrew from the ERM.

Consequences of withdrawal from the ERM

- The case for Britain's becoming involved in European monetary union was weakened.
- The argument of the **Euro-sceptics** against deeper integration with Europe was strengthened.
- The Conservatives' reputation for financial expertise was gravely damaged.
- Labour gained a fifteen-point lead in the opinion polls.
- Cabinet divisions widened between Euro-sceptics, principally Peter Lilley, Michael Portillo and Michael Howard, and pro-Europeans, principally Kenneth Clarke, Michael Heseltine and Douglas Hurd.

 **KEY TERM**

Euro-sceptics Those who doubted that the UK's closer integration into Europe would serve British interests.

Remarkably, the longer term economic effects proved far less disastrous. Indeed, some observers have called the event 'White Wednesday', a reference to the fact that, freed from its artificial ties, the pound began to recover. By 1996 the exchange rate of the pound was DM3, a higher rate than when the pound was in the ERM. What was true of finance was also true of the economy overall. Britain's growth rate outperformed that of its European partners, as Table 5.4 indicates. It prompted the Euro-sceptics to question again the supposed benefits of EU membership. Norman Lamont later remarked 'I know of no single benefit which has come to Britain solely because of its membership of Europe.'

These longer term effects were obviously of no immediate benefit to John Major's government. The truth was that Black Wednesday left its mark on the remainder of his administration to 1997. A divided Cabinet, uncertainty about Europe, a public who now doubted the government's financial competence and a Labour Party recovering its confidence: these were the legacies of the ERM crisis.

Parliamentary struggle over Maastricht 1993

John Major's signing of the Maastricht Treaty in 1992 had been only the beginning of the process. To become binding on Britain, it had to be ratified by Parliament. The ERM crisis had made this extremely problematic. Many in Major's own party, and a significant number of Labour MPs, were so concerned over the loss of sovereignty entailed by the Maastricht Treaty that they voted against the ratifying bills when they were introduced. The climax came in July 1993 when organised resistance by the **Euro-rebels** defeated a key bill necessary for the treaty to come into effect in November 1993.

Having committed his government to Maastricht, Major was not prepared to be thwarted by the Commons. In a hurried move, he reintroduced the proposal to accept the Maastricht Treaty and made it part of a formal vote of confidence in the government. In this way the proposal was forced through, since for the Euro-rebel Conservative MPs to have voted against it would have brought down the government. But the desperate means Major had used gave strength to the growing number of Euro-sceptics within and outside Parliament who claimed that Britain was being railroaded into European integration. They asserted that Europe and its supporters seemed frightened of democracy.

Calls for a national referendum, such as those held in Ireland, Denmark and France, were rejected by Major's government on the grounds that a referendum was 'unconstitutional'. The government was also well aware that it would very probably lose a referendum. Opinion polls indicated that the majority of the population were on the Euro-sceptic side. Having voted 'yes' in the 1975 referendum (see page 89), the British people were unlikely to do so again. Major's success later in 1992 in obtaining the EC's agreement to the principle of **subsidiarity** had done little to lessen Euro-sceptic fears.

Table 5.4 Comparative economic growth rates 1995–2005

France	1.5%
Germany	2.0%
Italy	1.3%
Eurozone	2.0%
Britain	2.7%

KEY TERMS

Euro-rebels A large group of Conservative MPs, led by Bill Cash and supported by most of the party's Euro-sceptics, who fought against the ratification of the Maastricht Treaty.

Subsidiarity The principle that in matters of special concern to a particular member state, that state had the right to ignore EU decisions.

Although the Labour Party (now led by John Smith, following Neil Kinnock's resignation after the election defeat) officially accepted Maastricht, there was no doubt it derived great satisfaction from the government's embarrassments. But it was the opposition within his own party that most offended John Major. In an unguarded moment, he was recorded on tape describing his critics within the Cabinet as 'bastards'. Although he would not give names when further questioned about this, it was widely assumed that he was referring to Peter Lilley, Michael Portillo, John Redwood and Michael Howard. Clearly, a prime minister who does not have the full support of his Cabinet and party is in a very difficult position and this was the case for Major throughout his period of office, which ran its full term until 1997.

In July 1995, in an effort to end the backstabbing to which he felt he was continually subjected, Major called a leadership election, which he easily won, defeating John Redwood by 218 to 89. But small though the vote against Major was, if the 22 abstentions were added in, it revealed the unwelcome fact that over 100 members were not fully committed to him as leader.

Foreign affairs

Whatever the reservations about Major's domestic record may have been, he had made a significant contribution to foreign policy.

The Gulf War 1991

John Major's conduct was certainly statesmanlike during the crisis over Kuwait, when he co-operated effectively with the USA in creating a coalition invasion force, which in 1991, in keeping with UN resolutions, successfully ended the illegal occupation of Kuwait by the forces of Iraq's leader, Saddam Hussein. Major's decision to keep the opposition leaders, Neil Kinnock and Paddy Ashdown, informed on the key moves in the Gulf War won him considerable respect.

Bosnia 1995

Major's government also became involved in the troubled Balkans. Following the break-up in the early 1990s of the former federal state of Yugoslavia, a bitter and complex civil war was fought between a set of fiercely competing national, religious and ethnic groups. Fighting had become so vicious in Bosnia between 1992 and 1995 that the international powers intervened in order to prevent the **genocide** of the largely Muslim Bosnians by the largely Christian Serb forces.

Britain contributed to a series of massive NATO aerial attacks on Serbian forces in August and September 1995. Over 3500 sorties were flown. 'Operation Deliberate Force', as it was codenamed, brought the Serbs to the negotiating table. In the Dayton peace agreement signed in December 1995, the warring parties agreed to keep to certain designated areas, which were to be monitored

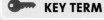

KEY TERM

Genocide The planned extermination of a people or a race.

by UN and NATO forces. John Major had the satisfaction of being one of the signatories when the Dayton agreement was ratified in Paris in December by the major powers: the USA, Britain, France, Russia and Germany.

John Major and Ireland 1990–7

Major had been in office for only two months when, early in 1991, in its most audacious act yet, the IRA fired mortar bombs at 10 Downing Street from a parked van. This was the prelude to a sustained IRA bombing campaign in Britain. In March 1993, a boy of three and another of twelve were killed and 50 people injured by bombs left in litterbins in a shopping mall in Warrington, Cheshire. In April, one person was killed and 40 were injured by a bomb planted in a lorry in Bishopsgate in the City of London. The bomb also caused over a billion pounds worth of damage to a number of bank and office premises.

The anger among ordinary people at these brutalities led to large peace rallies in London, Belfast and Dublin. Aware of how public opinion was turning against them on both sides of the Irish Sea, the IRA put out disclaimers saying that the deaths had not been intended and that it was the fault of the British police, who had failed to act on the detailed warnings that the IRA had given them about the location of the bombs.

The Downing Street Declaration 1993

Although the times did not seem propitious for a new political initiative, the Irish Republic and the UK had as premiers at this point two men with very similar characters and temperaments. Albert Reynolds and John Major shared an unflappable, practical attitude which enabled them quickly to agree on a common approach towards improving the chances of peace. The outcome of their agreement was the Downing Street Declaration, whose chief features were as follows:

- The British government announced that it had 'no selfish or strategic interest in Northern Ireland'; its sole concern was to accede to the democratically expressed wishes of the people there.
- It also accepted that it was 'for the people of the island of Ireland alone, North and South, to bring about a united Ireland, if that is their wish.'
- Reynolds declared that the Irish Republic accepted the right of the majority in Northern Ireland to decide its future and that, if a democratic settlement could be achieved there, the South was prepared to drop its traditional claim that Northern Ireland was part of the Republic.

Ceasefire 1994

Unofficial contacts between the British government and Sinn Féin eventually convinced the IRA that the declaration had indeed recognised the key republican and nationalist positions on the status of Northern Ireland and that Britain was not committed to indefinite control of the province. This was sufficient for the IRA to declare a ceasefire in August 1994.

The big issue was whether the loyalist paramilitary units could be persuaded to do the same. It was clear that the IRA would not keep the ceasefire for long if it remained a one-sided affair. The government's fear was that the precise point that had temporarily pacified the IRA, Britain's willingness eventually to allow Northern Ireland to determine its own status, might be seen by the unionists as a sell-out. Major took the step of assuring them that the British government had no intention of forcing the North into a united Ireland. This proved sufficient for the time being to quell unionist fears. In October the loyalist units announced that they would be observing their own ceasefire.

For the first time since the troubles re-ignited in late 1960s, the Northern Ireland sides were at peace. Given all the bitterness that had gone before, it could be only a fragile peace and how long it would hold depended on how long the IRA and the loyalist paramilitaries considered it served their respective interests. The ceasefire did not hold; between 1996 and 1998 there were frequent outbursts of renewed violence. The basic fact was that the two sets of paramilitaries did not trust each other.

The Mitchell Report, January 1996

It was at this point that the USA made an encouraging diplomatic contribution. In 1995 President Clinton was rapturously greeted on his visits to both Dublin and Belfast; in the following year, Senator George Mitchell chaired an international commission set up to consider the Irish issue. John Major showed a generous spirit in accepting the American move. Rather than see it as outside interference in a British problem, he welcomed the commission as offering a way forward.

Mitchell, in a report he presented in January 1996, laid down a set of principles on which a peace process might be developed, the principal ones being:

- the total disarmament of all paramilitary organisations and their renunciation of force
- the agreement by all parties concerned to accept as binding any agreement reached in an all-party negotiation.

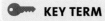

KEY TERM

Decommissioning
The giving up of weapons.

Mitchell's central conclusion was that real progress towards a settlement was ultimately impossible without **decommissioning**. However, to achieve this, both sides would have to be assured that laying down their arms could achieve the same results as using them. Peace had to be seen as being as politically profitable as violence. Yet the very fact that this tenuous peace existed at all when John Major left office in 1997 was a tribute to his diplomacy. He had shown what could be achieved by tact and patience.

Conservative defeat 1997

In 1993 John Major, seeking a unifying theme for the nation, had appealed to people 'to get back to basics; to self-discipline and respect for the law; to consideration for others'. No doubt sincerely meant, his call for moral improvement came back to haunt him. By the time of the general election in 1997, his position had been gravely weakened by a press campaign determined to expose leading Conservatives as being guilty of sexual scandal, corruption or 'sleaze', a term used to refer to such illicit or improper activities as '**cash for questions**'. Among the most damaging of the many scandals uncovered were the following:

KEY TERM

Cash for questions
The practice by which, in return for payment, a number of Conservative MPs asked questions in the Commons with the intention of promoting particular commercial interests.

- The heritage minister, David Mellor, resigned in 1992 over an affair with a Spanish actress, which, according to *The People* newspaper, involved his wearing the Chelsea football team kit while having sex.
- The environment minister, Tim Yeo, resigned in 1994 after it was revealed that his affair with a Conservative local councillor had produced a child.
- In 1994, a promising young Conservative MP, Stephen Milligan, accidentally throttled himself to death while engaging in an act of sexually stimulating self-strangulation.
- In 1994, *The Guardian* accused Neil Hamilton, a corporate affairs minister, of having received brown envelopes stuffed with money from Mohamed Al Fayed, the wealthy owner of the Harrods store in London, who hoped to obtain special commercial favours in return. Hamilton denied the allegations and a series of libel actions followed. In the 1997 election, Martin Bell, a BBC correspondent, stood as an independent against Hamilton in his Tatton constituency with the calculated aim of highlighting the lack of probity in government circles. The Labour and Liberal Democrat parties agreed not to field a candidate, which resulted in Bell's winning by a majority of 11,000. The media attention given to the campaign proved a great embarrassment to Major's government.

This mixture of the risible, the disreputable and the tragic spread a lengthening shadow over John Major's years in office and contributed significantly to his party's losing all the by-elections held during this time. The lowest point was reached in the general election of 1997 when his party suffered the heaviest defeat any government had undergone in the twentieth century.

Table 5.5 Results of the 1997 general election

Party	Votes	Seats	Percentage of vote
Labour	13,518,167	418	44.4
Conservative	9,600,943	165	31.4
Liberal Democrats	5,242,947	46	17.2
Northern Irish parties	492,992	14	1.8
Plaid Cymru	161,030	4	0.5
Scottish Nationalists	621,550	6	2.0

Reasons for the Conservatives' defeat in 1997

Historians and political scientists often observe that in modern British history, oppositions do not win elections, governments lose them. There are certainly grounds for applying this to the 1997 general election. The list of Conservative handicaps is a lengthy one:

- There were continuous divisions within the Cabinet and the Conservative Party between Euro-sceptics and pro-Europeans.
- The government's enforced withdrawal from the ERM undermined the Conservatives' reputation for responsible financial management.
- There was public distaste for the unseemly squabbles over the undemocratic ratification of the Maastricht Treaty in 1992.
- John Major's uninspiring leadership was a problem, given that he was never able to win the total loyalty of his colleagues and party.
- The Conservatives had already lost all the by-elections held since 1990.
- Throughout the 1990–7 period, the government had a very small majority, which had the inhibiting effect of obliging it do deals with the minority parties such as the Ulster Unionists in order to survive.
- The cumulative effect of a long series of sexual and financial scandals involving government ministers and Conservative MPs proved politically destructive.

To that list should be added two other influential factors. With hindsight, it can be seen that his unexpected victory in 1992 had been a mixed blessing for John Major. Long periods in government have a dispiriting and wearying effect on the holders. It might have been better for the Conservatives to have been defeated then, after thirteen years in office. It would have given them a chance to refresh themselves. But the government ran its full term to 1997, leading to mounting problems particularly within the Conservative Party itself. It was a tired and in many ways self-doubting party that went into the election of 1997.

The Conservatives had clearly outstayed their time. The 1997 result was in a sense a delayed reaction against Thatcherism. Although it was seven years since Mrs Thatcher had been prime minister, the shattering defeat of the Conservatives in 1997 was, arguably, a rejection not just of Major's government but of eighteen years of Thatcherite Conservatism.

Reason's for Labour's victory in 1997

The obverse of the Conservatives' weariness after eighteen continuous years in office was the eagerness and freshness with which the Labour Party approached the prospect of being in government again:

- Following Labour's defeat in the 1992 election and Neil Kinnock's resignation, John Smith became the Labour leader. His story is one of potential unrealised, since he died less than two years later. During his brief period of leadership, Smith had the following modernising achievements to his name. In 1993 he took a major step towards making the party more democratic, and thereby more electable, by replacing the trade union block vote at Labour Party conferences with a one member–one vote system. At the same party conference at which he introduced that reform, he formally pledged his party, when next in power, to the creation of a Scottish Parliament. By the time of his death in May 1994, Labour's lead in the opinion polls had risen to 23 per cent.
- As the new party leader, Tony Blair built on Smith's achievements by effectively using his spin doctors (see page 181) to put across Labour's message to the electorate.
- The Labour Party under Blair presented a more youthful and attractive alternative to Conservatism (see page 180).
- Blair skilfully projected himself and his party as representing 'cool Britannia' (see page 181).
- The results in Table 5.5 also illustrate another factor that contributed significantly to Labour's victory. The figures show the imbalance in the electoral system that at this point heavily favoured the Labour Party. There was a remarkable parallel with the great Labour victory of 1945. Despite its overwhelming number of seats, Labour was a minority government. The disparity the electoral system had produced is evident in the following ratios:
  - for each seat the Labour Party won, it had polled 32,340 votes
  - for each seat the Conservative Party won, it had polled 58,187 votes
  - for each seat the Liberal Democrats won, they had polled 113,977 votes.
- Notwithstanding these statistical anomalies, the fact remains that in terms of seats won, this was the Labour Party's greatest electoral success ever. Tony Blair, about to become the youngest prime minister of the twentieth century, had taken his party into power with an overall majority of 179. Since becoming party leader three years earlier, Blair had been working to modernise the party and make it electable. He was not working from scratch. The way had been prepared by his predecessors, Neil Kinnock and John Smith.

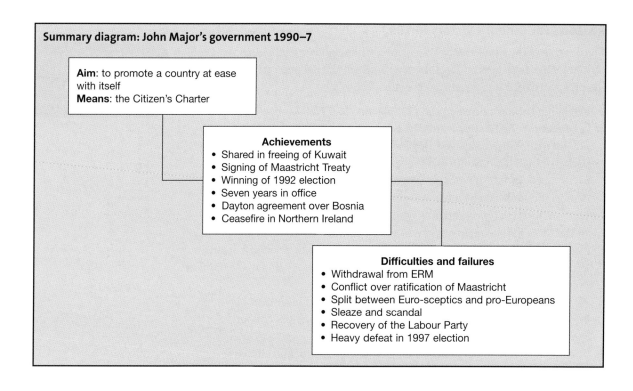

Summary diagram: John Major's government 1990–7

Aim: to promote a country at ease with itself
Means: the Citizen's Charter

Achievements
- Shared in freeing of Kuwait
- Signing of Maastricht Treaty
- Winning of 1992 election
- Seven years in office
- Dayton agreement over Bosnia
- Ceasefire in Northern Ireland

Difficulties and failures
- Withdrawal from ERM
- Conflict over ratification of Maastricht
- Split between Euro-sceptics and pro-Europeans
- Sleaze and scandal
- Recovery of the Labour Party
- Heavy defeat in 1997 election

5 New Labour 1994–7

▶ *In what sense was New Labour new?*

It is a matter of conjecture whether John Smith, but for his untimely death, would have led a regeneration of the party similar to that actually achieved under his successor, Tony Blair. What is undoubted is that Smith had begun to build on the reforms already introduced by Neil Kinnock and left a legacy that proved highly valuable to Blair in his restructuring of the party as an electoral force as **New Labour**.

Blair and New Labour

Tony Blair became leader in July 1994. It was later claimed by various commentators that shortly before the leadership election Blair had done a deal with his chief rival, Gordon Brown, the shadow chancellor of the exchequer. The story was that, at a meeting in May at the Granita Restaurant in Islington, London, Brown had agreed not to stand against Blair in the leadership contest, thus handing Blair the title, since the only other contender, John Prescott, lacked sufficient support in the party. Blair, in return, agreed to give Brown a wholly free hand at the exchequer once Labour was in government. In addition, Blair promised to pass on the premiership to Brown no later than 2003. Although

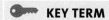
KEY TERM

New Labour Began as a slogan at the 1994 Labour Party conference, which was the first held with Tony Blair as leader, and became the name of the party from then on.

both men denied having made any such deal, the story was widely believed and certainly provides a plausible explanation of their strained political relationship during Blair's ten years as prime minister after 1997.

Despite its defeat in the 1992 general election, there were clear signs that the Labour Party's move away from the left, begun under Neil Kinnock and continued by John Smith, had begun to find favour with the electorate. Tony Blair picked up on this and continued the process of distancing the party from the policies that had perhaps deterred, rather than encouraged, support from the general public. As leader of the opposition during the final three years of Major's government, he skilfully and wittily played on the tired character of the Conservatives, who had been too long in government and who had become associated with corruption and scandal.

New Labour's programme

Blair complemented his attack on the government with the development of his programme for New Labour. The chief features of this were:

- Nationalisation was to be abandoned as a party objective.
- The City and the business world were to be wooed by the promise that capitalism would be safe in New Labour's hands.
- The legal restrictions on trade unions were to be maintained.
- Accepting that class-based politics were no longer relevant in Britain, New Labour would no longer present its policies in terms of class struggle.

The New Labour approach was expressed in a document which Blair himself had drafted and which was formally accepted by the party at a conference at Easter 1995 (see Source C).

SOURCE C

From a statement formally adopted by a Special Conference of the Labour Party, May 1995, http://en.wikipedia.org/wiki/Clause_IV.

The Labour Party organisation and procedures are democratic. They are designed to encourage the maximum amount of debate and free open exchange of opinion within the Party. The organisation and procedures which we use reflect our socialist values and distinguish the Labour Party as a uniquely democratic organisation. They provide a guarantee to all Party members that they have a right to be heard and that they will be listened to.

The Labour Party is a democratic socialist party. It believes that by the strength of our common endeavour we achieve more than we achieve alone, so as to create for each of us the means to realise our true potential and for all of us a community in which power, wealth and opportunity are in the hands of the many, not the few, where the rights we enjoy reflect the duties we owe, and where we live together, freely, in a spirit of solidarity, tolerance and respect.

In Source C, what is meant by the term 'the strength of our common endeavour'?

Tony Blair

1953	Born in Edinburgh
1966–71	Attended Fettes College, an independent school
1972–5	Studied Law at Oxford University
1975–83	Became active in left-wing politics
1983	Elected as an MP
1994	Became Labour Party leader
1997	Became prime minister
2007	Resigned after ten years in office

Tony Blair was educated at a Scottish private school and Oxford University. A lawyer by training, he entered politics and became an MP in 1983. As a young politician he was a member of CND and took a left-wing stance on most issues. However, once in Parliament, he moved to a centre position and aligned himself with Neil Kinnock's modernising programme. A great asset in his rapid rise up the party was his youthful style and appearance.

In 2001, after four years in office, Blair was riding high in the opinion polls. Sceptics suggested that his popularity was a reaction to his style rather than the content of his policies. Certainly presentation mattered. British politics had become presidential in style and Blair was in tune with the times. His popularity declined somewhat in the new decade, but he was still able to win comfortable victories in the 2001 and 2005 elections. In foreign affairs he skilfully juggled his sometimes contradictory commitments to Europe and the USA. Arguably, his greatest political achievement was his contribution to the peaceful settlement in Northern Ireland.

Three issues dominated the final four years of his premiership. One was the timing of his departure. Having held on to office longer than his obvious successor, Gordon Brown, had expected, he was the only modern prime minister to announce the date of his resignation a year before he intended to go. This gave his last year a 'lame duck' quality. Another issue was the 'cash for honours' scandal, which undermined the party's claim that its coming to power in 1997 marked the end of sleaze in government. His most hazardous step was the taking of Britain into war with Iraq in 2003 in the face of strong domestic and international censure. This was to cast a dark and lasting shadow over his reputation.

New Labour's policies were intended primarily to appeal to middle-class Britain where the bulk of the electorate were to be found. By avoiding extremes but by adopting progressive ideas, New Labour hoped to win over uncertain Conservative and floating voters. It was a recognition that the old working class, which historically had been the main supporters of Labour, had greatly shrunk with the decline of large-scale industry in Britain. It was also an implicit acceptance that Thatcherism had aroused aspirations and expectations that could not be ignored.

This new line of approach naturally upset the socialist wing of the party, who characterised it as a sell-out by the party to the forces of expediency. They were concerned that New Labour now lacked a distinct, radical ideology. Instead, it presented itself to the electorate as wanting to do the same things as the Conservatives, only more efficiently. The response of the supporters of New Labour within the party was to point out that the world had changed. Loyalty to old Labour values and refusal to modify policy had simply made the party unelectable for eighteen years. The argument was convincingly vindicated in the sweeping victory of New Labour in 1997.

Spin doctors

Tony Blair's style of government was typified by his use of spin doctors. The term was borrowed from the USA in the late 1990s to describe the special advisers employed by politicians to present their policies in the best light possible. At its best, 'spin' was essentially a form of public relations; at its worst it was telling lies. Blair relied on a team of advisers, most prominent of whom were **Alistair Campbell** and **Peter Mandelson**, to handle the media and help him judge the public mood, so that he could adjust his approach accordingly. The practice was not new. Margaret Thatcher, for example, had employed a well-organised press team. What was different about Labour's spin doctors was the large degree of influence they appeared to have not simply on the presentation but on the shaping of government policy.

New Labour's progressive image

It was his spin doctors who provided Tony Blair with the buzzwords and sound bites that he and the party used to convey New Labour's approach. Among these were the following terms:

- 'Cool Britannia': an already existing journalistic term appropriated by New Labour to describe how fashionable and in touch it was as a movement.
- 'Inclusiveness': referring to a society where nobody was left out, where there would be no 'social exclusion'.
- 'Stakeholder society': meaning in a practical sense ordinary people having state-protected investments and pensions, and in an abstract sense people feeling that they belonged collectively to society.
- 'Forces of conservatism': a blanket term, first used by Blair in a speech in 1999, to condemn everything that challenged his idea of progress.

Labour's women MPs

Arguably the most striking illustration of Labour's commitment to the political advancement of women was the election in 1997 of 101 female Labour MPs. This was complemented with thirteen Conservatives and three Liberal Democrats. There had been a residual resentment among the other parties when Margaret Thatcher, notwithstanding her lukewarm support for feminism, had blazed a trail for women by becoming the first woman to lead a British party and then the first woman to be prime minister. Determined not to be outdone by the Conservatives, Labour had adopted all-women shortlists in half the constituencies judged to be winnable in the 1997 election. Although successful in its outcome, there were claims that such shortlists were in breach of existing anti-discrimination laws. It was to prevent possible challenges on this front that Blair's government introduced a Sex Discrimination (Election Candidates) Act in 2002, which made it legal for all political parties to use the all-female shortlisting.

 KEY FIGURES

Alistair Campbell (1957–)

Tony Blair's special adviser and chief spokesman from 1994 to 2000. Although he held no official government post, he was so influential in presenting Blair and his policies to the public that some newspapers described him as the 'real deputy prime minister'.

Peter Mandelson (1953–)

MP and Tony Blair's highly successful 1997 election manager. He became trade minister in 1998 but resigned in the same year, then Northern Ireland minister in 1999 but resigned in 2001. He was Britain's European trade commissioner 2004–8.

The prime minister made much of the 1997 contingent, whom the press dubbed the 'Blair babes'. However, many of them disliked their experience at Westminster; they found the 'men's club' atmosphere distasteful and difficult to work under. This did not stop a number taking important government positions or making a significant impact from the backbenches. Prominent among these were Harriet Harman, Diane Abbot, Margaret Hodge and Tessa Jowell. Yet, by the time of the 2005 election, 31 of the original 101 were no longer MPs, although the overall number of women in the Commons had risen to 127. It has to be observed that many of the new intake of women MPs had performed unimpressively in the Commons. As some Labour Party members acknowledged, more had been expected from them than they had delivered. There were also suggestions that shortlisting, rather than promoting the equality of women, was in danger of patronising them. It was also the case that some were simply not prepared for the intrusive media scrutiny that politicians came under.

? What clues does Source D offer regarding the Labour Party's approach to the place of women in parliamentary politics?

SOURCE D

A famous photo of women Labour MPs after Labour's victory in 1997, with Blair waving in the middle.

Summary diagram: New Labour 1994–7

New Labour's programme	New Labour's style	New Labour's progressive image
• Nationalisation was to be dropped as an objective • The business world was to be wooed • Legal restrictions on trade unions were to be maintained • Policies would not be pursued as a class struggle • New Labour's policies were intended primarily to appeal to middle-class Britain where the bulk of the electorate were to be found • New Labour implicitly accepted that Thatcherism had aroused aspirations that could not be ignored • New Labour's supporters claimed it had made the party electable after eighteen years	• A response to the contemporary world of public relations • Spin doctors exemplified this • Campbell and Mandelson essential figures in this new presentation style	• *Cool Britannia*: suggestive of how fashionable and contemporary it was • *Inclusiveness*: referring to a society where there would be no 'social exclusion' • *Stakeholder society*: ordinary people having state-protected investments and pensions • *Labour's women MPs*: an illustration of Labour's commitment to the political advancement of women

---

6 Tony Blair's first administration 1997–2001

▶ *What were the key policies in Tony Blair's first administration?*

During its period in government, New Labour introduced a range of policies and measures that indicated its progressive intentions.

New Labour's economic policies

New Labour's first four years went well. The economy appeared healthy and Gordon Brown proved a major success as chancellor of the exchequer. One of his first moves was to give the Bank of England the authority to set interest rates. This appeared to take an important financial issue out of the political arena, although it could also be interpreted as a way for the government to avoid blame should mistakes later be made in the fixing of the rates. Brown also kept to a pledge, given before taking office in 1997, that Labour would keep within the spending plans the Conservatives had laid down. His prudent budgets swelled Britain's reserve funds while at the same time keeping inflation down.

Yet there is an argument that he could not have done this had he not inherited a strong economy. What is sometimes lost sight of is that the poor economic reputation Major's government had gained by 1997 was not entirely justified. Despite the ERM crisis of 1992, the fact was that, once Britain had withdrawn from the ERM, its financial and general economic situation considerably improved (see the figures in Table 5.4 on page 171). This, however, did not last.

By the time Gordon Brown moved from 11 to 10 Downing Street, it was clear that the success he had achieved in his early years as chancellor had not been sustained (see page 203).

Constitutional issues

When New Labour took office it was confronted by a set of constitutional questions.

Devolution

In its election manifesto, Labour had made a commitment to devolution, which it duly honoured by the creation of a Scottish Parliament and a Welsh Assembly. The Scottish Parliament was created in 1998, following a referendum in Scotland in the previous year. Three-quarters of the voters opted for a system in which Scotland, while remaining within the UK, would have its affairs run by a Scottish Parliament and a Scottish Executive with tax-raising powers.

The Welsh Assembly was also established 1998, following a referendum in the previous year which gave the pro-devolution voters a narrow 0.6% victory. Initially, the Assembly was simply a revising chamber, which examined UK measures that related to Wales, but later legislation gave Wales governmental powers, similar to those enjoyed in Scotland.

The House of Lords

The reform of the House of Lords, to which Labour was pledged, raised problems for the government. Ending the right of unelected hereditary peers to sit in the upper house was intended to strike a blow for democracy. But the problem was what form the new chamber would take and what powers it would have. By 2001 Blair had created more **life peers** in his four years of government than the Conservatives had in their eighteen. Critics complained that it was part of his scheme for consolidating New Labour's authority by packing the House of Lords with his own appointees. Even some of his own side were unhappy at this. Tony Benn, in his role as Labour's conscience, described the process as going back 700 years to the time when monarchs got their way by surrounding themselves with placemen.

Mayor of London

Following a referendum among the voters of London in 1998, the government introduced the Greater London Authority Act in 1999, under which arrangements were made for the election of a Mayor of London who (with the newly created London Assembly, made up of 25 members) was to be an executive figure responsible for governing Greater London. The winner of the first election, duly held in May 2000, was Ken Livingstone. He was a former Labour Party MP who stood as an independent, and held the office for the next eight years. A dynamic, if controversial, figure, Livingstone's personal style of leadership gave the mayoral role a high profile and suggested that governmental powers could be effectively and democratically devolved.

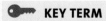 **KEY TERM**

Life peers Members of the House of Lords who are appointed to their positions, unlike hereditary peers who inherit their titles and their right to sit in the Lords.

Labour's New Deal

The 'New Deal' was the term the Labour government applied to its social policies. There was little that was truly new in regard to its social welfare programme; it necessarily built on existing structures, but after eighteen years in waiting it brought an enthusiasm and freshness to administration. The government's chief measures during its first period in office, 1997–2001, are outlined below.

Winter fuel allowance 1997

It was with a generosity of approach in social matters that the Blair government in 1997 introduced a winter fuel allowance for senior citizens. The measure, which initially granted £100 per person, was criticised on the grounds that as a universal payment made regardless of the recipient's income it was wasteful of public money which could have been directed to areas of greater need.

National Minimum Wage Act 1998

In accordance with its 1997 election promise, the Labour government introduced this measure in 1998, which established £4.85 as the minimum hourly wage for adult workers. Provision was made for that figure to be subsequently increased in line with the cost of living. When the Act came into force in 1999 it immediately raised the wages of over 1.5 million workers. The Conservatives initially opposed the measure as a threat to jobs, but came to accept it when in government themselves.

Human Rights Act 1998

The character of this measure had been summed up by Home Secretary Jack Straw when drafting the bill. He said that it was intended to achieve 'a better balance between rights and responsibilities, between the powers of the state and the freedom of the individual' and so oblige public authorities to be more attentive to the rights of ordinary people. The Act aroused some controversy as, according to some lawyers, it was essentially a matter of the UK putting itself under the pre-existing European Convention on Human Rights. However, Derry Irvine, the Lord Chancellor, Britain's leading legal authority, declared that British sovereignty was not an issue since the Act simply gave 'further effect in the United Kingdom to convention rights'.

Jobseeker's allowance 1998

This was an adjustment of the measure previously introduced by the Major government in 1996 which had replaced the existing unemployment benefit and income support with a single jobseeker's allowance. To qualify for the allowance, claimants were required to show evidence that they were actively looking for work. The Labour measures introduced in 1998 were meant to streamline this system by removing the means test attaching to applicants and allowing them greater time and flexibility in their search for work. Between 2003 and

2008, there were 2.5 million claims under the scheme. Labour's argument was that while it believed claimants should indeed be encouraged to seek work, they deserved to be treated with understanding and not as examples of the dependency culture.

Freedom of Information Act 2000

Passed in 2000 and coming into force in 2005, the Act required public authorities to grant 'right of access' to the information they held. Ordinary citizens were entitled to be told what information an authority had and to ask for its disclosure if it did not breach rules of confidentiality. It was this last clause that prevented the measure being as sweeping as originally intended. Libertarians complained that public bodies were still not fully accountable, since they could use the stipulations in the Act to avoid full disclosure. Although not intended to do this, a previous measure, the Data Protection Act (1998), allowing individuals and organisations to deny access to sensitive information, had somewhat qualified the effectiveness of the Freedom of Information Act.

Working families tax credit and child tax credit 1998

These two related measures were aimed at reducing child poverty. Under the working families tax credit arrangement, families with dependent children whose income from employment was below a minimum level, as judged by the price of essentials, were entitled to a tax allowance that in effect raised their wages. The government insisted that this was not to be thought of as a benefit since the extra money would appear as part of the actual wage received. As the Treasury statement put it, this form of payment 'would associate in the recipient's mind with the fact of working, a potentially valuable psychological change'. Although not specifically stated in the proposals, the child tax credit scheme was aimed at helping single parents. The tax credit was to be paid on a sliding scale according to parental income and the number of dependent children. The right to receive child tax credit did not exclude the parent from receiving benefits such as housing benefit.

Taken together, the two measures were part of New Labour's attempt to tackle what it referred to as 'social exclusion', the notion that, because of poverty and deprivation, sections of the community were shut off from the main society. In 1997, the government's Social Exclusion Unit had been set up to address this issue by integrating the various bodies and departments dealing with social welfare. The unit did not succeed in its attempt at integration, but its work was highly useful in defining the character of the problem. It confirmed that poverty was not simply an economic question. It was often as much a matter of lack of expectation and aspiration, and related to deprived areas, particularly in Britain's large cities, where a history of low incomes, poor education, chronic unemployment and poor diet had produced communities whose defining characteristics were lack of ambition, antisocial behaviour and petty crime, especially among the jobless young. The Social Exclusion Unit was lauded for its honesty in highlighting the problem, but a group of economists expressed disappointment that it had not given sufficient attention to the role that state benefits played in perpetuating Britain's dependency culture.

New Labour and Thatcherism

What was particularly notable about Tony Blair's government was that although it was very different in style and tone from the Thatcher–Major Conservatism that it replaced, in many areas it made no substantial effort to undo what had been done in the previous eighteen years. Margaret Thatcher's legacy proved a powerful one. She had weakened the trade unions, reintroduced the principle of accountability into the public services, and made the nation acknowledge that in economic matters nothing was for nothing. Although she was attacked for these policies in her time, those who came after her followed much the same path.

Blair and foreign affairs

Tony Blair made a strong impression abroad. EU ministers and officials warmed to him in personal meetings (see page 188), and the Clinton administration in the USA (1992–2000) admired him. Indeed, Bill Clinton had personal reason to be grateful to Blair for offering his moral support in 1999, when impeachment proceedings were instituted against the president over his sexual misdemeanours.

At the close of the century, Blair faced two particularly difficult problems in foreign affairs. One was the continuing war in former Yugoslavia, where the Dayton agreement had broken down (see page 172). The other was Iraq. Soon after becoming foreign secretary in Tony Blair's government, Robin Cook had declared that New Labour would pursue an 'ethical foreign policy'. The dilemma that this created was evident in the way the government handled these two issues.

NATO and Serbia

Tony Blair took an important initiative in the complex struggle that had broken out again in former Yugoslavia (see page 172). In 1999 he persuaded both NATO and President Clinton's USA to intervene militarily by relaunching air strikes against the Serbian forces under Slobodan Milošević. Blair's justification was that the Serbs had been engaging in the genocide of the Albanian people of Kosovo. However, there were critics who argued that the NATO action had led the Serbs to intensify their mistreatment of the Kosovans. There were also voices raised against the manner in which NATO bombing raids, carried out principally by the US and British air forces, had been conducted. To minimise the chance of casualties among themselves, the bomber crews had flown above 15,000 feet; this meant that, even with the sophisticated guidance systems available, bombs might well strike wrongly identified non-military targets. The Serbs produced evidence to show that this, indeed, had happened.

Initially, Blair had also wanted to send in ground troops. In a speech in Chicago, in 1999, he spoke of this as an act of necessary 'humanitarian intervention'. Clinton, however, was not prepared to go that far. Nevertheless, the combined air strikes did eventually achieve their objective; Milošević withdrew his forces. Later events were to show that this success in Kosovo convinced Blair that it could be used as a precedent for legitimate intervention elsewhere (see page 213).

Iraq

The accusation of indiscriminate bombing was also at the centre of the dispute in Iraq. In 1998, as part of a programme to make Saddam Hussein, the Iraqi leader (see page 212), comply with UN resolutions requiring him to open up his country to weapons inspections, Blair's government again joined with the USA in imposing sanctions. Observers reported that the effect of sanctions was not to hurt the Saddam regime but to deprive ordinary Iraqis of vital supplies such as medicines. It was also charged that the frequent nightly bombing raids that the allies carried out against military installations had caused the death of many innocent civilians. Iraq was to become the single biggest problem for Tony Blair in all his ten years in office.

Europe

Until the 1970s, the Labour Party had been far from pro-European and it was not until 1983 that it officially dropped its commitment to withdraw Britain from the EEC. Thereafter, as part of its reformation as New Labour, the party began to warm towards Europe. In part this was opportunistic. Labour was swift to exploit Mrs Thatcher's ambiguous European attitude and it made the most of Major's embarrassments over Maastricht and the ERM (see pages 171 and 172). But there was a more positive aspect to it. The party's earlier fears that Europe was essentially a club for capitalists had diminished. Labour could see, for example, the gains that workers could now derive from the generous European employment laws contained in the **Social Chapter**. The party declared its commitment to the European ideal. Tony Blair strove to impress the other European leaders with his sincerity.

KEY TERM

Social Chapter Sometimes referred to as the Social Charter, part of the Maastricht Treaty which committed EU member states to introducing extensive welfare schemes.

One of the first comments Blair made after becoming Labour Party leader in 1994 referred to Europe. He had declared: 'Under my leadership I will never allow this country to be isolated or left behind.' On becoming prime minister three years later, he kept his promise by immediately instructing British officials to address any unresolved issues with Europe. Blair's chief aim was to show the goodwill of the new government towards the EU. Some commentators have suggested that even at this early stage Blair had dreams of eventually becoming president of the EU and so wished to impress European colleagues with his dedication to the European ideal. Within two years Blair had attended a series of EU summit meetings at which he made a number of major concessions:

- Amsterdam 1997: Britain abandoned its opt-out on EU employment and social policy.

- St Malo 1998: Britain withdrew its objection to a common European defence policy which would operate independently of NATO. The French under president Chirac were delighted since it had long been a French aim to have a European force separate from the USA.

The question that confronted Bair and his government at the beginning of the new century was how far they should lead Britain down the path of European integration. The critical test would be whether the government would abandon the pound sterling and enter fully into the single currency system, a step which all the other EU members, apart from Denmark, had taken by 1999. Labour's interim answer was that it would prepare the ground for entry but would make a final commitment only if and when it could be established that entry was in Britain's economic interests. Its decision would then be put to a referendum of the British people.

Ireland

When Tony Blair became prime minister in 1997, he was the heir to the benefits that Major's accommodating diplomacy had brought, a fact that Blair willingly acknowledged. It was on the basis of the Mitchell principles (see page 174) that Blair, through his Northern Ireland team of ministers, gained Sinn Féin's agreement to persuade the IRA to accept decommissioning. A Sinn Féin delegation, including the party's leader, Gerry Adams, was invited to talks with the prime minister at 10 Downing Street. That such a meeting took place at all showed how far things had progressed and it eased the path towards the Good Friday Agreement of April 1998, the biggest constitutional advance since 1969.

The Good Friday Agreement, April 1998

The agreement owed much to the persistence of Blair and his Irish counterpart Bertie Ahern. Refusing to accept that the cycle of violence was unbreakable, both leaders used a mixture of charm and determination to bring the parties to the table. The agreement was accepted by the Ulster Unionists, the SDLP and Sinn Féin. Of the major parties only Ian Paisley's DUP rejected it. Under the Agreement:

- Northern Ireland's union with Britain was guaranteed for as long as the majority of the people of the province wanted it.
- The Irish Republic withdrew its territorial claim to Northern Ireland.
- A Northern Ireland Assembly with a new power-sharing executive government was created.
- As an act of goodwill, all terrorist prisoners would be released within two years.

The terms of the agreement were then put to the electorate in an all-Ireland referendum on the future of Northern Ireland. David Trimble, leader of the Ulster Unionists, and Gerry Adams of Sinn Féin urged their respective supporters to vote for it. The result was a large majority in favour of acceptance.

In the Irish Republic there was a 95 per cent yes vote, in Northern Ireland a 71 per cent yes vote. So, in return for their chance to share in government, the nationalists and republicans had given up their demand for a united Ireland. For their part, the Official Unionists had agreed to forgo their power to control Northern Irish politics and public affairs.

It was a remarkable study in direct democracy and gave renewed hope that peace could be achieved. The troubles did not immediately end. Republican and loyalist extremists rejected the agreement and violence continued, the worst instance being a car bomb explosion in Omagh in August 1998, which killed 28 people and injured 200. Yet it was evident that the perpetrators of such outrages were becoming isolated. Gerry Adams made a striking statement condemning the atrocity in which he said that 'violence must be a thing of the past, over, done with and gone'. International recognition of the progress being made in Northern Ireland came with the awarding in October 1998 of the Nobel Peace Prize jointly to David Trimble and John Hume, the SDLP leader.

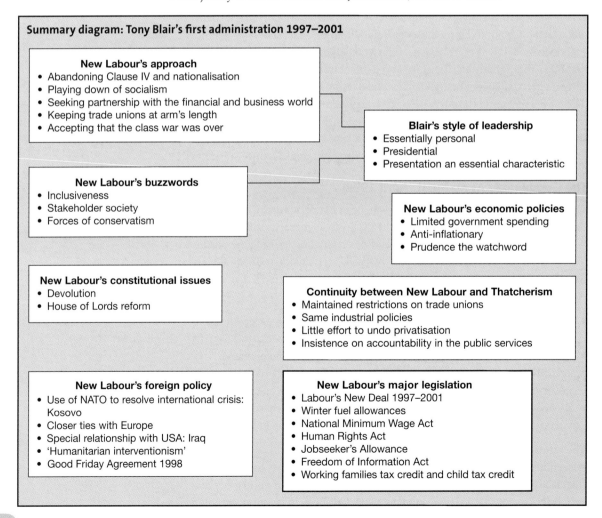

Summary diagram: Tony Blair's first administration 1997–2001

New Labour's approach
- Abandoning Clause IV and nationalisation
- Playing down of socialism
- Seeking partnership with the financial and business world
- Keeping trade unions at arm's length
- Accepting that the class war was over

Blair's style of leadership
- Essentially personal
- Presidential
- Presentation an essential characteristic

New Labour's buzzwords
- Inclusiveness
- Stakeholder society
- Forces of conservatism

New Labour's economic policies
- Limited government spending
- Anti-inflationary
- Prudence the watchword

New Labour's constitutional issues
- Devolution
- House of Lords reform

Continuity between New Labour and Thatcherism
- Maintained restrictions on trade unions
- Same industrial policies
- Little effort to undo privatisation
- Insistence on accountability in the public services

New Labour's foreign policy
- Use of NATO to resolve international crisis: Kosovo
- Closer ties with Europe
- Special relationship with USA: Iraq
- 'Humanitarian interventionism'
- Good Friday Agreement 1998

New Labour's major legislation
- Labour's New Deal 1997–2001
- Winter fuel allowances
- National Minimum Wage Act
- Human Rights Act
- Jobseeker's Allowance
- Freedom of Information Act
- Working families tax credit and child tax credit

Chapter summary

Margaret Thatcher's eleven years as prime minister ended when she was brought down by a series of crises largely of her own making. Her antipathy towards Europe caused divisions in her party. Her lack of political judgement was especially evident in her backing of the poll tax, which aroused fierce opposition across the social classes. Fearful of losing the next election, a group of senior colleagues openly challenged her authority. Having failed to win a convincing victory in the ensuing leadership election, Mrs Thatcher announced her resignation.

In her time she had changed the face of British politics.

Mrs Thatcher's successor, John Major, held office for seven years, making important decisions in foreign affairs and over Northern Ireland before being defeated in the 1997 election which brought Tony Blair and Labour into power. During its long years in opposition, the Labour Party had been transformed by the efforts of Blair's forebears, Neil Kinnock and John Smith. It was a modernising process that Blair embraced and, using his own populist flair, turned into New Labour. By 1999 Blair had already begun to tackle the demanding problem of Iraq. In Ireland he gained great credit for his role in the signing of the 1998 Good Friday Agreement.

 Refresher questions

Use these questions to remind yourself of the key material covered in this chapter.

1 What issues had weakened Mrs Thatcher's position by 1990?

2 Why did John Major win the Conservative Party leadership contest in 1990?

3 What were the main features of the Thatcher legacy?

4 Was the Thatcher legacy a negative or positive force in British politics?

5 How was John Major able to win the 1992 election?

6 What problems arose for the Major government over Europe?

7 How important an issue was 'sleaze' in the weakening of Major's government?

8 How effective was John Major's policy towards Northern Ireland?

9 Why did Labour win the 1997 election?

10 What was John Smith's contribution to the development of the Labour Party?

11 How effectively did political satire operate during the years of Conservative government 1979–97?

12 What were the main characteristics of New Labour?

13 What programme did New Labour adopt?

14 How important was Tony Blair's personality as a factor in New Labour's popularity?

15 What was New Labour's New Deal?

 Question practice

ESSAY QUESTIONS

1 'Mrs Thatcher fell from office in 1990 because of her own mistakes.' How far do you agree?

2 Assess the reasons for the defeat of the Conservatives in 1997 after eighteen years in office.

3 'Britain's acceptance of the Maastricht Treaty was achieved by the Major government's resorting to undemocratic means.' Explain why you agree or disagree with this view.

4 To what extent were public relations important in the development of New Labour?

SOURCE ANALYSIS QUESTION

1 With reference to Sources 1, 2 and 3, and your understanding of the historical context, assess the value of these sources to a historian studying the development of New Labour under Tony Blair.

SOURCE I

Tony Blair's speech to the Labour Party conference, 28 September 1999, www.theguardian.com/ politics/1999/sep/28/labourconference.labour14. Here Blair claims that New Labour under his leadership is changing Britain for the better by undoing the forces of conservatism.

Today at the frontier of the new Millennium I set out for you how, as a nation, we renew British strength and confidence for the 21st century; and how, as a Party reborn, we make it a century of progressive politics after one dominated by Conservatives. New Labour, confident at having modernised itself, now the new progressive force in British politics which can modernise the nation, will sweep away those forces of conservatism to set the people free.

100 years in existence, 22 in power, we have never, ever won a full second term. That is our unfinished business. Let us now finish it and with it finish the Tory Party's chances of doing as much damage in the next century as they've done in this one.

The frustration, the impatience, the urgency, the anger at the waste of lives unfulfilled, hopes never achieved, dreams never realised. And whilst there is one child still in poverty in Britain today, one pensioner in poverty, one person denied their chance in life, there is one Prime Minister and one Party that will have no rest, no vanity in achievement, no sense of mission completed, until they too are free. So I do not claim Britain is transformed. I do say the foundations of a New Britain are being laid.

SOURCE 2

From Peter Clarke, *Hope and Glory: Britain 1900–2000*, Penguin, 2004, p. 412. Clarke, a provocative modern historian, suggested there was a remarkable line of continuity between Blair's New Labour and Thatcherism.

Media attention flattered Blair; with his youthful demeanour often uncritically accepted as an earnest of wholesale political renewal. He played to a perception that he was not just another Labour politician. He came from a middle-class background, had attended a fee-paying school and had graduated from Oxford University. So had Attlee, Gaitskell and Foot before him. Blair, however, was the first to declare his lack of proletarian credentials as an asset. He claimed intuitive understanding of the fears and hopes of 'middle England' and sought to identify its professed values, whether flag-waving patriotism or upwardly-mobile aspirations, with New Labour as the party of 'one-nation'. These were, of course, traditional Conservative symbols and slogans, coolly appropriated in a vote-stealing exercise that self-consciously mirrored Thatcher's earlier success in appealing to a traditional Labour constituency.

SOURCE 3

From Tony Blair, *A Journey*, Random House, 2010, p. 101. Here, in his autobiography, Blair acknowledges the political debt he owed to Margaret Thatcher.

In what caused much jarring and tutting within the party, I even decided to own up to supporting changes Margaret Thatcher had made. I knew the credibility of the whole New Labour project rested on accepting that much of what she wanted to do in the 1980s was inevitable, a consequence not of ideology but of social and economic change. The way she did it was often very ideological, sometimes unnecessarily so, but that didn't alter the basic fact: Britain needed the industrial and economic reforms of the Thatcher period.

CHAPTER 6

New Labour in the new century 2001–7

Tony Blair's New Labour government entered the twenty-first century with considerable confidence. Its early years in power had gone well, particularly on the economic front. But there were problems that still needed resolution; Northern Ireland and the UK's relations with Europe were prominent among these. In 2002, however, a problem arose in foreign affairs that was to dominate the remainder of Blair's premiership: Iraq. This issue was to test Britain's special relationship with the USA and to result in Blair's leading Britain into a war on terror. The opportunity is also taken in this last chapter to examine a number of social issues that confronted Blair's government which had been building over the whole period covered by this book. The chapter examines the following themes:

★ The elections of 2001 and 2005

★ The New Deal continued 2001–7

★ New Labour and the economy

★ Tony Blair and Europe

★ Tony Blair and Ireland

★ Tony Blair, the USA and Iraq

★ Population change and social issues

Key dates

1998	Good Friday Agreement	2005	Labour won third successive election
1999–2002	Britain sold off half its gold reserves	2005	7/7 London bombings
		2006	St Andrews Agreement
2000	Blair's 'third way' speech		Blair gave in over rebate and CAP reform
2001	Labour won second successive election	2007	Northern Ireland Executive formed
2002	Euro adopted by EU		Brown succeeded Blair as prime minister
2004	Blair argued for reform of CAP		
	Treaty of Rome		Treaty of Lisbon

The elections of 2001 and 2005

▶ *Why was Labour able to win both these elections?*

New Labour's political success was evident in its consecutive election victories of 2001 and 2005.

The 2001 general election

In 2001, Labour maintained the massive majority it had gained in 1997, suggesting that the electorate considered the government had performed well over its four years in office. Labour lost only five seats. There was a fall of 3.7 per cent in its aggregate vote but this had a minimal effect on its overall strength. It is true that Labour lost nearly three million voters, but commentators put this down to a general apathy among the electorate which led to a turnout of 59 per cent compared with 71 per cent in 1997. The apathy was largely explained by the opinion polls giving the government such a clear lead that neither supporters nor opponents had an incentive to vote since the outcome was a foregone conclusion.

Table 6.1 Results of the 2001 general election

Party	Votes	Seats	Percentage of vote
Labour	10,724,895	413	40.7
Conservative	8,357,622	166	31.7
Liberal Democrats	4,812,833	52	18.3
Northern Irish parties	544,108	15	2.3
Scottish Nationalists	464,314	5	1.5
Plaid Cymru	195,893	4	0.6

Tony Blair's personal popularity was a major factor in Labour's success. Although William Hague, who had been elected as the Conservative leader in 1997, was a witty and trenchant performer in the House of Commons, his qualities did not translate into popularity in the country at large. The same was true of his party, which found it difficult to encroach on Labour's lead. The Conservatives at this stage lacked a distinct enough image to make them an attractive alternative in the eyes of the voters. Although they sniped at the government, they found it difficult to score a palpable hit. Britain's finances seemed secure in the hands of Gordon Brown as the chancellor of the exchequer and the economy was growing. In regard to Northern Ireland, Blair had taken a number of important initiatives (see page 189), leaving little room for the opposition to attack him. In foreign affairs, the government's record was sound and while there was some uncertainty about the government's attitude towards Europe, there was even more about the attitude of the Conservatives.

Reasons for Labour's victory in 2001

In the 2001 general election, the Labour Party maintained its lead; among the reasons were the following:

- Blair's continued personal popularity with voters.
- Improvements in the public services.
- Hague's inability to present himself as a better alternative to Blair.
- The perception that the government was handling the economy and foreign affairs effectively.
- Trust in Brown as a prudent chancellor of the exchequer.
- Lacking a clear set of targets on which they could attack the government, the Conservatives ran a poor campaign. Their main line was opposition to adopting the euro, which failed to attract floating voters.
- The opinion polls had concurred in forecasting a Labour victory, thus decreasing the incentive to vote.

The 2005 general election

In May 2005 Tony Blair achieved a remarkable first for a Labour prime minister; he won his third straight election victory in a row. The number of seats achieved by Labour was 57 fewer than the 2001 figure, 356 compared to 413, and its aggregate vote fell by over five per cent. The Conservatives gained 32 more seats than four years earlier. The Liberal Democrats did well in terms of popular support, gaining an aggregate of nearly 6 million votes, which was nearly two-thirds of Labour's total. However, this was not reflected in the number of seats they acquired, as the ratio of votes to seats indicated:

- For each seat the Labour Party won, it polled an average of 26,872 votes.
- For each seat the Conservative Party won, it polled an average of 44,373.
- For each seat the Liberal Democrats won, they polled an average of 96,538.

Despite losing some ground in the election, Blair's government had retained a comfortable overall majority. There was no reason for thinking it could not run another full term if it chose.

Table 6.2 Results of the 2005 general election

Party	Votes	Seats	Percentage of vote
Labour	9,566,618	356	35.3
Conservative	8,785,941	198	32.3
Liberal Democrats	5,985,414	62	22.1
Northern Irish parties	544,108	18	2.3
Scottish Nationalists	412,267	6	1.5
Plaid Cymru	174,838	3	0.6

Reasons for Labour's victory in 2005

- Although Blair's involvement in the Iraq war lost him some popularity (see page 211), he was still regarded by the electorate as the outstanding choice among party leaders.
- Since the Conservatives had supported the government's decision to go into Iraq, they were unable to gain from the mounting criticism of the war.
- Knowledge of the economic difficulties that were beginning to face Britain had not become sufficiently widespread for it to count as a factor against the government.
- Despite the Conservatives maintaining their vote and slightly increasing their aggregate support, they still could not make significant inroads into Labour's lead.
- The Conservative Party had had three different leaders within two years. William Hague had been replaced by Iain Duncan Smith after the 2001 election defeat. In 2003 Duncan Smith, having proved an uninspiring leader, was in turn replaced by Michael Howard. This did not impress the general public, who regarded the Conservatives as a divided party, lacking in confidence and unlikely to be able to govern well.
- Skilfully backed by his spin doctors, Blair by 2005 was an experienced political operator who knew how to project his image. Howard was a competent Conservative leader but he was no real match for Blair in the presidential-style campaign that the prime minister conducted.
- Howard made a bad choice of issues on which to fight the campaign. His emphasis on immigration and law and order, concerns on which his own record as home secretary in Major's government was not impressive, proved something of an embarrassment. As early as 1997, a colleague, Ann Widdecombe, had described Howard as having 'something of the night about him'. He tried to make light of her description but it proved a handicap thereafter. He was never quite able to rid himself of the sinister image that one of his own side had given him.

Summary diagram: The elections of 2001 and 2005

2001: Labour won second successive election

- Blair's continued personal popularity with voters
- Hague's inability to present himself as a better alternative to Blair
- Blair's successes in Northern Ireland
- Trust in Brown as a prudent chancellor

2005: Labour won third straight election victory in a row

- Despite Blair's involvement in the Iraq war, he was still regarded by the electorate as the outstanding choice for prime minister
- Since the Conservatives had supported the government's decision to go into Iraq, they were unable to gain from the criticism of the war
- Knowledge of the economic and financial difficulties that were beginning to face Britain had not become sufficiently widespread for it to count as a weakening factor against the government
- The Conservative Party had had three different leaders within two years
- Blair's spin doctors continued skilfully to project his image
- Howard made a bad choice of issues on which to fight the campaign

The New Deal continued 2001–7

> ▶ *What were the key measures and developments in Tony Blair's second administration?*

Tony Blair continued with the progressive policies he had adopted in his first administration. The emphasis again was on social reform as the government followed policies aimed at extending its New Deal.

Social inclusion 2001–7

The government's policies were based on the principle of creating and furthering social inclusion. Several key measures are outlined below.

Police Reform Act 2002

This measure created police community support officers (PCSOs) who were not legally police officers and, therefore, had very limited powers. The main aim was to suggest that there was a police presence in the local community, thereby lessening the 'them and us' attitudes existing between police and public.

Repeal of Section 28, 2003

A related measure which proved controversial was the government's repeal of Section 28 of the Local Government Act of 1988, which had declared that a local authority 'shall not intentionally promote homosexuality or publish material with the intention of promoting homosexuality or promote the teaching in any maintained school of the acceptability of homosexuality as a pretended family relationship'. Although delayed by resistance in the House of Lords, repeal was eventually achieved under the Local Government Act of 2003. Many people within and outside the Labour Party regarded this removal of the stigma on homosexuality as a further stage in the movement towards the tolerant society that the progressive policies of Roy Jenkins had begun in the 1960s (see page 72).

Civil Partnership Act 2004

The repeal of Section 28 helped to prepare the way for a further extension of gay rights. Although the Civil Partnership Act caused some controversy in the country at large, it created little dispute in Parliament. The Conservatives and Liberal Democrats gave their support to the bill, under which same-sex couples in a partnership were given the same legal rights and protections as couples in a male–female civil marriage.

Gender Recognition Act 2004

This Act gave transsexuals the right to change their gender legally and to marry someone of their newly assigned gender. The measure was a further practical example of New Labour's socially progressive approach, as was evident in the words of David Lammy when introducing the bill (see Source A).

SOURCE A

From David Lammy's speech introducing the Gender Recognition Act 2004 in the Commons, 23 February 2004, http://hansard.millbanksystems.com/people/mr-david-lammy/.

The Bill is part of the Government's commitment to reforming the constitution so that it better meets the needs of all people. It reflects, too, our commitment to social inclusion. Transsexual people are a small and vulnerable minority in our society and the Bill addresses one of the key problems that they face. It is essential that no one is left behind as we create the conditions for a credible and effective modern democracy.

There is a strong tradition of legislation in this country that has sought to respond to the concerns and needs of minority groups – whether they have been ethnic minorities, people who are disabled or, with this Bill, transsexual people. … I believe that the reformist tradition behind such measures is one that the country can be proud of. We, as a Government, are committed to continuing that tradition. The Bill provides transsexual people with the opportunity to gain the rights and responsibilities appropriate to the gender in which they are now living. At present, transsexual people live in a state of limbo. Their birth gender determines their legal status.

> In what ways does Source A illustrate the government's commitment to the principle of social inclusion?

Employment Act 2004

The Employment Act of 2004 was principally concerned with confirming trade union rights while at the same time improving industrial relations by requiring unions to hold a ballot before taking strike action.

Criticism from within the Labour Party

Despite these well-intentioned reforms under the New Deal, critics on the left of the party pointed to the uncomfortable statistic that during the Blair years, 1997–2007, the gap between the rich and poor in Britain had widened. From the right of the party, **Frank Field** argued that Labour's attempt at being more generous with social benefits was having the reverse effect from the one intended. It was increasing dependency and stifling work incentives. It was over this issue that Field had resigned from his position as minister of welfare reform in 1998. In contrast, the charge from the left of the party was that New Labour under Blair had merely tinkered with the system and continued to take an essentially Thatcherite approach to social problems. It was a repeat of the accusation that in reforming itself as New Labour, the Labour Party had abandoned genuine socialism.

> **🔑 KEY FIGURE**
>
> **Frank Field (1942–)**
> Labour MP for Birkenhead since 1979. Minister of welfare reform 1997–8. A specialist in social policy and a declared admirer of Margaret Thatcher.

SOURCE B

As stated in Source B, what obligations does the Act impose on both employers and trade unions?

From the Employment Act 2004, www.legislation.gov.uk/ukpga/2004/24/notes/contents.

The process [of recognition] is triggered by the union(s) writing to the employer, requesting recognition, and identifying the bargaining unit of the workers concerned.

The employer has a period in which to respond. If the employer agrees voluntarily to recognise the union (or unions), the statutory recognition procedure is regarded as closed.

Alternatively, if the employer agrees to negotiate, the parties have a time period to conclude discussions. The parties may call on the Advisory, Conciliation and Arbitration Service (Acas) to assist. If the employer refuses to negotiate or does not respond to the union's letter the union(s) may make an application for recognition to the CAC [Central Arbitration Committee].

A trade union that organises industrial action would, in the absence of statutory provision to the contrary, be liable under the common law for the civil wrong of inducing a breach of contract. However, the Act protects unions from the legal liability that would otherwise result if certain conditions are satisfied. One of these is that before inducing its members to take part in industrial action, the union must have held a properly conducted secret ballot of the members it is likely to induce to take part.

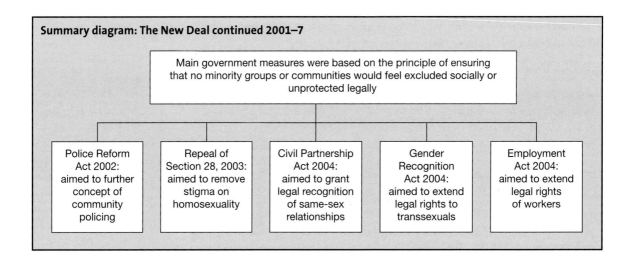

Summary diagram: The New Deal continued 2001–7

Main government measures were based on the principle of ensuring that no minority groups or communities would feel excluded socially or unprotected legally

| Police Reform Act 2002: aimed to further concept of community policing | Repeal of Section 28, 2003: aimed to remove stigma on homosexuality | Civil Partnership Act 2004: aimed to grant legal recognition of same-sex relationships | Gender Recognition Act 2004: aimed to extend legal rights to transsexuals | Employment Act 2004: aimed to extend legal rights of workers |

New Labour and the economy

▶ *What were the distinctive features of the Blair government's handling of the economy?*

Income and expenditure

During Tony Blair's first period in office from 1997 to 2001, the economy appeared to flourish and his government reaped the benefit politically, with another sweeping election victory in 2001. Gordon Brown gained an impressive reputation for restricting inflation and building up Britain's financial reserves. However, when the Conservatives lost office in 1997, the inflation rate had been 2.6 per cent; ten years later when Brown became prime minister, it was 4.8 per cent. The basic explanation for the rise was that after three years of tightly controlled spending, Brown had relaxed his prudent approach and engaged in large-scale government expenditure. Large amounts of money were spent on the public sector, particularly the National Health Service (NHS). While there was an obvious argument for this on social grounds, the effect financially was to increase inflation.

Pensions

There was another aspect of Brown's policy which created anger, particularly with elderly people. In order to build up the reserves of money for later expenditure, the chancellor began to tax pension savings. He did this by taxing the dividends which companies paid to their investors. Since the purpose of a having a pension is for holders to see a return in the form of interest on the money they pay in premiums, the taxing of dividends meant that the value of pensions fell. By 2007 the amount lost was over £8 billion. The British pensions industry, which had been one of the world's best funded and highest paying financial concerns, was despondent by 2007. One statistic that illustrates this is that the **savings ratio**, which stood at 9.7 per cent in 1997, had declined to 3.7 per cent ten years later.

An additional effect of the tax on pensions, known as a 'stealth tax', was that since share prices are dependent on dividend values, the cutting of dividend payments meant that total UK share values were some £120 billion lower than they would have been without government interference.

In the elections of 1997 and 2001 the Labour Party had promised a low taxation policy. In order not to appear to break that commitment, financial adjustments

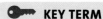 **KEY TERM**

Savings ratio The annual percentage of an individual's disposable income that is saved rather than spent.

were made, which, while not technically classed as taxation, were so in practice. Among these were the following:

- Raising National Insurance contributions.
- Removing the marriage tax allowance for couples aged under 65.
- Removing tax relief on mortgage payments.
- Reducing the level of tax-free savings that could be made each year under such schemes as **TESSA**s and **PEP**s. For example, in 1999 the untaxed amount an individual could save was £12,000; by 2007 that had been reduced to £7000.

Employment

One of the government's claims was that the number of people in employment in Britain grew during the Blair years. This is certainly true in overall terms; by 2007 there were 29.1 million people in work, 2.5 million more than in 1997. However, while there had been a growth in jobs this had not been in the areas where it was most needed, among the unskilled and the young. In 2007 there were 5.4 million people of working age, many of them between the ages of 16 and 30, who had never had a job, living on unemployment benefit.

Another consideration was that 37 per cent of the increase in jobs were in the public sector, which by 2007 was employing 7 million people, an increase of some 900,000 during Blair's ten years as prime minister. Britain had become a **client state** in which a quarter of workers were employed in the public sector; they did jobs that were paid for by the government out of public funds. There was the added problem that many of the positions in the public sector were in the state bureaucracies and had no productive value. This resurrected the situation which both James Callaghan and Margaret Thatcher had tried to end. Callaghan in 1978 had told the Labour Party conference: 'we are paying ourselves with money we have not earned'.

Borrowing

The government's justification for expanding the public sector was that it was a way of improving public services. However, the costs incurred tended to outrun the revenue received. The increase in government expenditure on the public sector, in areas such as the NHS, welfare services and education, could not be met entirely from taxation revenues. Over the period of his chancellorship, Golden Brown had borrowed heavily from foreign banks. The reason why this did not make headline news was that the ten years after New Labour came to power in 1997 were a period of relative stability and growth in the international economy. However, the ominous signs by the end of 2007 were that this period was coming to an end and that there was a likelihood of a serious world economic recession. In a period of decline, a country that has borrowed heavily has real problems, since its growth and revenues fall at the very time it needs them to rise so that it can meet its debts.

Judged by how much people spent, the decade after 1997 was in many ways a boom time in Britain. House buying and retail sales increased markedly. Mass buying of the products of new technologies, such as personal computers and mobile phones, showed great willingness among consumers to spend. However, the commodities and goods were paid for often not by money earned but by money borrowed. Encouraged by banks and loan companies, many ordinary people took out credit. The plastic credit card was a symbol of the times. The criticism made of this consumer boom by economists is that the government allowed it to run on too long in order to mask the difficulties it had created through its own borrowing. This was a recipe for recession.

'Golden Brown'

An important step taken by Gordon Brown, which went largely unnoticed at the time, was his decision was to sell off Britain's gold reserves. Between 1999 and 2002, when the price of gold fell on the international markets, the British government sold off 13 million ounces, nearly half of its reserves. In the same period the People's Republic of China bought up nearly 7 million ounces. With the subsequent recovery of gold prices by 2005 Britain found it had lost some £3 billion, equivalent to a penny on the basic tax rate. China, in contrast, had doubled its money. *The Scotsman* newspaper condemned what it called 'Brown's disastrous foray into international asset management', while one of the tabloids cuttingly referred to the chancellor as 'Golden Brown'.

It is interesting to note that China also proved far sharper at using the **WTO** system to its advantage than Britain. In 2006, the British government woke up to the fact that China was selling much more to Britain than it was buying and that Britain's European competitors had taken advantage. In 2005 Britain's exports to China were worth only £5 billion compared to Germany's £31 billion. In an effort to redress the balance, Britain embarked on a major campaign to increase its influence and trade with China. The effect diplomatically of this eagerness to develop commercial contact was that the government took care not to be too critical of China on other issues, such as human rights; it did not wish to risk losing trade with China's vast market of 1.4 billion people.

 KEY TERM

WTO World Trade Organisation, the international body responsible for negotiating and monitoring trade agreements between countries.

Summary diagram: New Labour and the economy

Income and expenditure

Policy: from 2001 the prudence of the earlier Blair–Brown years gave way to high public spending

Result
• Rising inflation

Pensions

Policy: government raid on pension funds

Results
• Rapid £8 billion fall in pension values
• Decline of British pensions industry
• Savings ratio fell

Employment

Policy: to reduce unemployment

Results
• 2.5 million more in work by 2007 than in 1997
• 5.4 million people of working age still living on unemployment benefit
• 37 per cent of the increase in jobs was in the unproductive public sector, which made Britain increasingly a client state

Borrowing

Policy: to borrow in order to fund the expansion of public services

Results
• Costs of services outran revenue returns, leading to increased borrowing
• Government borrowing encouraged a consumer credit boom
• Britain not well prepared for the international economic downturn that had set in by the end of 2007

Gold

Policy: to sell off half of Britain's gold reserves since gold prices were falling

Result
• Subsequent recovery of gold market meant Britain had sold at a heavy loss amounting to £3 billion

Tony Blair and Europe

▶ *What were Tony Blair's aims in his dealings with Europe?*

In 2008, on its official website, the Labour Party listed the government's 'top 50 achievements since being elected in 1997'. Europe did not feature in the list. Yet it had been one of Tony Blair's preoccupations. In his first years in office, Blair had made enthusiastic overtures to Europe (see page 188). To appease those in Britain, including many in the Labour ranks who thought he had gone too far, too soon, he tried from 2000 onwards to perform a balancing act.

Blair's third way

In a speech in Warsaw, Tony Blair said that attitudes towards Europe could be divided into two main types. On one side were those still totally committed to the nation state and the free market, who wanted the EU to have the minimum of power; opposite them were the 'superstaters', those who wanted the EU to supersede the nation state and have maximum powers of control. Blair argued for a **third way**. He spoke of an EU made up of friendly states, retaining their individual sovereignty, but collaborating on matters of common economic and political interest.

The third way notion was intended mainly for home consumption. It certainly made little impression on EU ministers and officials, who felt no obligation to make concessions to Britain simply because Britain had made concessions to them. For them, there was no room for a third way within the EU. As an organisation it was intent on greater integration and federalism. That indeed was its basic purpose; it was no longer really a matter for discussion. John Major's talk of Britain's 'being at the heart of Europe', which Blair repeated, was unrealistic. The EU was simply waiting for Britain to catch up and start conforming to the rules already drawn up.

Tony Blair was made aware of this when he tried to push for a reform of the expensive Common Agricultural Policy (CAP, see page 49). He declared that in exchange for the reform of CAP, he was willing to accept **majority voting** and the dropping of the veto principle. However, anticipating that he would do this, the French and German governments had previously got together to block any attempts to alter a system whose purpose from the beginning had been to protect French agriculture and was not negotiable.

The euro

The merits and disadvantages of Britain's membership of the EU again became a matter for public debate in 2002 over the issue of whether the UK should give up the pound sterling and join the euro. On New Year's Day 2002, the euro became the common currency of all but three of the members (Denmark, Sweden and

 **KEY TERMS**

Third way Suggesting the creation of a balance between left and right extremes, often associated with Blair and New Labour's policies in general.

Majority voting A system that attracted federalists since it enabled contentious resolutions to be passed without being blocked by a member state using its individual veto.

Eurozone Those countries that gave up their individual currencies for the euro.

Rebate The return of a proportion of Britain's budgetary payment.

the UK). Whether and when Britain should join were questions that divided Tony Blair from Gordon Brown, his chancellor of the exchequer. Blair was less concerned with the financial aspects of the case and more with the political implications. He calculated that to join the **eurozone** would help put the UK at the heart of Europe and enhance his own standing as a European statesman.

Brown's approach was more guarded and practical. He defined the problem in the form of a question: would joining the euro 'serve the long-term national economic interest?' He laid down five economic tests that the euro would have to pass before it could be adopted. These included judgements about its impact on jobs, inflation and trade.

Blair, however, was prepared to have a national referendum on the issue. He knew that opinion polls showed the British people to be currently against the euro but he believed that, as had happened with the 1975 referendum (see page 87), the people could be educated into saying 'yes'. Clare Short, a Cabinet minister at the time, later suggested that Blair at this point was even willing to step down as prime minister in favour of Brown, if Brown would commit himself to the euro. Whatever the truth of that suggestion, the fact was that in June 2003 Brown declared that the euro came nowhere near meeting the five tests and so there was a need for a referendum. Brown had economic and political logic on his side: since the economy was performing well under his stewardship, there was no point in putting it at possible risk by adopting the euro.

The rebate issue

A concern that had clouded Britain's relations with Europe since 1973 was the size of the annual budget paid by member states to Europe. Britain felt that it had been discriminated against from the beginning by being obliged to pay a disproportionately higher amount. It was true that in 1984 Margaret Thatcher had won an annual **rebate** for Britain, but there were strong complaints in many member states, most prominently France, which argued that rebates breached the various treaty obligations which members had signed. In 2004 this issue forced itself into the foreground when the EU was enlarged to include the states of Eastern Europe.

Blair told Europe that Britain was prepared to pay its 'fair share of the costs of enlargement', but he added that it could not give up its rebate and that he would use Britain's veto to block any EU attempt to force the UK to do so. One of Britain's strongest arguments was that the UK had never actually received its full rebate because, in accordance with European regulations, 66 per cent of any EU funding that it was granted was deducted from the rebate. The result was that in net terms the UK since joining in 1973, had received much less from the EEC/EU than it had paid to it.

In 2004 Blair further stated that 'the rebate and the Common Agricultural Policy are inextricably linked and there cannot be fundamental change in one unless there is fundamental change in the other'. He was on strong grounds. CAP had never worked in Britain's favour. In 2004, as the piechart in Figure 6.1 shows, Britain received less from CAP than any of the major member states.

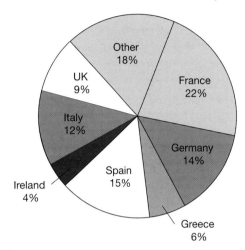

Figure 6.1 CAP beneficiaries in 2004.

Despite Blair's fighting words in 2004, he did not achieve the reform of CAP that he had wanted. When Europe closed ranks against Britain in 2005 and demanded that it increase its budget contributions, he gave in and complied. One of his last acts as prime minister on the European stage was in December 2006 when he negotiated away the UK's rebate, as a result of which Britain's annual contribution rose to £7 billion. There is an interesting aspect to Blair's eventually giving in to European pressure. Despite its odd-one-out image, Britain was the most compliant of all the EU member states. During 2006 the EU imposed over 3000 regulations and directives on Britain. Few of these were discussed, let alone modified, by the Westminster Parliament. Eighty per cent of the new regulations which came into force in Britain during Blair's years as prime minister were laid down by the EU.

The European constitution

Running parallel with the debate over CAP was the equally divisive issue of the adoption of a European constitution. In October 2004, the 27 EU member states met in Rome to sign the **Treaty Establishing a Constitution for Europe** (TCE). The treaty was scheduled to come into force in November 2006, provided it was ratified by each of the member states. Blair's government promised that, before the TCE was ratified by the UK, the question of whether it should be accepted would be put to the British electorate in a referendum. However, when in 2005, in separate referendums in France and Denmark, the electors there rejected the treaty, the government declared that ratification was now a dead issue, which made a referendum in Britain no longer necessary. This did not satisfy those who asked why the British people were to be denied a referendum which other member states had chosen to hold. Euro-sceptics claimed that the government had reneged on its promise because it knew the TCE would be rejected in Britain, an outcome strongly suggested by the opinion polls.

 **KEY TERM**

Treaty Establishing a Constitution for Europe
Brought together the existing EU treaties into one formal, binding document.

Undeterred by the failure to achieve ratification, the EU in June 2007 produced a replacement for the TCE. Technically, the new document was termed a 'Reform Treaty', a linguistic subtlety which meant that, although the new treaty was in every major respect the same as the TCE, it was not formally a constitution. As a consequence, when the Reform Treaty was subsequently accepted and signed by the EU members in Lisbon in December 2007, the British government (now led by Prime Minister Gordon Brown) declared that there was no need for a referendum on it. Claiming that its promise to hold a referendum applied only to a constitution, the government asserted that ratification was now solely a matter for parliamentary approval. This was duly granted in March 2008, when the government used its majority to push through ratification. It was all very reminiscent of the way John Major's government had achieved parliamentary acceptance of the Maastricht Treaty in 1993 (see page 171).

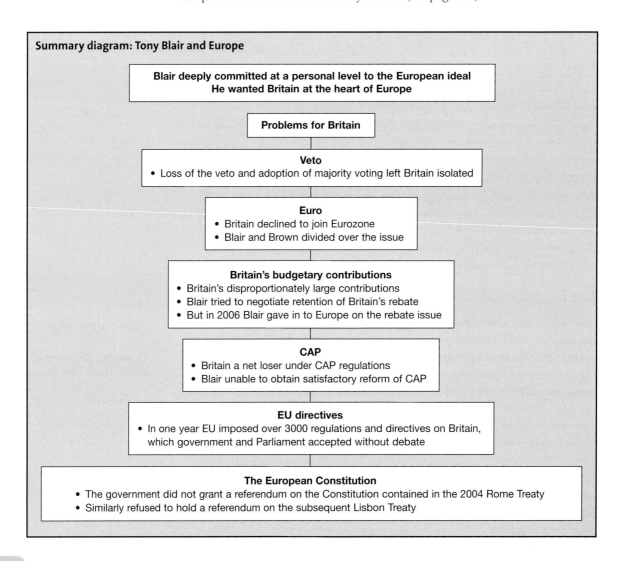

Summary diagram: Tony Blair and Europe

**Blair deeply committed at a personal level to the European ideal
He wanted Britain at the heart of Europe**

Problems for Britain

Veto
- Loss of the veto and adoption of majority voting left Britain isolated

Euro
- Britain declined to join Eurozone
- Blair and Brown divided over the issue

Britain's budgetary contributions
- Britain's disproportionately large contributions
- Blair tried to negotiate retention of Britain's rebate
- But in 2006 Blair gave in to Europe on the rebate issue

CAP
- Britain a net loser under CAP regulations
- Blair unable to obtain satisfactory reform of CAP

EU directives
- In one year EU imposed over 3000 regulations and directives on Britain, which government and Parliament accepted without debate

The European Constitution
- The government did not grant a referendum on the Constitution contained in the 2004 Rome Treaty
- Similarly refused to hold a referendum on the subsequent Lisbon Treaty

Tony Blair and Ireland

▶ *How did Tony Blair contribute to the settlement of the Northern Ireland issue?*

One of the achievements in which Tony Blair could take the greatest pride was his contribution to the peaceful settlement of the Northern Ireland issue.

Decommissioning

Following the Good Friday Agreement and the Omagh bombing in 1998 (see page 189), there was a growing sense among all but a few extremists that a political solution was the only answer. This sense of the futility of violence was quickened by the events of 9/11 in the USA in 2001 (see page 211). Many Irish-Americans who had previously given moral and financial support to the IRA campaigns in Northern Ireland now had a graphic example in their own homeland of what terrorism actually meant in practice. It was no coincidence that thereafter all the talk by responsible Americans, politicians and people, was of the need for a peaceful resolution of Northern Ireland's ills. In a similar way, the death and mutilation caused by the London bombings in July 2005 (see page 216) re-emphasised the illegitimacy in a civilised society of violent means being used to achieve political ends. In Northern Ireland itself, the main obstacle to peace remained the issue of decommissioning. Could the paramilitaries be brought to abandon their arms? On 28 July 2005, responding to a number of appeals by Sinn Féin, the IRA announced that, while it would remain in being as a force committed to defend nationalist Ulster, it was giving up its weapons and pledging itself to the use of 'exclusively peaceful means'.

The issue now was whether the loyalist paramilitaries, such as the Ulster Volunteer Force (UVF), would do the same. The UVF's claim had always been that they could not trust the IRA declarations of intent and, therefore, could not themselves disarm. Ian Paisley, although never an advocate of violence, had always proved a major obstacle to constitutional advance. His DUP (see page 99) had rejected the Downing Street Declaration and the Good Friday Agreement. As long as he held out, loyalist paramilitaries were unlikely to budge. However, the unionists were also undergoing a form of conversion. It was a matter of accepting reality. **Demography** was the key. Protestant unionists were fast becoming a minority in Northern Ireland. As Table 6.3 shows, the Catholic proportion of the population was growing, largely as a result of the birth rate being higher in the Catholic community than in the Protestant.

 KEY TERM

Demography Population analysis.

Table 6.3 Catholics and Protestants in Northern Ireland 1961–2001 (percentage of population)

Religion	1961	1991	2001
Roman Catholic	34.9%	38.4%	40.3%
Protestant	62.5%	50.6%	45.2%

Unless they adapted to these irreversible changes, Ulster unionists would become an increasingly embattled enclave. With few sympathisers anywhere beyond their own ranks, they could expect little help from outside. History was not on their side. It was such thinking that played a part in persuading Paisley and his DUP that it was far better to accommodate themselves to the situation, while they still had the chance to be part of a power-sharing government, than to continue with a resistance that might ultimately destroy their power altogether. The result was that in May 2006 the UVF renounced violence and pledged itself to give up its weapons. This opened the way for the St Andrews Agreement between the British and Irish governments.

The St Andrews Agreement, October 2006

- The Northern Ireland Assembly was restored.
- The DUP agreed to share power with republicans and nationalists in the Northern Ireland Executive.
- Sinn Féin accepted the authority of the Police Service of Northern Ireland (PSNI), which had replaced the Royal Ulster Constabulary (RUC).

Under the terms of the agreement, elections were held in March 2007. The numbers of seats gained by the main parties were as follows:

- DUP 36
- Sinn Féin 28
- Official Unionists 18
- SDLP 16.

The Northern Ireland Executive 2007

In May 2007, the new executive came into being with Ian Paisley, leader of the largest party, appointed first minister, and Martin McGuinness, leader of Sinn Féin, the second largest, deputy first minister. In July 2007, the British army announced the end of its mission in Northern Ireland, which it had been operating since 1969.

This was an extraordinary climax to nearly 30 years of intensely bitter rivalry, which had cost the lives of thousands. It was a tribute to those on both sides of the Irish Sea, most notably John Major, Bertie Ahern and Tony Blair, who had stayed committed to the peace process, no matter how many times it faltered. Perhaps most extraordinary of all were the amicable relations that developed in government between Paisley and McGuinness. At the end of 2007 McGuinness remarked, 'Up until the 26th of March this year, Ian Paisley and I never had a conversation about anything – not even about the weather – and now we have worked very closely together over the last seven months and there's been no angry words between us. This shows we are set for a new course.'

Summary diagram: Tony Blair and Ireland

Good Friday Agreement, April 1998	St Andrews Agreement, October 2006	Northern Ireland Executive formed, May 2007
• Northern Ireland's union with Britain guaranteed • The Republic of Ireland withdrew its territorial claim to Northern Ireland • Northern Ireland Assembly created	• DUP agreed to share power with republicans and nationalists • Sinn Féin accepted the authority of the Northern Ireland police	• British army withdrawn from Northern Ireland • Power-sharing, all-party executive formed

---

 Tony Blair, the USA and Iraq

▶ *How did 'the special relationship' develop between Tony Blair and George W. Bush?*

The 'war on terror'

On 11 September 2001 the USA was subjected to the deadliest act of terror that it had ever experienced on its own soil. The Islamist terrorist group **al-Qaeda** hijacked four commercial aircraft. Two of the planes were flown into the twin towers of the World Trade Center in New York, causing both to collapse. The third plane was piloted into the Pentagon building housing the US department of defence in Washington, DC, while the fourth crashed near Pittsburgh as the passengers fought with the hijackers. The death toll from the four crashes was over 3000; the victims were from nearly every race on earth. The reaction of the USA was to begin what became known as the 'war on terror'.

Tony Blair immediately committed himself to that war. He announced that Britain 'stood shoulder to shoulder with our American friends' in the struggle 'between the free and democratic world and terrorism'. The events of **9/11** and its aftermath turned him into President George W. Bush's closest and most dependable ally, a relationship that was to shape the remainder of Blair's premiership. A month after 9/11, Blair sent British troops to support the US forces in their attack on al-Qaeda bases in Afghanistan.

The Blair doctrine

The 9/11 attacks intensified Blair's sense of mission, but it did not create it. In a speech given in Chicago in 1999 the British prime minister had expressed what became known as the Blair doctrine. His position was that of a determined anti-appeaser; he believed that the best way to defeat tyranny in the world was not simply by using diplomacy to persuade oppressive regimes to behave better. Of course, diplomacy should be tried first, but, if this did not work, it was legitimate

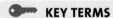 **KEY TERMS**

Al-Qaeda The Islamist terrorist organisation that organised 9/11.

9/11 The US formulation for the date 11 September 2001, typically used to refer to the terrorist attacks.

to use force to oblige aggressor states to conform to internationally agreed standards of conduct.

Tony Blair further believed that international action of the type he proposed should be carried out by those powers which were best fitted by experience and military capability for the task. In the nature of things, this necessarily meant the USA and the UK. The two major allies, therefore, had a special role in international affairs. Whenever possible, they should act with the sanction of the UN, since the UN was the ultimate international authority. But the reality was that there were times when the UN was simply too slow or too hamstrung by procedure to act effectively. Blair also held that NATO was entitled to act as an international peacekeeper. That had been the rationale for Britain's involvement, as part of NATO, in the attacks against Serbia in 1999 (see page 187).

Iraq 2002

It was in keeping with the Blair doctrine that, in September 2002, addressing a specially convened House of Commons, the prime minister set out to explain why it was essential that Saddam Hussein, still leader of Iraq eleven years after being defeated in the Gulf War (see page 188), be brought down. Blair quoted from a dossier (later referred to in the popular press as the 'dodgy dossier') passed to him by the **Joint Intelligence Committee (JIC)**, which claimed to have evidence that 'Saddam's weapons of mass destruction (WMD) programme is active, detailed and growing', and would have the capacity of launching air strikes against Britain within a 45-minute time span. It was this that would provide the justification for invading Iraq. However, at this stage Blair denied that an invasion was inevitable; he said it was the aim of the USA and the UK to work through the UN to bring about regime change in Iraq.

Anxious not to lose support at home, particularly among his own party, Tony Blair was initially insistent that Bush should take no action until the UN had formally resolved to back the Western allies. There had already been a first UN resolution (No. 1441, passed in November 2002) requiring Saddam Hussein to prove to UN inspectors that he had abandoned all his WMD, as he was required to do by the peace settlement that followed the Gulf War in 1991. Resolution 1441, however, did not authorise the armed invasion of Iraq; to achieve this there would have to be a second UN resolution.

The possibility of gaining a second UN resolution disappeared rapidly as Russia and China made it clear that they would block any attempt to push this through the Security Council. Bush, dismissing the opposition of those two countries as political rather than principled, decided to go ahead with the invasion plan. At a third key meeting between president and prime minister, Bush, aware of the difficulty Blair would have in convincing his Cabinet and party, offered the prime minister the chance to withdraw. But Blair, describing the fight against tyranny as 'the most fundamental issue of our time', declined to back out. He tried to gain support from Europe but failed; France and Germany found the

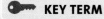

KEY TERM

Joint Intelligence Committee (JIC)
The government body principally responsible for providing ministers with national security information.

grounds for military intervention unconvincing. If Britain and the USA went ahead, they would be acting alone.

Anglo-American invasion of Iraq 2003

On 20 March 2003, US and British forces began the invasion of Iraq without formal UN sanction and, in Britain's case, in the face of fierce opposition at home. Mass anti-war demonstrations were held in London and other cities, and Robin Cook, the former foreign secretary, resigned from the Cabinet in protest at the invasion, declaring in his Commons' resignation speech that the war had 'neither international agreement nor domestic support'.

SOURCE C

Foreign secretary Robin Cook explains in his resignation speech in the Commons, 17 March 2003, why he cannot support Britain's invasion of Iraq, http://www.parliament.the-stationery-office.co.uk/pa/cm200203/cmhansrd/vo030317/debtext/30317.

On Iraq, I believe that the prevailing mood of the British people is sound. They do not doubt that Saddam is a brutal dictator, but they are not persuaded that he is a clear and present danger to Britain. They want inspections to be given a chance, and they suspect that they are being pushed too quickly into conflict by a US Administration with an agenda of its own. Above all, they are uneasy at Britain going out on a limb on a military adventure without a broader international coalition and against the hostility of many of our traditional allies.

From the start of the present crisis, I have insisted, as Leader of the House, on the right of this place to vote on whether Britain should go to war. It has been a favourite theme of commentators that this House no longer occupies a central role in British politics. Nothing could better demonstrate that they are wrong than for this House to stop the commitment of troops in a war that has neither international agreement nor domestic support. I intend to join those tomorrow night who will vote against military action now. It is for that reason, and for that reason alone, and with a heavy heart, that I resign from the Government.

> In Source C, what does Robin Cook give as his reasons for resignation?

Blair and Bush

The charge was made at the time, and has often been repeated since, that Blair was Bush's 'poodle', that he allowed himself to be dragged into the war. But this overlooks the driving sense of conviction and mission that inspired Tony Blair. His judgement may be faulted but it should not be denied that throughout he was his own man. Indeed, George Galloway, the rebel Labour MP who resigned to set up his own anti-war party, **Respect**, believed that the prime minister was the initiator rather than the follower in his relations with the president.

The military operation in Iraq was swift and successful. By the middle of April 2003 Saddam's forces were broken and the allies declared that the 'major

⚷ KEY TERM

Respect Founded in 2004 as a socialist breakaway group from the Labour Party, its initials represented the words Respect, Equality, Socialism, Peace, Environmentalism, Community and Trade Unionism.

combat' was over. It was then that the problems really started. In the rush to war, insufficient time had been devoted to planning what would follow victory. The toppling of Saddam Hussein may have removed a vicious oppressor but it did not lead to peace. Indeed, it could be said that civil war followed, with rival Muslim and regional factions fighting each other. The final capture of the fugitive Saddam Hussein in December 2003 brought rejoicing among Iraqis who had been victims of his regime but it did nothing to end the internal strife. The victorious allied forces which had been intended to liberate Iraq became its occupiers.

On 31 January 2006 in one of the saddest coincidences of the war in Iraq, the hundredth British serviceman to be killed was Corporal Gordon Prichard, who a month earlier had been photographed smiling with Tony Blair during one of the prime minister's visits to the troops. Eighteen months later when Blair stood down as prime minister, US and British forces were still in Iraq with no prospect of their leaving.

The WMD issue

The political problems that the war created for Blair were intensified by the failure to discover any evidence of WMD in Iraq. The suicide in July 2003 of Dr David Kelly, a weapons expert working for the government's defence ministry, deepened the gloom and stimulated the furore relating to the Iraq affair. Two months before his death, Kelly had confided to a BBC journalist his concern that the government had exaggerated the findings in the JIC dossier on which Blair had based his reasons for going to war. The journalist, Andrew Gilligan, then went public on radio and in the press, accusing the government of having 'sexed up' the report largely at the promptings of Alistair Campbell, the prime minister's chief spin doctor. It was after being revealed as Gilligan's source that Dr Kelly had taken his own life.

The government immediately set up an inquiry, which, under the chairmanship of Lord Hutton, examined the circumstances of David Kelly's death. Among the 70 witnesses were Alistair Campbell and the prime minister himself.

SOURCE D

? In Source D, on what grounds does Tony Blair defend his use of the September dossier?

Tony Blair testifies before the Hutton Inquiry, 28 August 2003. Here he answers a question concerning how much reliance he put on the JIC dossier in the build-up to the invasion of Iraq, quoted in David Aaronovitch _et al._, editors, _The Hutton Inquiry_, Guardian Books, 2004, pp. 177–8.

I think that we described the intelligence in a way that was perfectly justified and I would simply make this point. Although obviously people look back now on the September dossier in a quite different way, if I make these two points: the first is that the dossier, at the time, was not received as being particularly incautious in tone. On the contrary, a lot of people said that it was done in a fairly prosaic way. So the commentary at the time was not actually that it *seemed to be, you know, advancing the case in an adventurous way, if I can put it like that, at all. The commentary was rather to the opposite effect.*

Secondly, the 45-minute claim, I mention it in my statement. I think after then I do not think I mention it again in Parliament. And I think there is a sense in which it is important to recognise that the September dossier was not making the case for war, it was making the case for the issue to be dealt with and our preferred alternative was indeed to deal with it through the United Nations route.

When the inquiry published its findings in January 2004, it cleared the government of any direct involvement in Kelly's death. But what the Hutton report did not, and could not, do was lift the thickening cloud of doubt about the legality and morality of the Blair government's original decision to go to war.

SOURCE E

The summing up by Lord Hutton, who led the inquiry (held August to October 2003) into the circumstances of the suicide in July 2003 of Dr David Kelly, a weapons expert working for the defence ministry. Dr Kelly had apparently become depressed by the JIC dossier presented to the government, which he felt exaggerated his findings regarding Saddam Hussein's weapons programme. From Lord Hutton, *Report of the Inquiry into the Circumstances Surrounding the Death of Dr David Kelly C.M.G.*, The Stationery Office, 2004, pp. 320–1.

Why, in Source E, does Lord Hutton regard the term 'sexed-up' as an inappropriate description of the JIC dossier?

As the dossier was one to be presented to, and read by, Parliament and the public, and was not an intelligence assessment to be considered only by the Government, I do not consider that it was improper for … the JIC to take into account suggestions as to drafting made by 10 Downing Street and to adopt those suggestions if they were consistent with the intelligence available to the JIC. However I consider that the possibility cannot be completely ruled out that the desire of the Prime Minister to have a dossier which, whilst consistent with the available intelligence, was as strong as possible in relation to the threat posed by Saddam Hussein's WMD, may have subconsciously influenced Mr Scarlett [chair of the JIC] and the other members of the JIC to make the wording of the dossier somewhat stronger than it would have been if it had been contained in a normal JIC assessment. Although this possibility cannot be completely ruled out, I am satisfied that Mr Scarlett, the other members of the JIC, and the members of the assessment staff engaged in the drafting of the dossier were concerned to ensure that the contents of the dossier were consistent with the intelligence available to the JIC.

The term 'sexed-up' is a slang expression, the meaning of which lacks clarity in the context of the discussion of the dossier … However in the context of the broadcasts in which the 'sexing-up' allegation was reported and having regard to the other allegations reported in those broadcasts, I consider that the allegation was unfounded.

The London bombings, July 2005

On 7 July 2005, the reality of the war on terror was brought home to Britain when three co-ordinated bomb explosions in London killed 56 people and injured another 700. The dead included the suicide bombers, all of them young British Islamists. Two weeks later, a similar bomb plot was foiled at the last minute when police arrested the intended assassins, who, again, were all Islamist extremists. Muslim leaders were quick to condemn the assassins and plotters and to distance their faith from the perversion of Islam that the killers represented.

Some critics saw the bombings as a direct consequence of the Iraq War and the foreign policies of Bush and Blair. It was argued that:

- The removal of Saddam Hussein was not enough to justify the war. Britain and the USA had invaded Iraq for wholly inadequate reasons. Rather than being a war on terror, the Anglo-American action had encouraged its spread. The West had lost the moral high ground.
- By declaring a 'war on terror' and selecting particular targets to attack, as with Afghanistan and Iraq, the two leaders had in fact created or encouraged the very forces of terrorism that they were trying to defeat.
- The Anglo-American hostility to Islam which the war revealed led to retaliation by Islamist extremists who became **jihadists** in order to defend their faith against the 'corrupt Satanic' West.

KEY TERM

Jihadists Self-proclaimed warriors in the defence of their version of Islam.

The counter-response to such arguments by those sympathetic to the Bush–Blair alliance was to point to the facts that:

- Jihadist terrorism, as in the case of 9/11, pre-dated the Iraq War.
- The Anglo-American military campaigns fought since the 1990s had been undertaken largely to protect Muslim people and interests, for example in Kuwait in 1991, Bosnia in 1995 and Kosovo in 1999.
- Even though Iraq had not developed WMD, its leader, Saddam Hussein, had had the intention and means of doing so. Had he not been brought down by the Anglo-American invasion in 2003, the world at some point might well have had to deal with a nuclear-armed Iraq.

Yet, whatever the arguments for and against Blair's actions and policies towards Iraq and the 'war on terror', there is little doubt that they conditioned the character of his government after 2003. Notwithstanding his achievements on the domestic front, it was his foreign policy that defined his years in office.

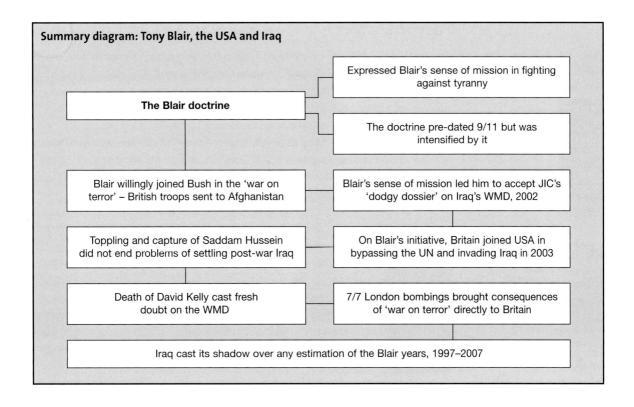

Summary diagram: Tony Blair, the USA and Iraq

7 Population change and social issues

▶ What impact had population change had on Britain between 1951 and 2007?

▶ What social issues confronted Britain by the early twenty-first century?

A dominant social feature of Britain in the first decade of the twenty-first century was the size and age distribution of its population.

Table 6.4 Population of Britain in 2006 (to the nearest 100)

Region	Population	Percentage of UK total
England	50,762,900	83.8%
Scotland	5,116,900	8.4%
Wales	2,965,900	4.9%
Northern Ireland	1,741,600	2.9%
Total	60,587,300	100%

Population change

Table 6.5 Total UK population 1951–2006 (to the nearest 1000)

1951	50,225,000
1961	52,709,000
1971	55,515,000
1981	56,337,000
1991	57,808,000
2001	58,789,000
2006	60,587,000

 **KEY TERM**

Life expectancy
The remaining number of years an individual is likely to live after a given age.

The total of 60.5 million (see Table 6.5) marked a growth in population of around 5 million since 1971 and towards 2 million since 2001. More significant than the simple aggregate increase was the rise in the average age of the population, going up from 34 in 1971 to 39 in 2006. Five years may not seem a large difference but it pointed to an important trend; Britain had a rapidly ageing population. The number of young people aged under 16 was shrinking in proportion to those aged over 65. By 2006, 10 million people, one-sixth of the population, were over 65, while a million were over 85. This was a result of the increase in **life expectancy** over the previous century, as depicted in Table 6.6.

Table 6.6 Life expectancy for males (M) and females (F) 1901–2001

	1901		1931		1961		2001	
	M	F	M	F	M	F	M	F
At birth	45.5	49.0	58.4	62.5	67.9	73.8	74.5	79.9
At age 1	53.6	55.8	62.1	65.1	68.6	74.2	74.0	79.3
At age 10	50.4	52.7	55.6	58.6	60.0	65.6	65.2	70.5
At age 20	41.7	44.1	46.7	49.6	50.4	55.7	55.4	60.6
At age 40	26.1	28.3	29.5	32.4	31.5	36.5	36.2	41.0
At age 60	13.3	14.6	14.4	16.4	15.0	19.0	18.7	22.7
At age 80	4.9	5.3	4.9	5.4	5.2	6.3	7.0	8.8

The social impact of the population shift

One result of the population changes illustrated above was that there were twice as many senior citizens in 2006 as there had been 50 years earlier. This tendency has been referred to as the 'demographic time-bomb'. The problem that this dramatic expression describes had the following components:

- Welfare services are funded by revenue raised in taxation from those in work.
- As the older, retired section of the population grew in number it made increasing demands on those services, for which it no longer helped to pay.
- The amount people paid in taxes and National Insurance while they were working seemed high at the time, but because of inflation and the ever-rising costs of medical technology, the original payments were inadequate to pay for welfare needs after retirement.
- It followed that to sustain welfare services at the expected level, the working population, which was in relative decline in numbers, would have to pay an ever-increasing burden in taxation.

The result of the growth and shift in the population was that the state had the increasingly difficult task of meeting ever-growing demands from ever-diminishing resources. How serious the trend was can be judged from Figure 6.2, which shows the projected rise in the population by 2050.

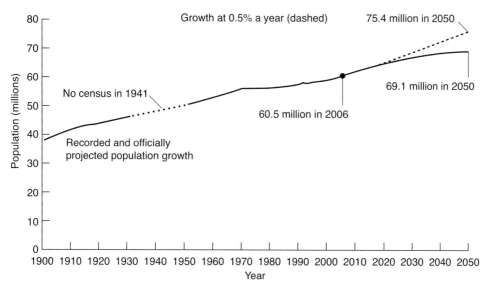

Figure 6.2 British population growth 1900–2006, with projections to 2050.

Immigration

The increase in population is not only a result of greater longevity; immigration is also a contributory factor. Figure 6.3 shows both the **natural change** that occurred and the impact of **net migration** in the years 1991–2006, which accounted for an increase of some 3 million in that period.

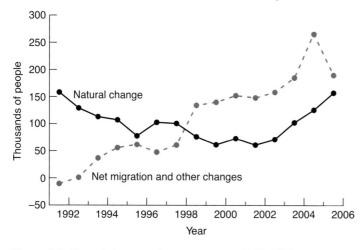

Figure 6.3 Natural change and net immigration 1991–2006.

Immigration had been a factor in population growth throughout the twentieth century. Significant numbers of people from the West Indies and India had arrived in the 1950s and 1960s, in response to the government's appeal for workers in the public services (see page 41). Another important contingent were the ethnic Asians who came to Britain in the 1960s and 1970s after being driven

KEY TERMS

Natural change The net difference between the number of deaths and the number of births.

Net migration The net difference between emigration, the number who left Britain, and immigration, the number who entered it.

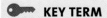

Census An official recording of population figures, held every ten years in the first year of the decade.

from where they had settled in such African countries as Kenya and Uganda. The **census** of 2001 revealed the following details:

- Indians were the largest single ethnic minority group in Britain, with 984,000 people.
- People of Caribbean or African descent numbered 969,000.
- Pakistanis and Bangladeshis numbered 932,000.
- Ethnic minority groups represented just over seven per cent, much less than one in ten, of Britain's population.
- The 2001 census was the first time that religious affiliation had been measured. One of the findings was that there were 1.6 million Muslims in Britain, making them the largest British non-Christian faith group.

Overall numbers were not the only pertinent factor. Where there was opposition in the host nation to the presence of immigrants it was not usually in regard to aggregate numbers, but to their concentration in particular urban areas where there were poor or limited resources (see page 41). As to the role that recent immigrants played in the life of the country, there were two main and opposed views:

- One argument was that immigrants played a vital role in the economy by taking unpleasant, but essential, low-paid jobs that the indigenous workers would not consider. By working and paying taxes they contributed to the nation's revenue and gave an object lesson in hard work and responsibility.
- A counter-argument was that while the first point about filling vacant positions was true, it was only a stop-gap measure since once immigrants became settled they began to demand the better wages and conditions enjoyed by host workers. As to taxation, since immigrant workers mainly had low-paid jobs the revenue they contributed was smaller than the added costs of providing them and their families with health, welfare and educational services.

Multiculturalism

The big social question that Britain faced in the early twenty-first century was no longer about race. The argument for racial equality was accepted by all responsible people. No one but a bigot could claim that one race was superior to another and that people's worth and rights were to be determined by the ethnic group to which they belonged. The issue that remained to be resolved was not a racial but a cultural one. Were all cultures to be regarded as morally equivalent? Was there such an identifiable concept as British culture? If there was, what were its main features? And if, for example, these included freedom of speech, religious tolerance, and race and gender equality, how were other cultures to be treated that did not accept or practise these values? Could a liberal society accept, for example, female genital mutilation, a practice to be found among some groups in Britain?

Riots in 2001 in Bradford, Manchester and Oldham in which black, white and Asian groups clashed were a disturbing sign that integration had not taken place in the more deprived urban areas. Significantly, Trevor Phillips, the Chairman of the **EHRC**, acknowledged that the multicultural policies which successive governments had followed had largely failed and that integration was not taking place in the way that had been hoped.

In 2005, Phillips expressed fears that multiculturalism could cause Britain to 'sleepwalk towards segregation' and argued that a key way of preventing segregation hardening was not to allow it in British education in the form of exclusive faith schools. He had in mind particularly the exclusively Muslim schools where children were trained in an Islamic way of life. Not unnaturally, the supporters of the madrassas responded by pointing out that:

- Catholic and Jewish faith schools had long been established in Britain.
- The teaching of Islamic values was wholly compatible with preparing young Muslims to become responsible British citizens.

Phillips' comments aroused anger on the left. Ken Livingstone, the Labour mayor of London, attacked him for giving currency to racist ideas by 'pandering to the right'. Phillips replied by saying it was essential 'to ask hard questions about multicultural Britain', adding in a memorable phrase that the basis of free speech was the right 'to allow people to offend each other'. Interestingly, Phillips was supported in principle by two prominent Christian clerics, Michael Nazir-Ali, the Pakistani-born Bishop of Rochester, and John Sentamu, the Ugandan-born Archbishop of York, both of whom expressed strong doubts about multiculturalism, arguing that, whatever its intentions, in practice it had created social division, not social harmony.

Religious Hatred Act 2006

That people of such obvious goodwill and informed experience were so concerned over the effect of multiculturalism indicates that it had become one of the most demanding and contentious of issues. The New Labour government's awareness of this and its desire to set the right example led it in 2006 to introduce a Religious Hatred Act, intended to protect people from being abused and attacked for their religious beliefs. What had pushed the government into introducing it had been the wish to calm the tensions created by two events which had illustrated in a dramatic and tragic form that, far from being integrated into society, there were religious groups in Britain who felt deeply alienated from the mainstream culture.

The first was the London bombings of July 2005 (see page 216). The second was the violent reaction to cartoons in a Danish newspaper. In 2005 the paper had published of a set of satirical cartoons which, according to many Muslims, insulted the prophet Mohammed, the founder of the Islamic faith. In London, in February 2006, some 300 Muslims demonstrated against their publication in the previous year. Four of the demonstrators were arrested and subsequently

KEY TERM

EHRC The Equality and Human Rights Commission, successor to the Commission for Racial Equality.

tried and imprisoned for incitement to violence and murder. One of the convicted four had whipped up the crowd by leading a repeated chant, 'Bomb, bomb the UK'. Disturbingly, the four convicted demonstrators, like the July suicide bombers, had all been brought up in the UK.

The Religious Hatred Bill met stiff criticism from both believers and non-believers, who suggested that religious hatred was too imprecise an attitude to legislate against and that existing laws against incitement already gave adequate protection. In the end, the Act went through in a watered-down form and added little to existing laws on incitement.

Extra-parliamentary movements

An important development that began in the final quarter of the twentieth century was the growth of **extra-parliamentary** groups and campaigns which sought to achieve their ends by direct action rather than through party politics.

Environmentalism

The environmentalist movement was an attempt to preserve the world from the harmful effects of uncontrolled economic growth. Through the work and propaganda of such movements as **Friends of the Earth**, founded in 1969, and **Greenpeace**, founded in 1971, the attention of the public was drawn to a range of ecological issues. But environmentalism also aroused contrary ideas. Doubters emerged who challenged the basic environmentalist premise that

KEY TERMS

Extra-parliamentary
Not relying on conventional party politics.

Friends of the Earth and **Greenpeace** Similar movements which originated in the USA but quickly spread to Europe. They believed in direct action as a way of spreading their ideas about the threat to the planet.

? How might the depiction in Source F have helped stimulate the environmental movement?

SOURCE F

'So it wasn't the H-Bomb that finished off the earth people, after all!'
A newspaper cartoon from November 1969 drawing attention to the pollution that followed from a number of accidents in which damaged tankers had leaked their cargo of oil; the most disturbing case for Britain had occurred two years earlier when the tanker *Torrey Canyon* hit a reef off the coast of Cornwall and discharged over 100,000 tonnes of crude oil into the sea, resulting in over 100 miles of Cornish coastline being seriously polluted.

global economic trends were leading the world to disaster. The arguments and counter-arguments were particularly fierce over the issue of climate change (see box below).

These opposing schools of thought often argued their case with fervour. A difficulty was that since they were concerned with what may or may not happen in the future, neither side could deal solely in facts. Both viewpoints were based on projection, conjecture and differing scientific analyses; they were foretelling the future, a hazardous venture in any context. Yet it is notable that the environmental lobby, though relatively small in the number of its adherents, had a large measure of success in persuading Western governments into going 'green'. All the major British parties accepted that climate change constituted a danger that had to be tackled by sustained government action. Much of the legislation in regard to environmental issues was influenced by green

The environmentalists' case

- The emission of greenhouse gases, caused by the burning of fossil fuels, was raising the earth's temperature.
- Ice caps and glaciers were melting, sea levels were rising and rivers were drying up.
- Rising temperatures were destroying animal and plant species, thus threatening the whole ecosystem.
- If this trend went unchecked, animal and human life would become unsustainable.
- Measurements of carbon dioxide (CO_2) emissions showed that it was the advanced industrial economies, chiefly those in the Western world, which were the main culprits in the polluting of the atmosphere.

- Unless the West changed its economic ways and put sustainability before economic growth there was no future for the planet and its inhabitants.
- National governments individually and nations collectively had to impose binding restraints on industrial production.
- These conclusions were based on the findings of the UN's Intergovernmental Panel on Climate Change (IPCC).
- The IPCC drew its information from the findings of scientific researchers, the great majority of whom accepted the forecasts of the environmentalists.

The deniers' case

- The notion of warming is based in selective measurements. In reality, the earth has warmed less than 1°C degree overall in the past 100 years.
- Human-produced CO_2 has played only a minor role in this. CO_2 is an effect of warming, not a cause.
- In the Antarctic, which holds 90 per cent of the world's glaciers, ice mass has grown, reversing a 6000-year melting trend. World sea levels have risen less than 1 inch.
- The sun is the main determinant of whether the earth cools or heats. Solar heat is not a constant.

- In any case, an increase in temperature would have more beneficial effects than harmful, for example, lower death rates from hypothermia, greater food production.
- The IPCC is not a neutral scientific body but a pressure group which rejects any research that challenges its fixed position. Its projections are computer based and are programmed to produce the desired results.
- Environmentalism is a front for left-wing anti-capitalists and will damage not only the West but developing countries which will be denied the industrial growth they needed.

Green Party In 1985 a number of environmental groups came together as the Green Party. Although it would not have its first elected MP until 2010, the party proved highly active and successful in pressing its arguments on Parliament and the general public.

Landfill Directive A measure for standardising the practice in the EU countries in regard to the disposal of waste in landfill sites, the main purpose being to limit the emissions of methane, a greenhouse gas. A related measure which affected all premises in Britain from 2003 onwards was the EU requirement that household waste be collected in a regulated way so that appropriate materials could be recycled.

British National Party An anti-immigration party.

Countryside Alliance An amalgam of landowners, land workers, vets, riding schools and those involved in the commercial side of fox hunting.

KEY FIGURE

Richard Dawkins (1941–) Oxford 'Professor of the Public Understanding of Science' and media celebrity, who for decades had been developing powerful intellectual arguments to undermine traditional religious beliefs.

arguments, a tribute to the work of the **Green Party**. The directives issued by the EU testified to the impact environmentalism had had on it. An example of this was its **Landfill Directive** of 1990, which Britain implemented.

Authoritarianism

The growth of a new form of non-parliamentary politics may also be seen as a reaction against the permissiveness that had come in since the 1960s (see page 107). But it was never as clear-cut as that. Some of those who had been the strongest advocates of the abolition of censorship, for example, were among the foremost in demanding that restrictions be placed on activities to which they objected, such as smoking and hunting. In the political field, few liberals were happy with the thought of extremist groups like the **British National Party** being allowed to operate unfettered. It is a dilemma that has always troubled the liberal conscience; how to reconcile freedom and conviction. It tested the limits of how far liberals would allow others to go in expressing ideas of which they disapproved.

There is also a case for interpreting the spread of environmentalism and related movements as being an aspect of the decline of organised religion in Britain in the second half of the twentieth century. There was certainly a growth in secularism and religious scepticism. One of the most powerful expressions of this was the publication in 2006 of *The God Delusion* by **Richard Dawkins**. Figures for all the major Western faiths and denominations showed a fall in formal worshippers, a trend which was slowed but not reversed by the coming of religiously minded immigrant groups, such as Polish Catholics and Pakistani Muslims. As the number of church attenders decreased there was an inclination for many people to turn to modern causes to fill the gap. For example, it may not be entirely accidental that the fervour with which environmentalists hold their views is reminiscent of the passion of some religious believers.

The Countryside Alliance

An interesting extra-parliamentary group that appeared on the right rather than the left of politics was the **Countryside Alliance**. Angered by the Labour government's declared intention to outlaw fox hunting with hounds, the Alliance resolved to resist. It argued that New Labour was an urban party that had no understanding of the true nature of the land or of the people who worked on it; hence its willingness to ban hunting without thinking through the harmful effects this would have on the livelihoods of those who depended on it. At a demonstration in London in September 2002, the Alliance was able to amass 400,000 supporters. This was nearly half the number of those who in February 2003 protested against the war in Iraq (see page 213). Tony Blair thus had the odd distinction of presiding over the two largest anti-government protests in British history. Nevertheless, the Alliance failed. In September 2004 the government pushed its ban on fox hunting through the Commons and it became law two years later.

Focus groups

The government's ignoring of the massive protests against the Iraq War and the outlawing of hunting suggested that popular direct democracy had little effect if it contradicted government planning. Much more influence was exerted by focus groups and lobbies. These were representatives of a particular viewpoint who advised government on policy decisions. Such groups often represented only themselves rather than the wider public.

Scepticism about traditional politics

A further possible explanation for the spread of extra-parliamentary activity was the loss of faith in traditional politics, which by the end of the twentieth century could be regarded as having become stale and self-satisfied. Peter Hennessy, a distinguished political analyst, spoke in 2001 of the cult of 'celebocracy' affecting politics as much as popular culture. This referred to a lack of substance in the new generations of MPs who had made politics a career but had no experience of life and work. Many now went straight from university into politics without ever having done a proper job. Largely gone were the days of workers and trade unionists with their real knowledge of the world of work or of business people who had run successful enterprises, providing employment in the process.

A further factor was that, with the growth of central government power, Parliament had declined in influence. Decisions were made by the government. That is why MPs were anxious to obtain government posts. Opinion polls suggested that at the end of Tony Blair's term in office, MPs were not held in high esteem by the general public. One reason is that they were seen to be earning easy money; MPs' salaries were well above the national average, with many perks in the form of generous expenses and secure pension rights. A more telling reason, however, for their unpopularity is that they were not regarded as being particularly useful. MPs had become lobby fodder, casting their votes as dictated by their parties.

Yet the system had its defenders. It was arguable that 'lobby fodder' was exactly what was wanted. Since the parties represented broad blocks of public opinion, it was appropriate that MPs elected on a party label should see it as their primary duty to vote in accordance with their party's wishes. That was the form that modern democracy had taken. Politics does not stand still, so there was little point bemoaning the passing of a system that was only ever transitory.

Education

In 1997 Tony Blair had declared that his priority in government would be 'Education, Education, Education'. In keeping with this, there was a stream of measures during his ten-year administration. Among the main educational changes and schemes introduced were the following.

Schools

- Special attention given to failing schools.
- Reduction of class sizes.
- Under an 'Excellence in Cities' plan, special funding was provided to raise standards in underachieving schools in deprived areas.
- The assisted places scheme introduced by the Conservatives in 1980, under which children whose families could not afford to send them to fee-paying schools were provided with free places, was withdrawn. Pupils currently in the scheme would continue to be financed until they had finished their schooling. The money saved was redirected to reducing class sizes in state schools.
- Labour restated its conviction that comprehensive schools were the socially fairest form of secondary education but accepted that streaming, the grouping of pupils by ability within certain subjects, was acceptable. In fact, although this was never openly declared, the comprehensive school system underwent a transformation under Blair. In 2000, under the Learning and Skills Act, plans were laid for turning the majority of state secondary schools into 'academies', whose main purpose was 'to improve pupil performance and break the cycle of low expectations'. The academies would be funded through both local authority grants and private and commercial sponsorship.
- 1000 new schools had been opened during Blair's ten years as prime minister.
- Between 1997 and 2007, the Labour governments raised the amount spent on education to 5.6 per cent of GDP, which put the UK on a level with most of the other advanced Western economies.
- By 2007, the number of qualified teachers in state schools had risen by 35,000. This was supplemented by an increase in the number of ancillary workers, such as teaching assistants, to 170,000.

Higher education

- Tony Blair had expressed a hope that in time, half of Britain's school leavers would go on to university. This has yet to be achieved but as a preliminary step towards this, former polytechnics and higher education colleges became universities.
- Tuition fees were introduced in 1998. The average annual fee in 2006 was £3000.
- By 2004, the number of university students stood at 2.4 million, more than double the figure for 1990.
- The number of women in higher education in 2006 was twice the number for 1995 and seven times greater than in 1970.
- As in schools, league tables of performance were introduced into universities as a way of determining how much central funding each of them was to receive. It was an interesting extension of the Thatcherite requirement that institutions receiving public money should be accountable.

- In 2001 the government began to give financial support to the University of the Third Age (U3A), an independent body providing learning opportunities for people over retirement age.

New Labour's achievements in education make impressive reading, but it was not a story of unqualified success. While it was true that more money had been devoted to education and that exam results improved each year, there was still an underlying feeling that the education system had largely failed in its social objective of providing equal educational opportunity for all, the reason being that the quality of a school or academy was largely determined by the quality of the area in which it was located. The poorest schools educationally were invariably to be found in the most socially deprived areas. Social historians and commentators such as Arthur Marwick and Katherine Watson also pointed to an anomaly in higher education; only three per cent of the growing number of university places were filled by students from disadvantaged sections of society. University expansion predominantly benefited the middle classes.

The government did not always help its own cause of ending privilege in education. Some of the leading figures in the Labour Party were either products of private schools or sent their children to them. Other Labour MPs used their high incomes to move homes so as to be able to send their children to a reputable school. The complaint, here, was not that it was wrong for them to do so – it was natural for parents to wish to do the best for their children – but that it was improper for them to follow educational policies that denied the same right to others.

Corruption

The people's confidence in their leaders is invariably diminished when they fall short of the expected standards of integrity. Labour in opposition had been quick to taunt and condemn the Major government when it became mired in accusations of sleaze (see page 175). But this came back to haunt Labour. The difficulty for any party adopting a moral stance is that it is likely to be let down by its own members. Human nature means that scandal and impropriety are always just around the corner. Labour in opposition had justifiably attacked the follies and scandals of the Conservatives (see page 176). However, in office, it was to find that it was just as open to the charge of impropriety. Sleaze was matched by the **cash for honours** scandal.

It was not simply a matter of some behaving illegally. MPs generally seemed willing to take advantage of their access to privilege. In 2006 there was a sense of public dismay at Parliament's voting itself copper-bottomed pensions at a time when ordinary pensioners were seeing a sharp decline in the value of their contributions. Official figures also revealed that in 2007, £337,000 of public money had been claimed by MPs in travelling expenses.

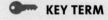 **KEY TERM**

Cash for honours There were various accusations during the Blair years that government figures were engaged in giving out honours in return for cash donations to the Labour Party. A police inquiry eventually concluded in 2007 that there was insufficient evidence to warrant prosecutions.

The Conservatives during the Blair years

It could not be said that the opposition distinguished itself during the Blair years. After a series of leaders, William Hague, Iain Duncan Smith and Michael Howard, had failed to grab the attention of the country or the full support of party members, the Conservatives elected David Cameron as their leader in 2005. He made it his task to become more Blairite than Blair. His main line of approach was to offer more of the same. No new policies emerged; on health, welfare, European integration, education and the economy, Cameron promised to do the same as Labour only better. It many ways it was a striking echo of the way New Labour had transformed itself by becoming more Thatcherite. Just as Labour's left had complained that, by shifting its ground to the centre, New Labour had deprived the party of its socialist credentials, the Conservative right complained that Cameron was depriving the party of its distinctive Tory character.

Britain's international position in 2007

In 2007 Britain remained a major international power. The following list provides the justifications for this claim:

- Britain was one of a small group of nations with the resources to use nuclear power for domestic and military purposes.
- Britain's retention of its independent sterling currency enabled it to avoid the crises that periodically afflicted the eurozone.
- The City of London was one of the world's major finance and commercial exchange centres. The flow of international money through the City and the sale of financial services helped to keep the UK solvent.
- Despite decolonisation, Britain, because of its imperial past, had a knowledge and experience of other countries that could be highly valuable when called on to play a peacekeeping role.
- Largely because of the Queen's position as head of the Commonwealth since the beginning of her reign in 1952, Britain retained an influential role in Commonwealth affairs.
- Although in many respects a reluctant participant, Britain remained a member of the EU. Tony Blair regarded himself as a good European and proudly claimed Britain's closer ties with Europe as one of his legacies.
- As a member of the G8 (with Canada, France, Germany, Italy, Japan, Russia and the USA), Britain ranked as one of the world's major industrial powers, capable of influencing international economic decisions.
- Following the return of Hong Kong to the PRC in 1997, in keeping with the joint declaration negotiated by the Thatcher government in 1984, Britain had developed close commercial and financial links with China.
- The UK devoted two per cent of its GDP to foreign aid.

Britain's membership of international peacekeeping organisations was made more significant by the fact of its military capacity:

- It was Britain's military prowess and reputation that made it a leading member of NATO.
- As a permanent member of the UN Security Council, Britain was a major player in international peacekeeping affairs.
- Notwithstanding the controversy over its legitimacy, the UK's participation in the wars in the Gulf, Afghanistan and Iraq indicated that Britain's armed services were still a formidable military force among the Western powers.
- As Blair's joining George W. Bush in the war on terror had shown, Britain continued to regard its special relationship with the USA as a vital necessity.

Summary diagram: Population change and social issues

Phenomenon:
- Increase in size and distribution of British population through natural increase and immigration

Problem:
- Ageing population made increasing demands on diminishing revenue sources

Phenomenon:
- Multiculturalism

Problems:
- Segregation
- Racism
- Religious tensions and extremism
- Challenges to liberal values from some groups

In 2007 Britain remained a major diplomatic and military power in the world

Phenomena:
- Growth in extra-parliamentary politics
- Environmentalists and deniers
- Extremist groups
- Focus groups

Problems:
- Pressure from unrepresentative lobbies created a democratic deficit
- Authoritarianism

Phenomena:
- Decline in social values
- Decline in traditional religion
- Scepticism about traditional politics
- Parliament tainted by corruption

Problems:
- A disordered society?
- Dispute over education
- Maintenance of privilege
- Low standards in public life
- Parliamentarians out of touch with people

Chapter summary

New Labour's handling of the economy in its early years proved impressive. Chancellor Gordon Brown's policies saw inflation and unemployment fall. However, job creation was largely in the unproductive public sector and after three years Brown relaxed his prudent approach and allowed a period of high government spending and borrowing to set in. A consumer boom increased the government's popularity, as reflected in comfortable Labour victories in the 2001 and 2005 elections. However, by 2007 the signs of an economic recession had begun to appear.

Blair followed a co-operative 'third way' towards Europe, but his efforts to do a deal over CAP were unproductive; he lost Britain's budget rebate without gaining the reform of CAP. It was largely at Brown's insistence that Britain declined to adopt the euro. Blair was far more successful over Ireland, where he played a key diplomatic role in bringing the sides together in the power-sharing Northern Ireland Executive in 2007. However, his reputation as a statesman sank when his partnership with US President Bush in their 'war on terror' led to an Anglo-American invasion of Iraq, a move that aroused opposition at home and abroad. The chapter concludes with a survey of the social features of Britain as they had developed by Blair's time.

Refresher questions

Use these questions to remind yourself of the key material covered in this chapter.

1 How prudent was Gordon Brown as chancellor of the exchequer?

2 Why did the Labour Party win the elections of 2001 and 2005?

3 What was Tony Blair's attitude towards the EU?

4 Why was Tony Blair unable to achieve the reform of CAP?

5 Why did Blair's policy towards Northern Ireland prove so successful?

6 Why did Tony Blair and George W. Bush share a common outlook in the 'war of terror'?

7 What was the 'Blair doctrine' in foreign affairs?

8 How big a factor was the supposed existence of WMD in Iraq in Blair's decision to invade Iraq in 2003?

9 What problems have the growth and changing composition of the population created in Britain?

10 Why did multiculturalism become such a disputed issue?

11 Why was there a significant turning to non-parliamentary ways to achieve political ends?

12 Why had the Blair government become tainted by suggestions of corruption by 2007?

13 What reforms and advances in education were achieved by Tony Blair's government?

14 What was the UK's international standing and status in 2007?

Question practice

ESSAY QUESTIONS

1 'Gordon Brown's greatest mistake as chancellor of the exchequer was to abandon prudence in favour of spending.' Assess the validity of this view.

2 To what extent did Tony Blair in office follow essentially Thatcherite policies?

3 'The creation of the Northern Ireland Executive was Tony Blair's outstanding achievement as prime minister.' Assess the validity of this view.

4 How far was the UK's invasion of Iraq in 2003 'a gross misjudgement' on Tony Blair's part?

SOURCE ANALYSIS QUESTION

1 With reference to Sources C (page 213), D (page 214) and E (page 215), and your understanding of the historical context, assess the value of these sources to a historian studying the issues relating to Britain's invasion of Iraq in 2003.

AQA A level History

Essay guidance

At both AS and A level for AQA Component 2: Depth Study: Britain 1951–2007, you will need to answer an essay question in the exam. Each essay question is marked out of 25:

- for the AS exam, Section B: answer **one** essay question from a choice of two
- for the A level exam, Section B: answer **two** essay questions from a choice of three.

There are several question stems which all have the same basic requirement: to analyse and reach a conclusion, based on the evidence you provide.

The AS questions often give a quotation and then ask whether you agree or disagree with this view. Almost inevitably, your answer will be a mixture of both. It is the same task as for A level – just phrased differently in the question. Detailed essays are more likely to do well than vague or generalised essays, especially in the Depth Studies of Paper 2.

The AQA mark scheme is essentially the same for AS and the full A level (see the AQA website, www.aqa.org.uk). Both emphasise the need to analyse and evaluate the key features related to the periods studied. The key feature of the highest level is sustained analysis: analysis that unites the whole of the essay.

Writing an essay: general skills

- *Focus and structure.* Be sure what the question is asking and plan what the paragraphs should be about.
- *Focused introduction to the essay.* Be sure that the introductory sentence relates directly to the focus of the question and that each paragraph highlights the structure of the answer.
- *Use detail.* Make sure that you show detailed knowledge – but only as part of an explanation being made in relation to the question. No

knowledge should be standalone; it should be used in context.

- *Explanatory analysis and evaluation.* Consider what words and phrases to use in an answer to strengthen the explanation.
- *Argument and counter-argument.* Think of how arguments can be balanced so as to give contrasting views.
- *Resolution.* Think how best to 'resolve' contradictory arguments.
- *Relative significance and evaluation.* Think how best to reach a judgement when trying to assess the relative importance of various factors, and their possible interrelationship.

Planning an essay

Practice question 1

To what extent was the ability of the Conservative Party to remain in office between 1979 and 1997 due to the weakness of the Labour Party?

This question requires you to analyse why the Conservative Party was able to stay in power. You must discuss:

- How the weakness of the Labour Party helped the Conservative Party to retain power (your primary focus).
- The other factors that allowed this to happen (your secondary focus).

A clear structure makes for a much more effective essay and is crucial for achieving the highest marks. You need three or four paragraphs to structure this question effectively. In each paragraph it is best to deal with one factor. One of these *must* be the factor in the question.

A very basic plan for this question might look like this:

- Paragraph 1: The effects of the weaknesses of the Labour Party.

- Paragraph 2: The effects of events beyond the control of the Conservatives, such as the Argentinian seizure of the Falklands and the ERM crisis in Europe.
- Paragraph 3: The policies and achievements of the Conservatives in government.

It is a good idea to cover the factor named in the question first, so that you don't run out of time and forget to do it. Then cover the others in what you think is their order of importance, or in the order that appears logical in terms of the sequence of paragraphs.

The introduction

Maintaining focus is vital. One way to do this from the beginning of your essay is to use the words in the question to help write your argument. The first sentence of question 1, for example, could look like this:

The Conservatives were successful in maintaining power between 1979 and 1997 partly because of the weakness of the Labour Party, but there were also other factors to explain this.

This opening sentence provides a clear focus on the demands of the question.

Focus throughout the essay

Structuring your essay well will help with keeping the focus of your essay on the question. To maintain a focus on the wording in question 1, you could begin your first main paragraph with 'weakness'.

The weakness of the Labour Party was one very important factor in allowing the Conservatives to retain power.

- This sentence begins with a clear point that refers to the primary focus of the question (the Conservatives' retention of power) while linking it to a factor (the weakness of the Labour Party).
- You could then have a paragraph for each of your other factors.
- It will be important to make sure that each paragraph focuses on analysis and includes

relevant details that are used as part of the argument.
- You may wish to number your factors. This helps to make your structure clear and helps you to maintain focus.

Deploying detail

As well as focus and structure, your essay will be judged on the extent to which it includes accurate detail. There are several different kinds of evidence you could use that might be described as detailed. These include correct dates, names of relevant people, statistics and events. For example, for question 1 you could use terms such as the 'deregulation' and 'the velvet revolution'. You can also make your essays more detailed by using the correct technical vocabulary.

Analysis and explanation

'Analysis' covers a variety of high-level skills including explanation and evaluation; in essence, it means breaking down something complex into smaller parts. A clear structure which breaks down a complex question into a series of paragraphs is the first step towards writing an analytical essay. The purpose of explanation is to provide evidence for why something happened, or why something is true or false. An explanatory statement requires two parts: a *claim* and a *justification*.

For example, for question 1, you might want to argue that one important reason was the internal division within the Labour Party. Once you have made your point, and supported it with relevant detail, you can then explain how this answers the question. For example, you could conclude your paragraph like this:

So, because[1] of its failure to present a united front, the Labour Party was unable to exploit the mistakes made by Margaret Thatcher or take advantage of her unpopularity[2]. This was especially evident in economic matters where Labour's commitment to nationalisation[3] lost it electoral support.

1 'Because' is a very important word to use when writing an explanation, as it shows the relationship between the claim and the justification.
2 The first part of this sentence is the claim while the second part justifies the claim.
3 Justification.

Evaluation

Evaluation means considering the importance of two or more different factors, weighing them against each other, and reaching a judgement. This is a good skill to use at the end of an essay because the conclusion should reach a judgement which answers the question. For example, your conclusion to question 1 might read as follows:

Clearly, there were times when the Conservatives were in difficulties. However, the weakness of the Labour Party meant that many voters, while not strongly pro-Conservative, were not attracted to Labour as an alternative. This gave the Conservatives greater freedom to pursue policies they might otherwise not have risked. Therefore, the weakness of the Labour Party provided an opportunity for the Conservatives.

Words like 'however' and 'therefore' are helpful to contrast the importance of the different factors.

Complex essay writing: argument and counter-argument

Essays that develop a good argument are more likely to reach the highest levels. This is because argumentative essays are much more likely to develop sustained analysis. As you know, your essays are judged on the extent to which they analyse.

After setting up an argument in your introduction, you should develop it throughout the essay. One way of doing this is to adopt an argument–counter-argument structure. A counter-argument is one that disagrees with the main argument of the essay. This is a good way of evaluating the importance of the different factors that you discuss. Essays of this type will develop an argument in one paragraph and then set out an opposing argument in another paragraph.

Sometimes this will include juxtaposing the differing views of historians on a topic.

Good essays will analyse the key issues. They will probably have a clear piece of analysis at the end of each paragraph. While this analysis might be good, it will generally relate only to the issue discussed in that paragraph.

Excellent essays will be analytical throughout. As well as the analysis of each factor discussed above, there will be an overall analysis. This will run throughout the essay and can be achieved through developing a clear, relevant and coherent argument.

A good way of achieving sustained analysis is to consider which factor is most important.

Here is an example of an introduction that sets out an argument for question 1:

During its eighteen years in opposition, the Labour Party struggled to agree on policy and to unite behind its leaders[1]. However, this was not the only reason for the ability of the Conservatives to win four consecutive general elections. The Thatcher and Major governments often showed skill and judgement in dealing with economic, Irish and international problems[2]. Yet the fact remains that the most important reason why the Conservatives succeeded in retaining office was the failure of the Labour Party to organise itself in such a way as to present itself to the electorate as a credible alternative government[3].

1 The introduction begins with a claim.
2 The introduction continues with another reason.
3 Concludes with the outline of an argument of the most important reason.

- This introduction focuses on the question and sets out the key factors that the essay will develop.
- It introduces an argument about which factor was most significant.
- However, it also sets out an argument that can then be developed throughout each paragraph, and is rounded off with an overall judgement in the conclusion.

Complex essay writing: resolution and relative significance

Having written an essay that explains argument and counter-arguments, you should then resolve the tension between the argument and the counter-argument in your conclusion. It is important that the writing is precise and summarises the arguments made in the main body of the essay. You need to reach a supported overall judgement. One very appropriate way to do this is by evaluating the relative significance of different factors, in the light of valid criteria. Relative significance means how important one factor is compared to another.

The best essays will always make a judgement about which was most important based on valid criteria. These can be very simple, and will depend on the topic and the exact question.

The following criteria are often useful:

- Duration: which factor was important for the longest amount of time?
- Scope: which factor affected the most people?
- Effectiveness: which factor achieved most?
- Impact: which factor led to the most fundamental change?

As an example, you could compare the factors in terms of their duration and their impact. A conclusion that follows this advice should be capable of reaching a high level (if written, in full, with appropriate details) because it reaches an overall judgement that is supported through evaluating the relative significance of different factors in the light of valid criteria.

Having written an introduction and the main body of an essay for question 1, a concluding paragraph that aims to meet the exacting criteria for reaching a complex judgement could look like this:

Thus there are several interrelated explanations for the Conservatives' eighteen-year retention of power. It was not simply a matter of the leadership skills of Margaret Thatcher and John Major; it also resulted from the particular circumstances of the time, relating to financial, European, Irish and international issues. These offered opportunities for successful government responses, which raised the esteem of the Conservatives at home and abroad. Yet the Conservatives also pursued social and financial projects that proved deeply unpopular. It was in this respect that the weakness of the Labour Party proved so significant. Its own internal dissensions and disputed leadership freed the Conservatives from effective opposition, enabling them to remain in power for eighteen years.

Sources guidance

Whether you are taking the AS exam or the full A level exam for AQA Component 2:
Depth Study: Britain 1951–2007, Section A presents you with sources and a question
which involves evaluation of their utility or value.

AS exam	A level exam
Section A: answer question 1, based on two primary sources. (25 marks)	Section A: answer question 1, based on three primary sources. (30 marks)
Question focus: with reference to these sources and your understanding of the historical context, which of these two sources is more valuable in explaining … ?	Question focus: with reference to these sources and your understanding of the historical context, assess the value of these three sources to a historian studying …

Sources and sample questions

Study Sources 1–3. They are all concerned with Britain's first application to join the EEC. Practice questions
relating to the sources are on page 238.

SOURCE 1

From Harold Macmillan's speech in the House of Commons, 2 August 1961.

In this, as in most countries, there is a certain suspicion of foreigners. There is also the additional division between us and Continental Europe of a wholly different development of our legal, administrative and to some extent political systems. Nevertheless, it is perhaps worth recording that in every period when the world has been in danger of tyrants or aggression, Britain has abandoned isolation.

There are, as I have said, some to whom the whole concept of our working closely in this field with other European nations is instinctively

disagreeable. Others feel that our whole and sole duty lies with the Commonwealth. If I thought that our entry into Europe would injure our relations with and our influence in the Commonwealth, or be against the true interest of the Commonwealth, I would not ask the House to support this step.

I think, however, that most of us recognise that in a changing world if we are not to be left behind and to drop out of the main stream of the world's life, we must be prepared to adapt and change our methods. All through history this had been one of the main sources of our strength.

SOURCE 2

From a speech by President de Gaulle at a press conference in Paris, 14 January 1963, giving his reasons for vetoing Britain's application.

One might sometimes have believed that our English friends, in posing their candidature to the Common Market, were agreeing to transform themselves to the point of applying all the conditions which are accepted and practised by the Six. But the question is whether Great Britain can now place herself like the Continent inside a tariff

which is genuinely common, to renounce all Commonwealth preferences, to cease any pretence that her agriculture be privileged, and, more than that, to treat her engagements with other countries of the free trade area null and void – that question is the whole question. It cannot be said that it is yet resolved.

SOURCE 3

From the minutes of a Cabinet meeting in July 1960. Derick Heathcoat-Amory, the chancellor of the exchequer, describes the concerns with which the government approaches the question of whether Britain should join the EEC.

A decision to join the Community would be essentially a political act with economic consequences, rather than an economic act with political consequences. The arguments for joining the Community were strong. If we remained outside it, our political influence in Europe and the rest of the world was likely to decline. By joining it we should not only avoid tariff discrimination by its members against our exports, but should also be able to participate in a large and rapidly expanding market.

However, the arguments against United Kingdom membership were also very strong. We should be surrendering independent control of our commercial policies to a European bloc, when our trading interests were world-wide. We should have to abandon our special economic relationship with the Commonwealth, including free entry for Commonwealth goods and the preferential system, and should instead be obliged to discriminate actively against the Commonwealth. We should have to devise for agriculture and horticulture new policies under which the burden of support for the farmers would be largely transferred from the Exchequer to the consumer, thus increasing the cost of living. Finally, we should sacrifice our loyalties and obligations to the members of the European Free Trade Association (E.F.T.A.), some of which would find it impossible to join the E.E.C. as full members.

AS style question

With reference to Sources 1 and 2 (page 236), and your understanding of the historical context, which of these two sources is more valuable in explaining why France vetoed Britain's application to join the EEC in 1963?

AS mark scheme

See the AQA website (www.aqa.org.uk) for the full mark schemes. The summary of the AS mark scheme below shows how it rewards analysis and evaluation of the source material within the historical context.

Level 1	Describing the source content or offering generic phrases.
Level 2	Some relevant but limited comments on the value of one source or some limited comment on both sources.
Level 3	Some relevant comments on the value of the sources and some explicit reference to the issue identified in the question.
Level 4	Relevant well-supported comments on the value and a supported conclusion, but with limited judgement.
Level 5	Very good understanding of the value in relation to the issue identified. Sources evaluated thoroughly and with a well-substantiated conclusion related to which is more valuable.

A level style question

With reference to Sources 1, 2 and 3 (pages 236–7), and your understanding of the historical context, assess the value of these sources to a historian studying the difficulties that confronted Macmillan's government in framing a policy towards the EEC between 1960 and 1963.

A level mark scheme

The summary of the A level mark scheme below shows how it is similar to the AS, but covers three sources. The wording of the question means that there is no explicit requirement to decide which of the three sources is the most valuable. Concentrate instead on a very thorough analysis of the content and evaluation of the provenance of each source, using contextual knowledge.

Level 1	Some limited comment on the value of at least one source.
Level 2	Some limited comments on the value of the sources or on content or provenance, or comments on all three sources but no reference to the value of the sources.
Level 3	Some understanding of all three sources in relation to both content and provenance, with some historical context; but analysis limited.
Level 4	Good understanding of all three sources in relation to content, provenance and historical context to give a balanced argument on their value for the purpose specified in the question.
Level 5	As Level 4, but with a substantiated judgement.

Working towards an answer

It is important that knowledge is used to show an understanding of the relationship between the sources and the issue raised in the question. Answers should be concerned with the following:

- provenance
- arguments used (and you can agree/disagree)
- tone and emphasis of the sources.

The sources

The two or three sources used each time will be contemporary – probably of varying types (for example, diaries, newspaper accounts, government reports). The sources will all be on the same broad topic area. Each source will have value. Your task is to evaluate how much in terms of its content and its provenance.

You will need to assess the *value of the content* by using your own knowledge. Is the information accurate? Is it giving only part of the evidence and ignoring other aspects? Is the tone of the writing significant?

You will need to evaluate the *provenance* of the source by considering who wrote it, and when, where and why. What was its purpose? Was it produced to express an opinion; to record facts; to influence the opinion of others? Even if it was intended to be accurate, the writer may have been biased – either deliberately or unconsciously. The writer, for example, might have only known part of the situation and reached a judgement solely based on that.

Here is a guide to analysing the provenance, content and tone for Sources 1, 2 and 3 (pages 236–7).

Analysing the sources

To answer the question effectively, you need to read the sources carefully and pull out the relevant points as well as add your own knowledge. You must remember to keep the focus on the question at all times.

Source 1 (page 236)
Provenance:

- The source is from a speech by Harold Macmillan, the Conservative prime minister. He will have a particular view on Britain's relationship with Europe.
- It is taken from a speech in the House of Commons – it will therefore be addressing that particular parliamentary audience.

Content and argument:

- There are certain suspicions in Britain towards foreigners.
- Britain's Commonwealth ties must be considered.
- The source argues that Britain must be prepared to adapt.

Tone and emphasis:

- The tone is conciliatory. Macmillan wishes to assure his audience that his primary concern is to protect British interests.

Own knowledge:

- Use your own knowledge to agree/disagree with the source, for example: Britain's economic decline and difficulties in foreign affairs since the Suez crisis in 1956 have persuaded many in the Conservative Party to consider European entry.

Source 2 (page 236)
Provenance:

- The source is from a French press conference address made by President de Gaulle.
- It provides a contemporary account of what de Gaulle thought at the time.

Content and argument:

- The source argues that Great Britain is not yet ready to be a member of the Common Market.
- Britain is unwilling to introduce the measures necessary for it to be an acceptable member.
- Britain's links with the free trade area are not compatible with the Common Market's tariff policy.

Tone and emphasis:

- The tone is firm but not unfriendly. De Gaulle emphasises that Britain's historical links with non-European countries restrict its freedom of choice.

Own knowledge:

- Use your own knowledge to agree/disagree with the source, for example: behind de Gaulle's statement is his fear that British entry would challenge French dominance in Europe and be the thin end of a US wedge in Europe.

Source 3 (page 237)

Provenance:

- The source is from Cabinet minutes.
- It is a record of the chancellor of the exchequer's views.

Content and argument:

- The source describes the differing opinions within the Cabinet over Europe.
- The source refers to the gains and losses that would follow membership.

Tone and emphasis:

- The tone is balanced. The chancellor attempts to present the pros and cons relating to the European question.

Own knowledge:

- Use your own knowledge to agree/disagree with the source, for example: detailed knowledge about the British economy and the hopes and fears among Britain's political parties about the consequences of joining Europe.

Answering AS questions

You have an hour to answer the question. It is important that you spend at least one quarter of the time reading and planning your answer. Generally, when writing an answer, you need to check that you are remaining focused on the issue identified in the question and are relating this to the sources and your knowledge.

- You might decide to write a paragraph on each 'strand' (that is, provenance, content and tone), comparing the two sources, and then write a short concluding paragraph with an explained judgement on which source is more valuable.
- For writing about content, you may find it helpful to adopt a comparative approach, for example when the evidence in one source is contradicted or questioned by the evidence in another source.

At AS level you are asked to provide a judgement on which is more valuable. Make sure that this is based on clear arguments with strong evidence, and not on general assertions.

Planning and writing your answer

- Think how you can best plan an answer.
- Plan in terms of the headings above, perhaps combining 'provenance' with 'tone and emphasis', and compare the two sources.

As an example, if you are answering the AS level practice question on page 238, here is a comparison of Sources 1 and 2 in terms of provenance, and tone and emphasis:

The two sources have distinct viewpoints. Source 1 is concerned with the safeguarding of British interests as a condition of Britain's entering the Common Market. Source 2 is similarly concerned with the protection of interests but in this case with safeguarding the existing Common Market structure which de Gaulle feels would be damaged were Britain to join while still retaining its free trade links with the Commonwealth.

Then compare the *content and argument* of each source, using your own knowledge. For example:

Source 1 is arguing for Britain to abandon its suspicion of foreigners and, with the proviso that its existing economic ties are protected, adapt to the changing world by entering Europe. Behind Macmillan's appeal is his perception that Britain can no longer stand apart from Europe, a notion strongly put to him by Edward Heath.

Source 2, however, focuses on the impossibility of Britain's genuinely accepting the Common Market tariff while at the same time insisting on maintaining its Commonwealth and overseas commitments. Behind de Gaulle's objections is his desire to prevent Britain's challenging French dominance and becoming an outpost of US influence in Europe.

Which is *more valuable?* This can be judged in terms of which is likely to be more valuable in terms of where the source came from; or in terms of the accuracy of its content. However, remember the focus of the question – in this case, why France vetoed Britain's application.

With these sources, you could argue that Source 2 is the more valuable because it is a direct statement of the principal reasons for the French veto. They are the words of de Gaulle, spoken at a critical time after Britain had applied, whereas Source 1 is more limited to a consideration of whether Britain should apply for membership.

Then check the following:

- Have you covered the 'provenance' and 'content' strands?
- Have you included sufficient knowledge to show understanding of the historical context?

Answering A level questions

The same general points for answering AS questions (see 'Answering AS questions') apply to A level questions, although of course here there are three sources and you need to assess the value of each of the three, rather than choose which is most valuable. Make sure that you remain focused on the question and that when you use your knowledge it is used to substantiate (add to) an argument relating to the content or provenance of the source.

If you are answering the A level practice question on page 238 with Sources 1, 2 and 3 (pages 236–7):

- Keep the different 'strands' explained above in your mind when working out how best to plan an answer.
- Follow the guidance about 'provenance' and 'content' (see the first two points of the AS guidance).
- Here you are *not* asked to explain which is the most valuable of the three sources. You can deal with each of the three sources in turn if you wish.
- However, you can build in comparisons if it is helpful, but it is not essential. It will depend to some extent on the three sources.
- You need to include sufficient knowledge to show understanding of the historical context. This might encourage cross-referencing of the content of the three sources, mixed with your own knowledge.
- Each paragraph needs to show clarity of argument in terms of the issue identified by the question.

OCR A level History

Essay guidance

The assessment of this OCR Unit Y113 Britain 1930–1997 depends on whether you are studying it for AS or A level:

- for the AS exam, you will answer one essay question from a choice of two, and one interpretation question, for which there is no choice
- for the A level exam, you will answer one essay question from a choice of two and one shorter essay question, also from a choice of two.
- The guidance below is for answering both AS and A level essay questions.

For both OCR AS and A level History, the types of essay questions set and the skills required to achieve a high grade for Unit Group 1 are the same. The skills are made very clear by both mark schemes, which emphasise that the answer must:

- focus on the demands of the question
- be supported by accurate and relevant factual knowledge
- be analytical and logical
- reach a supported judgement about the issue in the question.

There are a number of skills that you will need to develop to reach the higher levels in the marking bands:

- understand the wording of the question
- plan an answer to the question set
- write a focused opening paragraph
- avoid irrelevance and description
- write analytically
- write a conclusion which reaches a supported judgement based on the argument in the main body of the essay.

Understanding the wording of the question

To stay focused on the question set, it is important that you read the question carefully and focus on the key words and phrases. Unless you directly address the demands of the question, you will not score highly. Remember, in questions where there is a named factor, you must write an analytical paragraph about the given factor, even if you argue that it was not the more or most important.

Types of AS and A level questions you might find in the exams	The factors and issues you would need to consider to answer them
1 Assess the reasons why Britain applied to join the EEC in 1963.	Weigh up the relative importance of a range of factors as to why Britain applied to join the EEC in 1963.
2 How far were economic fears the main motive for Britain's application to join the EEC in 1963?	Weigh up the relative importance of a range of motives, including comparing the importance of economic fears with other motives.
3 'The leadership of Harold Macmillan was the most important reason for Britain's applying to join the EEC in 1963.' How far do you agree?	Weigh up the relative importance of a range of factors, including comparing the importance of Macmillan's leadership with other issues, to reach a balanced judgement.

Planning an answer

Many plans simply list dates and events – this should be avoided as it encourages a descriptive or narrative answer, rather than an analytical answer. The plan should be an outline of your argument; this means you need to think carefully about the issues you intend to discuss and their relative importance before you start writing your answer. It should therefore be a list of the factors or issues you are going to discuss and a comment on their relative importance.

For question 3 in the table, your plan might look something like this:

- The relative decline of Britain's economy when compared with EEC.
- EFTA's failure to match EEC.
- Britain's post-war economic commitments.
- UK's sense of isolation after the Suez crisis.
- Doubts about Britain's special relationship with USA.
- The reliance of Britain's nuclear programme on the USA.
- Change in the attitude of City-orientated Conservatives towards Europe.
- Macmillan's leadership as prime minister.
- Heath's personal commitment to Britain's membership of the Six.

The opening paragraph

Many students spend time 'setting the scene'; the opening paragraph becomes little more than an introduction to the topic – this should be avoided. Instead, make it clear what your argument is going to be. Offer your view about the issue in the question – was Macmillan's leadership the main factor? – and then introduce the other issues you intend to discuss. In the plan it is suggested that economic fears were critically important. This should be made clear in the opening paragraph, with a brief comment as to why – perhaps that Macmillan judged the British economy to be in decline in comparison with that of the Six. This will give the examiner a clear overview of the argument in your essay. For example:

There are a number of reasons why Britain applied to join the EEC in 1963; among them are Britain's economic decline, its doubts about its international position after Suez, its uncertain relationship with the USA[1]. *However, the most important reason was Macmillan's belief that it was his government's responsibility to lead Britain into Europe*[2]. *This conviction was confirmed for him by the findings of Edward Heath who, as specially appointed minister for Europe, reported back to Macmillan that Britain's entry into the EEC was a necessity*[3].

1 The answer is aware that there were a number of important reasons.
2 The answer offers a clear view as to what it considers to be the most important reason – a thesis is offered.
3 There is a brief justification to support the thesis.

Avoid irrelevance and description

Well used, the plan will stop you from simply writing all you know about Britain and Europe and will force you to weigh up the role of a range of factors.

Write analytically

This is the most important skill you need to develop. An analytical approach can be helped by ensuring that the opening sentence of each paragraph introduces an idea, which directly answers the question and is not just a piece of factual information. In a very strong answer it is possible, simply by reading the opening sentences of all the paragraphs, to know what argument is being put forward.

If we look at question 3 on the importance of Macmillan's leadership (see page 242), the following are possible sentences with which to start paragraphs:

- Britain had become aware by the early 1960s that its economy was in relative decline and that the best way to address this decline was by joining the EEC.
- The economies of the Six in the EEC appeared to be growing stronger, while Britain's was stagnating.
- Following the Suez crisis in 1956, a feeling grew that Britain could no longer stand alone internationally and that membership of the EEC would be a way of avoiding isolation.
- Influential businessmen in the Conservative Party were beginning to suggest that Britain's economic future lay in Europe since this where they judged the expanding markets to be.
- Reflecting on the various concerns, Macmillan asked Heath to examine the possible consequences of Britain's joining Europe and report back as to whether it might be in the nation's best interests for it to be in the EEC.

- Having become convinced that Britain should join the EEC, Macmillan and Heath presented a powerful case for membership to their government and party colleagues.

You should then go on to assess the importance of the various factors mentioned in the opening sentence. The final sentence of the paragraph should be a direct response to the requirement to assess. This approach should ensure that the final sentence of each paragraph links back to the actual question you are answering. If you can do this for each paragraph, you will have a series of mini-essays, which discuss a factor and reach a conclusion or judgement about the importance of that factor or issue. For example:

In approaching the question of membership, Macmillan considered the economic, political and international concerns relating to Britain's position and came to the conclusion that Britain should make a formal application to join the Six[1]. In assessing the various factors it should be stressed that Macmillan's leadership proved critical. It was his decision to accept the advice of Edward Heath that joining the EEC was in Britain's best interests that began the application process[2].

1 The sentence puts forward a clear view that Macmillan came to his decision after careful and considered reflection on the issues.
2 The claim that it was Macmillan who made the crucial decision is provided to support the argument.

The conclusion

The conclusion provides the opportunity to bring together all the interim judgements to reach an overall judgement about the question. Using the interim judgements will ensure that your conclusion is based on the argument in the main body of the essay and does not offer a different view. For the essay answering question 1, asking you 'to assess the reasons', you need to distinguish between the varying levels of importance which you attach to each reason you introduce in explaining the 1963 application, but for questions 2 and 3 you will need

to comment on the importance of the named factor – Macmillan's leadership – as well as explain why you think a different factor is more important, if that has been your line of argument. Or, if you think the named factor is the most important, you will need to explain why that was more important than the other factors or issues you have discussed.

Consider the following conclusion to question 2: How far were economic fears the main motive for Britain's application to join the EEC in 1963?

Although there were certainly other motives for the British application in 1963 to join Europe, such as Britain's concerns regarding its diplomatic isolation, its overdependence on the USA, its defence commitments and its international role post-Suez, the main motive remained British government anxieties over the nation's relatively poor economic growth[1]. After all, Britain's attempts to arrest its economic decline by creating EFTA had not produced the hoped-for results. A strong conviction had grown within the government, principally as a result of Edward Heath's strongly pro-European campaigning, that EEC membership would create greater opportunity for economic recovery and growth by attaching Britain to a clearly successful European trade bloc[2].

1 This is a strong conclusion because it considers the importance of the named reason – economic fears – but weighs that up against a range of other factors to reach an overall judgement.
2 It is also able to show links between the other factors to reach a balanced judgement, which brings in a range of issues, showing the interplay between them.

Glossary of terms

9/11   The US formulation for the date 11 September 2001, typically used to refer to the terrorist attacks.

The Aeneid   An epic poem by the Roman writer Virgil (70–19BC).

Al-Qaeda   The Islamist terrorist organisation that organised 9/11.

Apartheid   In theory, the notion of separate and equal development for different racial groups in South Africa; in practice, the subjection of the majority black and Cape-coloured races to minority white rule.

Aswan Dam   Intended to modernise Egypt by providing a huge supply of hydroelectric power.

B Specials   A wholly Protestant reserve police force on which the full-time police could call.

Backbench   The area in the House of Commons where MPs sit who hold no official position in the government or opposition.

Balance of payments   The equilibrium between the cost of imports and the profits from exports; when import costs outstrip income from exports, financial crisis follows.

Bevanites   Followers of Aneurin Bevan, a hero of the left. Bevan was not always as radical as his followers. At the 1957 Labour Party conference, he rejected unilateralism as an 'emotional spasm'.

The big five   USA, USSR, Britain, France and China.

Birmingham pub bombings   On 21 November 1974, in separate explosions in two public houses in Birmingham's city centre, 21 people were killed and 180 seriously injured.

Blitz   The German aerial bombing of London and other British cities, which was at its most intense between September 1940 and May 1941.

Block vote   Labour Party procedures allowed individual trade union leaders to cast their conference votes on behalf of all the members of their union, which could number millions.

British National Party   An anti-immigration party.

Cannabis   A mildly addictive recreational drug; in a parliamentary debate in 1969 it was asserted that there were a million cannabis users and nearly 3000 users of the more damaging heroin.

Capitalism   The predominant economic system in the Western world according to which individuals and companies trade and invest for private profit.

Cash for honours   There were various accusations during the Blair years that government figures were engaged in giving out honours in return for cash donations to the Labour Party. A police inquiry eventually concluded in 2007 that there was insufficient evidence to warrant prosecutions.

Cash for questions   The practice by which, in return for payment, a number of Conservative MPs asked questions in the Commons with the intention of promoting particular commercial interests.

CBI   Confederation of British Industry. Representing Britain's leading manufacturers and industrialists; although officially neutral in politics, it tended to side with the Conservatives.

CDS   Campaign for Democratic Socialism. Made up of Labour supporters who wanted the party to distance itself from the trade unions, nationalisation and unilateralism; a number of CDS members went on to break from Labour in 1981 and form a new political party, the Social Democratic Party.

Census   An official recording of population figures, held every ten years in the first year of the decade.

City-orientated   Relating to the money markets in London's international financial centre, known as 'the City'.

Client state   A society in which a significant number of the population work directly for the government or its agencies.

CND   Campaign for Nuclear Disarmament. Founded in 1958 to agitate for unilateral nuclear disarmament.

Coalition   A government formed of opposing parties who agree to work together for the greater good.

COHSE   Confederation of Health Service Employees.

Cold War   The period of tension between the USSR and its allies and the USA and its allies 1945–91.

Collectivism   The people and the state acting together with a common sense of purpose, which necessarily meant a restriction on individual rights.

Common market   A trading system between equal states with the minimum of regulation.

Commonwealth Immigrants Act   This aimed to limit immigration by creating a voucher scheme, restricting the right of entry to those who had actual jobs to go to.

Consensus   Common agreement on major issues.

Conviction politician   Someone with strong opinions who acts out of principle rather than political expediency.

Counter-culture   A lifestyle based on the rejection of traditional social norms.

Countryside Alliance   An amalgam of landowners, land workers, vets, riding schools and those involved in the commercial side of fox hunting.

Cuban Missile Crisis   In October 1962 the USA, having discovered that Soviet nuclear missiles were being installed on the island of Cuba, ordered their removal. After days of acute tension, the USSR gave way and ordered their dismantling and withdrawal.

Cultural Revolution   A movement, which was at its fiercest between 1966 and 1971, to rid China of all opposition to Mao and thereby leave his permanent mark on the PRC.

Decolonisation   The granting of independence by Britain to the majority of its colonies and dependencies.

Decommissioning   The giving up of weapons.

Deficit budgets   The government's spending more than it raised in revenue.

Demography   Population analysis.

Détente and coexistence   An easing of antagonisms and a mutual recognition of each side's right to live in its own way.

Devolution   Granting to Wales and Scotland a significant measure of control over their own affairs by the creation of a separate parliament or national assembly.

Dictators   Chiefly Adolf Hitler (German leader 1933–45) and Benito Mussolini (Italian leader 1922–43).

Diplock Courts   Set up in 1972 to hear cases without a jury, the aim being to avoid the problem of jury members' being intimidated.

Dollar gap   Since sterling was weaker than the dollar, the goods that Britain desperately needed from North America had to be paid for in dollars.

DUP   Democratic Unionist Party, which had broken away from the Official Unionist Party in 1971.

East of Suez   A traditional shorthand way of referring to Britain's military commitments in the Middle East and Asia.

EFTA   The European Free Trade Association formed by Britain, Norway, Sweden, Austria, Portugal, Switzerland and Denmark.

EHRC   The Equality and Human Rights Commission, successor to the Commission for Racial Equality.

Embargo   Prohibition on sale and purchase.

ERM   The Exchange Rate Mechanism introduced by the EEC in 1979 as a system for bringing European currencies much closer together in value as preparation for the eventual adoption of a single European currency.

Etonians   'Old boys' of Eton, one of Britain's most prestigious public schools, which traditionally provided a high number of Britain's government ministers and statesmen.

Euro-rebels   A large group of Conservative MPs, led by Bill Cash and supported by most of the party's Euro-sceptics, who fought against the ratification of the Maastricht Treaty.

Euro-sceptics   Those who doubted that the UK's closer integration into Europe would serve British interests.

Eurozone   Those countries that gave up their individual currencies for the euro.

Extra-parliamentary   Not relying on conventional party politics.

Fait accompli   An irreversible position already established.

Federation   An organisation in which the member states surrender a significant degree of individual sovereignty for the union of states to have effective executive power.

Fellow travellers   Secret Communists and Soviet sympathisers.

Flying pickets   Teams of union members ready to rush to areas where strikes had been called to help dissuade or intimidate workers from going to work.

Free market   An economic system in which the forces of supply and demand are allowed to operate naturally without regulation by the government.

French Algeria   A French colony, the majority of whose indigenous Arab population supported the Algerian independence movement. French forces became involved in a bitter struggle (1954–62) against Algerian nationalists.

Friends of the Earth and **Greenpeace**   Similar movements which originated in the USA but quickly spread to Europe. They believed in direct action as a way of spreading their ideas about the threat to the planet.

Gay   A term adopted by homosexuals themselves as a word that was free of connotations of stigma or disapproval.

GDP   Gross domestic product: the annual total value of goods produced and services provided.

Genocide   The planned extermination of a people or a race.

Gerrymandering   Manipulating constituency boundaries.

GNP   Gross national product: the annual total value of goods produced and services provided by Britain at home added to the profits from overseas trade.

Green Party   In 1985 a number of environmental groups came together as the Green Party. Although it would not have its first elected MP until 2010, the party proved highly active and successful in pressing its arguments on Parliament and the general public.

Greenham Common   Became the site of a women's peace camp which picketed the base from 1981 to 2000, a graphic example of the extra-parliamentary protests against government policy that were a feature of late twentieth-century politics.

Hippy   Unconventional in appearance, language and behaviour.

Hong Kong   The Chinese city-port that had been a British Crown colony since 1898 and was not scheduled to return to China until 1997.

IMF   The International Monetary Fund. A scheme intended to prevent countries going bankrupt. It began in 1947 and by 1990 had been joined by over 150 countries. Each member state paid into a central fund from which it could then draw in time of need.

Imperialism   The nineteenth-century takeover by separate European powers, such as Britain and France, of many parts of Africa and Asia.

Inflation   A decline in the value of money, which means countries have to spend more money to buy imports.

INLA   Irish National Liberation Army, whose republicanism was part of its programme for Marxist world revolution.

Interest rates   A mechanism for raising or lowering the cost of borrowing money by adjusting the amount of interest charged on financial loans.

Invisible exports   The sale of financial and insurance services to foreign buyers, traditionally one of Britain's major sources of income from abroad.

IRA   Irish Republican Army. Dedicated to the creation through violence of an all-Ireland republic. Its political front was Sinn Féin, a legitimate political party. At the end of 1969 the movement split into the Official IRA and the Provisional IRA.

Israelis   The people of Israel, which became a sovereign state in 1948, taking most of Palestine.

Jihadists   Self-proclaimed warriors in the defence of their version of Islam.

Joint Intelligence Committee (JIC) The government body principally responsible for providing ministers with national security information.

KGB The Soviet Union's espionage network.

Landfill Directive A measure for standardising the practice in the EU countries in regard to the disposal of waste in landfill sites, the main purpose being to limit the emissions of methane, a greenhouse gas. A related measure which affected all premises in Britain from 2003 onwards was the EU requirement that household waste be collected in a regulated way so that appropriate materials could be recycled.

League of Empire Loyalists Formed in 1954 as a pressure group to agitate against Britain's adopting a policy of decolonisation.

Lib–Lab pact A 1977 agreement committing the Liberals to vote with the government in the Commons in return for the government's agreement to consult the Liberals on key issues. The pact lapsed in the autumn of 1978.

Liberal The principles of equality and freedom of the individual.

Life expectancy The remaining number of years an individual is likely to live after a given age.

Life peers Members of the House of Lords who are appointed to their positions, unlike hereditary peers who inherit their titles and their right to sit in the Lords.

Londonderry A disputed place name; republicans call it Derry.

Loyalist Anti-republican, pro-unionist.

Majority voting A system that attracted federalists since it enabled contentious resolutions to be passed without being blocked by a member state using its individual veto.

Mandate Popular backing for a particular policy.

Market forces The natural laws of supply and demand operating without interference by government.

Marxist The views of Karl Marx, the nineteenth-century revolutionary, who believed in the inevitable destruction of capitalism by the workers.

Militant tendency A Marxist group founded in 1964 with the aim of infiltrating the Labour Party and forcing revolutionary policies on it.

Mixed economy A system in which the private and public sectors of the economy both operate.

Mod cons Short for modern conveniences; for example, central heating, and household accessories such as vacuum cleaners, refrigerators and washing machines.

Mods and rockers Mods drove motor scooters and were rather more smartly dressed than rockers, who rode motorbikes; their prearranged fights usually took place in seaside resorts on bank holidays.

Mons and Dunkirk Occasions in the First and Second World Wars when British forces recovered from initial defeats to win the final military struggle.

NATO The North Atlantic Treaty Organisation, a defensive alliance formed in 1949 by Britain, France and the Benelux countries as a safeguard against Soviet expansion into Western Europe. The USA became a member by invitation.

Natural change The net difference between the number of deaths and the number of births.

Nazi The period of National Socialist rule under Adolf Hitler, 1933–45.

NCB The National Coal Board, the body with overall responsibility for running the industry.

Net migration The net difference between emigration, the number who left Britain, and immigration, the number who entered it.

New Commonwealth Bangladesh, India, Pakistan, West Indies.

New Labour Began as a slogan at the 1994 Labour Party conference, which was the first held with Tony Blair as leader, and became the name of the party from then on.

Niche market A particular section of society targeted by advertisers and manufacturers.

Night of the Long Knives A deliberate overdramatic phrase used by the press to compare Macmillan's Cabinet reshuffle with an episode in Nazi Germany in

1934 in which Hitler had massacred a number of his leading supporters.

North Sea oil   This resource had begun to be tapped in the late 1970s and turned Britain from a net importer to a net exporter of oil.

NUPE   National Union of Public Employees.

OPEC   Organisation of Petroleum Exporting Countries. Formed in 1961, it came to represent all the leading oil-producing nations, including the strategically vital Arab states of Bahrain, Iraq, Kuwait, Libya and Saudi Arabia.

Opium War   In a series of wars in the middle years of the nineteenth century, Britain had forced China to buy large quantities of opium, a humiliation which remained a basic historical reference point for many Chinese in explaining their suspicion towards the West.

PEP   Personal Equity Plan.

Poll tax   A flat-rate levy to fund local services, to be paid by all adults resident in the local area, not just owners of property; introduced into Scotland in 1989 and into England and Wales in 1990.

Populist   A way of appealing directly to ordinary people that bypasses normal party politics.

Poverty trap   The dilemma facing the low paid; if they continued working they were penalised by being taxed, which reduced their net income to a level little higher than if they simply drew unemployment benefit.

Prevention of Terrorism Act   Gave the police and authorities considerably extended powers of search and arrest.

Prime minister's questions   A twice-weekly session (weekly from 1997) when selected members of the House of Commons put direct questions to the prime minister.

Print workers   Among the highest paid workers in British industry, they were reluctant to accept work practices based on new technology that threatened their job security.

Privatisation   The selling of nationalised (government-owned) concerns fully or in part to private buyers and investors.

Property-owning democracy   A society in which people are encouraged to become homeowners, on the principle that the ownership of property is a necessary part of democracy.

Protectionist   Making non-common market goods uncompetitive by denying them entry or placing tariffs on them.

PSBR   Public sector borrowing requirement. The public sector includes the whole of national and local government and the nationalised industries. The costs of running these is met from government revenue. If the revenue is insufficient, the difference is made up by borrowing. The gap between government revenue and government needs is known as the PSBR.

Psephologist   An expert on election trends and voting patterns.

Psychedelic   Hallucinatory drugs like LSD (lysergic acid diethylamide).

R&D   Research and development in the economic sphere.

Reaganism   The conservative social and economic policies followed by the Reagan administration in the USA 1981–9.

Real wages   The purchasing power of earnings when set against prices. When prices are high money will buy less; when prices are low the same amount of money will buy more.

Rebate   The return of a proportion of Britain's budgetary payment.

Respect   Founded in 2004 as a socialist breakaway group from the Labour Party, its initials represented the words Respect, Equality, Socialism, Peace, Environmentalism, Community and Trade Unionism.

RUC   Royal Ulster Constabulary; an almost exclusively Protestant armed police force.

SAS   Special Air Service, a special forces regiment of the British army whose duties include counter-terrorist operations.

Satellites   Smaller states that are dependent on a larger state for economic, diplomatic and military assistance, often in alliance – in this case, the Eastern European states under Soviet control.

Savings ratio   The annual percentage of an individual's disposable income that is saved rather than spent.

Selsdon Man   A symbolic anti-Keynesian, pro-market individual.

Shareholders   Investors in companies or public utilities, such as electricity and gas.

The Six   France, Germany, Italy and the Benelux countries (Belgium, the Netherlands, Luxembourg).

Social Chapter   Sometimes referred to as the Social Charter, part of the Maastricht Treaty which committed EU member states to introducing extensive welfare schemes.

Social contract   An informal 1972 agreement between Wilson and Vic Feather, the TUC general secretary, to the effect that when Labour was returned to power, the unions would follow a wage restraint policy in return for the adoption of pro-worker industrial policies by the government.

Social reconstruction   Shaping society so as to provide protection and opportunity for all its citizens.

Socialism   In its British form, a programme for creating equality for all by means of government-led economic and social reforms.

Soviet bloc   The satellite countries of Eastern Europe under the domination of the USSR, for example, Poland, Hungary and Czechoslovakia.

Soviet invasion of Afghanistan   In 1980 Soviet forces began occupying parts of Afghanistan in an attempt to install a pro-Soviet regime there; a ten year war ensued before the Soviet withdraw having failed in its aim.

Soviet invasion of Czechoslovakia   In August 1968, the USSR, angered by the Prague Spring, the Czech government's attempt to liberalise its form of communism, sent forces into Czechoslovakia to suppress what it regarded as an anti-Soviet rebellion.

Soviet Union   Formed in 1922, the Union of Soviet Socialist Republics (USSR, or Soviet Union) was a single-party Communist state that existed until it was dissolved in 1991.

Special relationship   The term coined by Winston Churchill in 1946 to describe the common values that, he believed, made the USA and Britain natural allies.

Stormont   The building which housed the Northern Ireland Parliament.

Subsidiarity   The principle that in matters of special concern to a particular member state, that state had the right to ignore EU decisions.

Supranational   An organisation having power over its individual member states.

'Sus' law   A regulation that allowed police to 'stop and search' people suspected of criminal behaviour.

Taoiseach   Gaelic for prime minister.

Teddy boys   Young men of the 1950s with a strong tendency to violence when gathered in numbers; they took their name from their style of dress which recalled the fashions of Edward (Teddy) VII (king from 1901 to 1910).

TESSA   Tax-exempt Special Savings Account.

The smack of firm government   Eden had a habit, when emphasising a point, of smacking the palm of one hand with the back of the other. It was this image that the press used to mock his indecision.

Think-tank   A body of specialists working together in a research organisation.

Third way   Suggesting the creation of a balance between left and right extremes, often associated with Blair and New Labour's policies in general.

1921 Treaty   The Anglo-Irish agreement that had partitioned the island of Ireland between an independent south Ireland and Northern Ireland (loosely referred to as Ulster), which remained part of the UK.

Treaty Establishing a Constitution for Europe   Brought together the existing EU treaties into one formal, binding document.

Truman Doctrine   In 1947 President Truman pledged the USA 'to support free peoples who are resisting attempted subjugation by armed minorities or by outside pressure'. Although he did not mention the Soviet Union by name, he clearly had it in mind as the aggressor. Two particular developments indicated the willingness of the Labour government to support the USA in the growing Cold War: the Berlin Airlift and the Korean War.

TUC   Trades Union Congress: a federation of individual trade unions.

UDI   Unilateral Declaration of Independence.

UN Security Council   The United Nations' body responsible for maintaining international peace, using military force where necessary.

Unilateralists   Those who believed that Britain should give up its atomic weapons without waiting for a multilateral agreement between the nuclear powers to do so.

Velvet revolution   In the face of popular nationalist opposition, the USSR abandoned its authority over the countries of Eastern Europe without a fight; this culminated in the collapse of the USSR itself in 1991.

Veto   Each individual member of the UN Security Council had the right to block the collective decisions of the others.

Vietnam War   Fought from 1963 to 1975, it became the longest military struggle of the Cold War years. The USA sent forces to support the South Vietnamese governments in their resistance to invasion by Communist North Vietnam.

'Wets'   Applied during the Thatcher years to those in the government and Conservative Party who opposed or were uncertain about the tough measures that Mrs Thatcher adopted.

White Defence League   A racist organisation formed in 1957 in Notting Hill and modelled on Oswald Mosley's Union of Fascists, which had been active in the 1930s.

White Paper   A preliminary parliamentary statement of the government's plans in regard to a bill it intends to introduce.

Winter of discontent   The term comes from the first line of Shakespeare's *Richard III*: 'Now is the winter of our discontent.'

WTO   World Trade Organisation, the international body responsible for negotiating and monitoring trade agreements between countries.

Yuppy   An acronym for 'young upwardly mobile professional person'.

Further reading

Books of overall relevance

Robert Blake, *The Conservative Party from Peel to Major* (Arrow Books, 1997)
An authoritative survey by the outstanding historian of Conservatism

Brian Brivati and Richard Heffernan, editors, *The Labour Party: A Centenary History* (Macmillan, 2000)
A very useful survey of developments within the Labour Party across the period

Francesca Carnevali, editor, *Twentieth-Century Britain: Economic, Cultural and Social Change* (Routledge, 2007)
An illuminating collection of scholarly essays covering the themes in the subtitle

Nicholas Crafts *et al.*, **editors,** *Work and Pay in 20th Century Britain* (Oxford University Press, 2007)
A fascinating study of the change in the conditions of British workers during the twentieth century

Andrew Marr, *A History of Modern Britain* (Macmillan, 2007)
A popular approach by a popular journalist who enlivens the big issues by the skilful use of anecdote and quotation

Arthur Marwick, *A History of the Modern British Isles 1914–1999* (Blackwell, 2000)
An important and absorbing book by a pioneering social historian

Kenneth O. Morgan, *The People's Peace, British History Since 1945* (Oxford University Press, 1999)
A highly regarded study by one of the leading authorities in this field

Malcolm Pearce and Geoffrey Stewart, *British Political History 1867–1995* (Routledge, 1996)
A very useful survey illustrated with well-chosen documents

Robert Pearce and Graham Goodlad, *British Prime Ministers from Balfour to Brown* (Routledge, 2013)
A very helpful set of individual essays describing all the premierships from 1945 onwards

Bernard Porter, *Britannia's Burden: The Political Evolution of Modern Britain 1851–1990* (Edward Arnold, 1994)
Particularly strong on the post-1945 years

Alan Sked and Chris Cook, *Post War Britain* (Penguin, 1992)
Takes an interesting right-of-centre approach

Anthony Sutcliffe, *Economic & Social History of Western Europe since 1945* (Longman, 1997)
Specially written for students, it puts British post-war social history in its European context

Hugh Thomas, *Armed Truce: The Beginnings of the Cold War* (Hamish Hamilton, 1986)
Effectively sets the period's foreign affairs in perspective

Nick Tiratsoo, editor, *From Blitz to Blair: A New History of Britain since 1939* (Phoenix, 1997)
A stimulating set of essays from a left-of-centre viewpoint

S. Wichert, *Northern Ireland since 1945* (Longman, 1999)
Covers the major developments in the Northern Irish story after 1945

Ina Zweiniger-Bargielowska, *Women in Twentieth-Century Britain: Social, Cultural and Political Change* (Routledge, 2001)
A detailed account of the experiences of British women in the twentieth century

Chapter 1

Corelli Barnett, *The Audit of War* (Macmillan, 1986)
An important and controversial book that seeks to explain Britain's post-war decline

David Kynaston, *Austerity Britain 1945–51* (Bloomsbury, 2007)
The first volume of a series, 'Tales of a New Jerusalem', an absorbing social history based largely on the words of the people themselves

Robert Pearce, *Attlee's Labour Governments 1945–51* (Routledge, 1997)
A short but well-informed essay on the achievements of Attlee's groundbreaking government

Chapter 2

Vernon Bogdanor and Robert Skidelsky, *The Age of Affluence 1951–64* (Penguin, 1970)
Highly recommended study of the thirteen years of Conservative government

Martin Gilbert, *Churchill: A Life* (Minerva, 1992)
The best study of Churchill in his declining years after 1951 is this distillation into one book of Gilbert's multi-volume biography

Alistair Horne, *Macmillan 1957–86* (Papermac, 1991)
The second volume of a detailed, sympathetic biography

Dennis Kavanagh and Peter Morris, *Consensus Politics from Attlee to Major* (Blackwell, 1994)
A detailed and authoritative study of the workings of consensus

David Kynaston, *Family Britain 1951–57* (Bloomsbury, 2009) and *Modernity Britain 1957–59* (Bloomsbury, 2013)
The second and third in the 'Tales of a New Jerusalem' series in which contemporaries describe their experiences

John Ramsden, *The Age of Churchill and Eden, 1940–57* (Longman, 1996)
An illuminating assessment of the first two post-war Conservative prime ministers

D.R. Thorpe, *Supermac: The Life of Harold Macmillan* (Pimlico, 2011)
A spirited treatment of Macmillan and the major issues in which he was involved

Chapter 3

John Campbell, *Roy Jenkins* (Jonathan Cape, 2014)
A sympathetic study of a key figure in the shaping of 'the permissive society'

David Dutton, *British Politics since 1945: The Rise and Fall of Consensus* (Blackwell, 1991)
A brief but very helpful study of the character of consensus

Bernard Donoghue, *Prime Minister: Conduct of Policy Under Harold Wilson and James Callaghan, 1974–79* (Jonathan Cape, 1987)
A very valuable account by an insider who worked under Wilson

Dominic Sandbrook, *Seasons in the Sun: The Battle for Britain 1974–1979* (Allen Lane, 2012)
A fascinating, highly detailed and witty study of the Wilson and Callaghan governments

Philip Ziegler, *Edward Heath: The Authorised Biography* (HarperPress, 2011)
A study of an enigmatic Conservative leader who, arguably, took more momentous decisions than any other prime minister post-1945

Chapter 4

Charles Moore, *Margaret Thatcher. Volume 1: Not for Turning* (Penguin, 2014)
A very detailed and very readable study, which is likely to become the definitive account of its subject and her times

Margaret Thatcher, *The Downing Street Years* (HarperCollins, 1995)
The author's reflections on the movement that bore her name; well worth consulting

Richard Vinen, *Thatcher's Britain* (Pocket Books, 2009)
Concentrates less on Margaret Thatcher herself and more on the issues and struggles that characterised her time in government

Hugo Young, *One of Us* (Pan, 2013)
A highly critical and very entertaining biography of Margaret Thatcher

Chapter 5

Jad Adams, *Tony Benn: A Biography* (Macmillan, 1992)
A very readable study of the man regarded by many as the Labour Party's conscience

Stephen Driver and Luke Martell, *New Labour* (Polity Press, 2006)
Examines the origins of New Labour and assesses its record in government

Mervyn Jones, *Michael Foot* (Victor Gollanz, 1994)
A sympathetic study which challenges the notion that Foot's leadership of the Labour Party made it unelectable

Peter Mangold, *Success and Failure in British Foreign Policy 1900–2000* (Palgrave, 2001)
A stimulating assessment of some of the key issues in British foreign policy

Chapter 6

Tony Blair, *A Journey* (Arrow, 2001)
A very readable account of the author's own view of the issues and problems he faced

Steve Richards, *Whatever it Takes: The Real Story of Gordon Brown and New Labour* (Fourth Estate, 2010)
Essentially a study of the problematic political relationship between Blair and Brown

Anthony Seldon and Peter Snowdon, *Blair Unbound* (Pocket Books, 2008)
A balanced account of Blair's achievements as New Labour leader and prime minister

Geoffrey Wheatcroft, *Yo, Blair! Tony Blair's Disastrous Premiership* (Politico's Publishing, 2007)
True to its title, the book is heavily biased against Blair but is certainly thought provoking

Index

Acknowledgements: Arrow Books, *The Conservative Party from Peel to Major* by Robert Blake, 1998. Conservative Party Archive, www.bodleian.ox.ac.uk/cpa. Guardian Books, *The Hutton Inquiry* by David Aaronovitch *et al.*, editors, 2004. Guardian News and Media. HarperCollins, *The Downing Street Years* by Margaret Thatcher, 1993. harvard-digital.co.uk. Hodder & Stoughton, *Suez 1956* by Barry Turner, 2006. Hutchinson, *Our Times* by A.N. Wilson, 2008. labour-party.org. uk. Longman, *The Conservative Governments 1951–1964* by Andrew Boxer, 1996. MacGibbon & Kee, *The Suez War* by Paul Johnson, 1957. Macmillan, *Macmillan 1957–1986* by Alistair Horne, 1989. Margaret Thatcher Archive Trust. National Archives (Open Parliament Licence v3.0). Oxford University Press, *Consensus Politics from Attlee to Thatcher* by D. Kavanagh and P. Morris, 1989. Oxford University Press, *The People's Peace* by Kenneth O. Morgan, 1999. Penguin, *Hope and Glory: Britain 1900–2000* by Peter Clarke, 2004. Penguin, *Margaret Thatcher* by Charles Moore, 2014. Phoenix, *From Blitz to Blair* by Dilwyn Porter, 1997. Random House, *A Journey* by Tony Blair, 2010. Routledge, *Global Capitalism and National Decline* by Henk Overbeck, 1989. The Stationery Office, *Report of the Inquiry into the Circumstances Surrounding the Death of Dr David Kelly C.M.G.*, 2004. Times Newspapers, *The Times*, 12 July 1984. UK Parliament (Open Parliament Licence v3.0). ukpolitics.org.uk. Western European Union, *Political Union of Europe*, 1964.